# A PERPETUAL WITNESS

# A PERPETUAL WITNESS

## A Story of Grace and All Saints

### GORDON CHASTAIN

authorHOUSE®

AuthorHouse™
1663 Liberty Drive
Bloomington, IN 47403
www.authorhouse.com
Phone: 1-800-839-8640

James Tomlinson- Executive Publisher
Tim Jensen-Cover Photos
Lars Lawson Timber Design Co.-Jacket design

Special thanks to Indiana Historical Society and Bass photo archive.

First published by AuthorHouse    09/27/2011

ISBN: 978-1-4670-2495-2 (sc)
ISBN: 978-1-4670-2494-5 (hc)
ISBN: 978-1-4670-2493-8 (ebk)

Library of Congress Control Number: 2011917231

Printed in the United States of America

*The Cathedral Church of All Saints, in the city and Diocese of Indianapolis, erected as a perpetual witness to the Faith of our Lord Jesus Christ, and to the glory of God; and in loving memory of the bishops, clergy and laity of the Diocese, who having finished their course in faith, do now rest from their labors; stands for the following purposes:*

*... It shall ever be a House of Prayer, where all persons, of whatever race or nation, may have opportunity to worship God, the Father, Son and Holy Spirit; to draw near to Him in prayer and praise, and to hear the good tidings of the Gospel of Jesus Christ.*

From the Statutes of Governance, All Saints Cathedral, 1912

# A Note on Sources

A fire in 1978 destroyed almost all the existing records of All Saints. Only one parish register and some vestry minutes were saved. Three previous histories of the parish exist. The **Autobiography of a Cathedral** is a charming book, published in 1927, in which Louis Howland adopts the technique of having the cathedral speak in the first person. In 1964 Richard Mote wrote a **History** to celebrate the parish centennial. Several typewritten copies were found. Gloria Kemper, who worshipped at All Saints for more than 75 years, contributed the entry for All Saints in the sesquicentennial **History of the Diocese of Indianapolis, 1838-1988.** Following the fire, parishioners (especially Gloria Kemper) contributed their files of saved bulletins, annual meeting materials, newsletters and miscellaneous other documents. In addition, the parish has a scrapbook of newspaper clippings (not always identified by date and name of publication). A complete set of vestry minutes has been kept since the fire.

The stories of the founding and early years are intertwined with the personalities and policies of the bishops of the diocese. Addresses of the bishops and minutes of diocesan conventions are particularly useful for understanding the early history of Grace Church and All Saints. Correspondence and reports relating to All Saints from and to Bishops Francis, Kirchhoffer and Craine are in the diocesan archives. In those archives are also files for the Talbot Fund, which provided support for the parish and Episcopal Community Services. Other materials in the archives include documentation of the "Arkansas Lands" sold to build the cathedral and a 1941 booklet called **Forward in Faith with All Saints Cathedral.**

Also useful are the histories of other Indianapolis parishes—Christ Church, St. Paul's, and Trinity. Two memoirs by Indianapolis residents, Charlotte Cathcart and Sarah S. Pratt, provide charming details and impressions of Grace Church and All Saints from persons who knew the parish even though they were not members. Mrs. Pratt's book was the source for some of the quotes from Bishop Upfold's diary. Eli Lilly's history of Christ Church (**Little Church on the Circle**) was the source for quotes from the diaries of Bishop's Kemper and Talbot.

# CHAPTER ONE

## Digging a Cornfield with a Fountain Pen:
## The Episcopal Church in Indianapolis
## 1835-1863

The "mother church" for the Episcopal parishes in Indianapolis is Christ Church on Monument Circle, which was officially organized in 1837. At that time, Indianapolis itself was in its infancy. Commissioners had decided on the location of what was to become the new state capitol only a few years before in 1820. The plan for the capitol, with some inspiration from the plan of Washington, D.C., was of streets radiating out from a circle in a square one mile wide on each side. At first Monument Circle was the site of a wooden market building. It was soon replaced (in 1827) by a Governor's mansion, "in which no governor could induce his family to live." (Eli Lilly, **Little Church on the Circle**, Indianapolis, 1957, p. 30.)

In the years between 1820 and 1830, the population of Indiana increased significantly, as pioneer immigrants crossed the Cumberland Mountains fleeing soil exhaustion, taxes, inflation, and in some cases religious intolerance and slavery.

The 1820's and 1830's were also turning points in the young nation's life. John Adams and Thomas Jefferson died on the same 4th of July in 1826, signaling the end of the Founding Father's leadership. Internal improvements—roads and canals—became a major focus of public attention. Inspired by the success of the Erie Canal, the Indiana Legislature created the Mammoth Internal Improvements Bill, which envisioned a network of canals into Indianapolis. The financial panic of 1837, however, meant that the only portion completed was that between Broad Ripple and Indianapolis.

A covered bridge over the White River at Washington Street was completed in 1834, and permission was granted by the Pottawatomi Indians to construct the Michigan (toll) Road north from Indianapolis. Other roads connected the town to Fort Wayne, Crawfordsville, and Lafayette. The expansion of the National Road (later Highway 40) from Washington, D.C., to Indianapolis in 1827 was the most significant of all early roadway construction projects in the state.

Rail transportation reached Indianapolis in 1847. By 1855 several lines connected to the city. The nation's first Union Station was built in Indianapolis in 1853. With the railroad came businessmen and industrialists who would be attracted to the Episcopal Church

In this atmosphere of beginnings and change, The Rev. Melancthon Hoyt, a graduate of Yale University, appeared as the missionary of the Episcopal Church to Indianapolis. His appointment by the national church in Philadelphia on March 9, 1835, marked a step in a new direction for the Episcopal Church. The early days of Indiana's planned city coincided with the first planned missionary work of Episcopalians in the United States.

The church in each of the original 13 colonies had formed itself into a diocese in the years following the Revolutionary War. As each diocese organized and obtained a bishop (no easy feat for the first dioceses, since the established church of the nation with which we had just fought a war was not eager to consecrate bishops for the ex-colonies), it joined the Protestant Episcopal Church which had been formed in Philadelphia in 1789. The Episcopal Church, however, had been weakened by the war. Many of the Anglican clergy and parishioners had fled to Canada or England, having chosen loyalty to England and Prayer Book (with its compulsory prayers for the king) over independence. Although many of the new leaders of the United States (Washington and Jefferson among them) were at least nominal members of the church, Episcopalians were often looked upon with suspicion. The country had just gotten rid of a king. What did it want with bishops—the ecclesiastical version of kings?

All during the colonial period, there had been no Church of England bishops in America. In other words, a church whose very name (Episcopal) implies that it needs the presence of bishops (*episkopoi* in Greek) had been cut off from that source of identity. From the founding of the first parish in Jamestown, Virginia, in 1607 until after the Revolution, there had been no confirmations or ordinations in America. Consequently, Episcopal clergy were few and far between. At times a priest would act as a representative of the Bishop of London and some priests were sent to American shores by the English Society for Propagation of the Gospel, but there was neither organizational unity nor supervision of the colonial church.

Following the Revolution, the dioceses of the former colonies

> made a confederation under a constitution, but the doctrine of diocesan rights went along with the doctrine of state rights ... There was no clear general conception of an American Church. As a result there was no sense of common initiative ... The church did not consider itself as a single church responsible for the extension of the Kingdom of God ... Accordingly, that portion of the continent which we now call the Middle West had been left to go its own way. Among the settlers were many churchmen, who desired the service of the Church. Occasional pioneer priests ventured into the new places, and did what they could. But they were few in number, and the sheep, for the most part, had no shepherd. In the meantime, the Methodists, the Baptists, the Presbyterians, having ecclesiastical organizations easily adaptable to the frontier conditions, were building churches. And to these churches, as good Christians having no choice, the sons and daughters of the church were going. (George Hodges, **Three Hundred Years of the Episcopal Church in America,** George W Jacobs & Co., 1906, pp 121-123.)

In 1818 the five clergy of Ohio met with a few lay persons and chose The Rev. Philander Chase as their bishop and formed the first diocese outside the original colonies. Within a dozen years a disagreement arose between Chase and his clergy, so he moved to Illinois. Then in 1835 the three clergy and parishes in Illinois elected Chase as their bishop, leaving Indiana as an empty space on the map of the Episcopal Church.

Partly motivated by the example of Bishop Chase, the 1835 General Convention of the Episcopal Church moved from a passive to an active stance of mission planning. The new vision was for the entire church to be a missionary society (thus the name of The Domestic and Foreign Missionary Society, which still serves as the corporate title of the church). As an expression of this new missionary vision, Bishop Jackson Kemper was consecrated as the Bishop of the Northwest (including Indiana) on September 1, 1835.

The Rev. Mr. Hoyt, who had just arrived in Indianapolis, now had a bishop. Mr. Hoyt seems to have been received as something of a novelty because he wore a gown and was invited to preach at the Methodist Church.

> He could learn of only four or five Episcopalians, but set to work immediately securing the courthouse for services, even though he was warned that it would be disagreeably cold in the winter. Mr. Hoyt was much impressed by the potential importance of the town and wrote the Right Rev. Mr. Kemper of its many advantages, reporting that during the last year upwards of four thousand travelers had stopped in one of the three or four public houses. (**Little Church**, p. 33.)

Bishop Kemper's own arrival in Indiana followed shortly thereafter on November 13, 1835; however, on this visit he gave his attention to the southern part of the state where the prospects for the church seemed brighter in the more established towns along the Ohio River. The southern third of the state was settled first because the Ohio provided a natural "highway" to the west. In addition, treaties with Native Americans closed the northern portion of Indiana to settlement before 1821.

Following his visit to the Ohio River area, Bishop Kemper moved on to the other parts of his jurisdiction (Missouri).

On December 2, 1835, Mr. Hoyt wrote to Bishop Kemper that he had found 13 families who would "take pews in the church" (that is, support the church when it was formed by renting a pew) and "about 6 who will become communicants." (**Little Church**, p. 35.) But he found that could expect no more than $25 from the congregation, whereas Crawfordsville promised him four times that amount. He went to Crawfordsville, promising to conduct services in Indianapolis from time to time.

Bishop Kemper next tried to convince The Rev. Jehu C. Clay to become missionary to Indianapolis. Mr. Clay came to town and was well received, but declined to take the job.

The bishop himself came to Indianapolis in 1837 for two weeks in which he met many of the people who would become the leaders of Christ Church. His diary contains details of his trip from Madison to Indianapolis, details that illuminate the hardships of a frontier bishop and the hazards of travel in Indiana.

> A rough wagon covered over drove up about 9 ... & on a cold, windy lowering morning we started ... brot (*sic*) nothing but saddle bags, buffalo boots, umbrella & over-coats. The road thus far had been hard and rough ... our meals were eaten with chattering teeth in consequence of the want of fire. I sat till 9 in the bar room & only found an opportunity to read a little Greek ... I had a bed in a room with two others—no fire—but I slept well ... I washed at an early hour out of doors and succeeded in getting a little soft soap ... My bill for supper, bed & breakfast was 62 ½ cents ... the landlord was greatly mortified at the want of politeness towards me ... The horses being tired we did not start til ten ... The road icy but railed or corderoyed (*sic*) the whole way ... I had my room to myself & slept comfortably [in Browning's Hotel on Washington Street in Indianapolis] ... Smoke of the chimney drove me from my room & I went to the bridge over the White river.

On February 7, the bishop performed a wedding for the daughter of the owner of Browning's Hotel. He received $20 and gave it to Arthur St. Clair, grandson of General Arthur St. Clair, as a contribution for the building of the future Christ Church.

The Rev. James B. Britton (a native of Philadelphia who had been ordained in Kentucky in 1836) was in Indianapolis in April, 1837. He advertised that on the 15th he would officiate and preach at the courthouse at 11 a.m., 3:30 p.m., and 7:30 p.m. Afterwards he wrote Bishop Kemper that, if the Domestic and Foreign Missionary Society would appoint him with a salary of $400, he would go to Indianapolis.

On June 2, Mr. St. Clair wrote the bishop that a contract had been completed for the purchase of a lot on the Circle to build the church. $800 had been raised towards the contract of $1,000. The next step towards Christ Church took place on July 13, when 31 persons signed an agreement to form a parish and to recognize the jurisdiction of Bishop Kemper.

Mr. Britton took up residence that same July, at first holding services in the Presbyterian and Baptist churches. On July 30, Bishop Kemper returned to confirm four persons. On August 6, Mr. Britton administered Holy Communion to five persons and baptized one adult and two infants. The Episcopal Church had arrived to stay in Indianapolis.

Sarah S. Pratt, whose family played a role in the development of the Episcopal Church in Indiana for several generations, summarized the difficulties of foundation in the state:

> Planting the Episcopal Church in the Indiana of that day seemed about as hopeless an undertaking as digging a cornfield with a fountain pen. Bishop Kemper was the gold pen with which the digging began. It was easy to understand why Indiana presented physical and spiritual barriers to the introducing of such a complex institution as the Church. This state was a densely-wooded, immense, malarious waste. The settlers made their way into it by wagon and ox team; they fought every difficulty of beast, insect, and reptile. While the peasantry of England knew the Prayer Book by heart and kept every Holy Day, the same class in this country had rarely heard of our church. Sectarian churches were born in a day. All they needed was a room in a log cabin and an exhorter with a Bible. It is to them that Indiana owes most of its stalwart religion of today. The Methodists and Baptists brought their religion with them; but were any Churchmen migrating to Indiana? Very few. Virginia was a Church stronghold, as were some of the Eastern communities, but few of such Churchmen left a settled country for a new, unknown territory. (**Episcopal Bishops in Indiana: A Churchwoman's Retrospect**, Indianapolis, The Pratt Poster Co, 1934, p 1.)

Yet the Church was planted. There would, of course, be difficulties ahead. But there would be growth, too—especially when Indianapolis began to spread outward from its center on the Circle, creating opportunity for the birth of what would one day become All Saints Episcopal Church.

THE RT. REV. JACKSON KEMPER, D.D., LL.D.
Missionary Bishop of Indiana and Missouri,
later Missionary Bishop of the Northwest

# CHAPTER TWO

## A Neat, Unpretentious, and Inexpensive Shack: The Founding of Grace Church: 1864-1866

Before there was an All Saints, there was a Grace Church. And before Grace Church stood at 16th and Central, it "graced" the southeast corner of Pennsylvania and St. Joseph Streets.

Richard Mote in his **History of All Saints** says that "Grace Church was organized due to the overcrowded conditions existing at Christ Church" and that the founding of Grace Church was "surrounded by doubt and lacking diocesan unanimity." Nevertheless, the beginnings of the parish are also rooted in what appears to have been some diocesan planning.

In 1857, Bishop George Upfold purchased two lots (numbers 110 and 190) on the corner of Pennsylvania and St. Joseph Streets. The Bishop used funds he had received from friends "abroad" and cash from the Episcopal Fund of the Diocese of Indiana. The Diocesan Convention of 1865 admitted the new Grace Parish, which was at the time constructing a building on one of the lots, and seated D. E. Snyder as its first lay delegate The 1865 convention also heard a proposal to build a residence for the bishop adjacent to Grace Church since that lot was "entirely unproductive and ... subject to considerable taxation." The estimated cost of a "suitable dwelling" was between $6,000 and $8,000.

Bishop Upfold's address to convention provides us with more details of the process leading up to the admission of the new parish into the diocese. On September 17, 1864, he had consented to the organization of Grace. Then on November 27, he had admitted Martin V. Averill, a student of General Theological Seminary to the Holy Order of Deacons in a service at Christ Church. Mr. Averill was then made the minister of Grace. The bishop described his newest parish to the convention: "This Parish has been engaged in the erection of a neat and comparatively inexpensive church edifice in the northern portion of the city, which will soon be completed and ready for consecration."

Mr. Averill, in addition to distributing elements of Holy Communion at the opening service and serving as Assistant Secretary of convention, also gave his own report to the diocese. Since his ordination, he had officiated at 76 services, preached 22 times, officiated at five funerals and one marriage, and baptized one infant. But none of these acts had taken place in Grace Parish! "Being unable to procure a room in which to hold Divine Service, we have never met in public worship," he says. So Mr. Averill had officiated at Madison, Lafayette, Crawfordsville, and Christ Church in Indianapolis. He says that he had received a call to Grace Church on November 28, the day after his ordination, and that Grace had been organized with the consent of the vestry of Christ Church (as was required by the canons of the church for a new parish organized within an existing parish). He continues,

> Consent of the Trustees of the Diocese was then procured for the use of the lot, belonging to the Diocese … Plans for the church edifice were adopted in January, 1865. The main building is fifty five feet in length by thirty in width—built of wood—Gothic style with a vestibule in front, and a belfry on the front gable end. There is also a Vestry room 14 feet square, on the south rear corner. The church will seat two hundred and forty persons. It will in all probability be ready for occupation by the first of July.

The fresh young minister of Grace also reported that 12 families had joined the parish, and that others had stated their intention to do so. The organizing members included Deloss Root, J.O.D. Lilly and Nelson Kingman, with their families—all from Christ Church. Others were James Starrett, N.W. Ferguson, W.J. Holliday, D.E. Snyder, R.F. May, John Harkness and George W. Geiger. In other words, the parish had a minister, an almost completed building, and members—all before meeting together as a congregation in public worship!

Mr. Averill's date for completion of the building seems to have been on target because consecration took place on July 27, 1865. A description in a newspaper clipping found in the parish archives describes the structure as

> a frame building of the modified Gothic style, and particularly neat and tasteful in its ensemble, finish and appointments. It is doubtful if at a like expense a better effect in respect of a house of worship could be produced. The aspects of the interior are inviting and suggestive of comfort. The windows are of stained glass; the ceiling of the open-roofed construction. The chancel in the ornamentation of its triple windows and its appointments is artistic, the symbols typifying, with fine effect, the idea expressed in the name, Grace church.

Some descriptions of the building in later years would be less kind. Louis Howland, in his whimsical **Autobiography of a Cathedral**, calls it a "shack" and says there was some regret that it did not burn down completely in the course of its two fires.

A Frederick Polley drawing of the original Grace Church as it look from 1864-1869 appears in Eli Lilly's **Little Church on the Circle.** The vertical boards, steeply pitched roof, and arched windows of "carpenter Gothic" are evident. To the side is an entry with a steeple over it. Next door is the bishop's two story residence.

Was overcrowding at Christ Church the primary motivation for the creation of the new parish, as Richard Mote suggested?

Indianapolis had increased more than 10,000 in population in the decade preceding the Civil War. With the new railway system, which had become functional just before the war, the city was in position to become an important communications, assembly and supply center during the course of the war. Expansion and growth continued after the war. The rail network now made the city a center the processing and shipping of farm products. The value of manufactured products also increased from $890,000 in 1860 to $16,384,000 in 1870.

This same decade saw growth in the Episcopal Church. As a matter of fact, another congregation made its appearance in Indianapolis even before Grace Church. In the fall of 1863, Episcopal families living south of Pogue's Run formed St. Luke's Church, which was admitted into the diocese in June, 1864. This congregation, however, was not to prosper. It made no report to the 1865 convention (the year when Christ Church reported 29 adult baptisms, 65 infant baptisms, 21 confirmations, 199 communicants, a Sunday School of 200, and income of $3,538.65). At the 1867 convention, the connection of St. Luke's to the diocese was dissolved. Therefore, Grace/All Saints, even though the third parish to be organized in Indianapolis, is the second oldest surviving congregation.

Another congregation that would indeed prosper, St. Paul's, was founded in 1867. The cornerstone of St. Paul's was laid (at the corner of Illinois and New York Streets) during the same convention (1867) which ended the brief life of St. Luke's. The beginnings of St. Paul's involve the political and emotional divisions of the Civil War. The charter members of the new parish were prominent "Copperhead" Democrats. The congregation of Christ Church included equally prominent Republicans. The first minister of St. Paul's was to be The Rev. Horace Stringfellow, who had resigned as rector of Christ Church under accusations of "sympathy with the detestable Southern Cause." (Alice Ashby Roettger and Joseph F. Thompson, M.D., **Blessings on Thee Old St. Paul's**, Guild Press, Carmel, Indiana, 2000.) Bishop Upfold supported the creation of St. Paul's, citing crowded conditions at Christ Church as the reason. Indeed the membership of Christ Church had increased dramatically, from 199 in 1865 to 317 in 1866, despite the fact that 27 persons transferred from Christ Church to Grace in that year. By June, 1867, (when Bishop Upfold gave his approval for its organization) St. Paul's had 87 communicants. One of them seems not to have come from Christ Church, but from Grace. David (D.E.) Snyder, who had been the lay delegate to convention from Grace in 1865, was one of petitioners for the organization of St. Paul's on July 7, 1866. Along with Snyder, J.O.D. Lilly's name appears on the first vestry list of St. Paul's; this Mr. Lilly (not of the pharmaceutical company's family) was at various times also associated with Grace.

In addition to lay folks, clergy moved back and forth between Indianapolis parishes. The Rev. Horace Stringfellow returned to Indianapolis in 1866 after service as a chaplain with the Confederate

Army and a move to Ontario, Canada. He preached at Grace Church and at Christ Church. His return to Indianapolis reflected a nation and a church trying to heal its divisions and to seek unity after the Civil War. David Snyder was responsible for Stringfellow's return. "Snyder, a cashier in the Indiana Banking Company, had traveled to Canada to find a man who had defaulted on some notes held by the bank" and met Stringfellow at the same time. (**Blessings on Thee**, p. 9) During the visit of Stringfellow to Indianapolis, he agreed to become the first rector of St. Paul's.

The name of yet another congregation, Holy Innocents, appears during the years immediately after the Civil War. On January 26, 1866, the "Sabbath School" of Christ Church donated $50 to Holy Innocents Mission. Property at Fletcher Avenue and Cedar Street was donated by Stoughton Fletcher, Jr., for this mission; and in October of that year, a contract was let to build a structure for $1,725. This mission became independent of Christ Church in 1869, but it was not to last long.

> Unfortunately this mission did not survive, for the diocese was not strong, and the machinery for permitting missions to become parishes was consequently weak. They were often allowed to do so on pitifully inadequate self-support which did not allow enough for clergy stipend and other operational expenses, and the marginal backing could be quickly wiped out by poor choice of leadership or depression. (**Little Church on the Circle**, p. 182)

In the year 1865-1866, Bishop Upfold was ill and unable to perform many official duties. He did, however, report to the diocese in June, 1866 (in written form, since he was too ill to attend the convention) that

> On the 27th of July [1865] I consecrated the beautiful, commodious, and comparatively inexpensive church edifice erected by the parish of Grace Church which, it is gratifying to report, is entirely free from debt, and is usually well filled by a respectable and gradually increasing congregation. On this occasion the request to consecrate was read by the minister in charge, Mr. Averill, and the Sentence of Consecration by the Rev. Mr. Ingraham, the Rector of Christ Church. Morning Prayer was read by the Rev. Mr. Martin of Terre Haute and the Rev. Mr. Runcie of Madison, and the sermon preached by myself.

A second official act of the Bishop during the year of his illness was the ordination of Mr. Averill to the priesthood on August 24, 1865, in Christ Church.

Mr. Averill's own report to the convention of 1866 says that "Grace Church, Indianapolis, has erected an excellent frame church and expended for parochial purposes over $7000"; one assumes that this amount includes the cost of construction. In his statistical report, Averill lists 10 baptisms, 10 confirmations, 41 communicants, three marriages, six funerals, 95 Sunday School students with 15 teachers, 143 services, 89 sermons, 12 celebrations of the Holy Communion, and income of $7,120.50. The 12 celebrations of Holy Communion are indicative of the practice then current of offering the sacrament only once a month.

Although Bishop Upfold was absent from the 1866 convention, a new assistant Bishop, The Rt. Rev. Joseph Cruikshank Talbot, was there. He had been elected because of Upfold's failing health. By June, 1866 Talbot had already visited Grace twice.

Other actions of the convention of 1866 illustrate a problem which was soon to plague Grace Church. A resolution was passed to "deprecate the frequent and unreasonable changes [in ministers] which result in discouragements to a parish." Yet another resolution reflects the hopeful mood of the Episcopal Church as it emerged from the Civil War; the resolution "hails with great joy and returns thank to Almighty God for the entire unity of the Church within these United States."

In the wake of the Civil War, Indianapolis would experience another spurt of growth. Industrialization and transportation had already brought the growth that crowded Christ Church and furnished motivation for the founding of "daughter" parishes. Yet we have already seen that not all of the first five Episcopal congregations would survive. And at many times in the years ahead, survival for Grace would become doubtful.

Bishop Upfold's description in 1865 of Grace, located at the corner of Pennsylvania and St. Joseph Streets, as being in the "northern portion" of the city seems odd to All Saints parishioners of the 21st century.

Nevertheless, at the end of the Civil War, that corner was at the edge of the city, just beyond the original mile square (which ended at North Street). What would happen when the city's edge moved even further north? Would the parish move, too? And if so, how many times? And if it did not move, how would it deal with the demographic and economic changes brought by events in the nation and the world beyond? Born at a time of national crisis and economic expansion, Grace Church and All Saints would become very familiar with change and crisis.

GRACE CHURCH AND THE BISHOP'S RESIDENCE, 1864-1869

# CHAPTER THREE

## Frequent Changes, Discouragement, and Desecration Grace Church: 1867-1884

The infant parish had been born. However, would this child named Grace survive? The outline of its early history can be told quickly. An article in an Indianapolis newspaper ("All Saints Cathedral Had Beginning Indianapolis at Close of Civil War", by Ethel A. Wynne, unknown date) puts it this way:

> A Sunday School was organized with George W. Geiger as superintendent, and the Rev. Martin V. Averill, Crawfordsville, was called to the rectorship. The Rev. Mr. Averill, "an energetic as well as able rector", served well and the prosperity of the parish is attested by the fact that during the period of his service the number of communicants increased from ten to sixty. The Rev. Mr. Averill was succeeded in 1867 by the Rev. C.V. Davidson, who accepted the call on September 9 and served until 1870. For a time after the Rev. Mr. Davidson left, the parish was without a rector, but in 1871 the Rev. James Runcie was called and entered on his duties March 1. A proposition was made the following year for the church to buy the lot on which the church was built, a courageous undertaking for so young and untried a parish. In 1874 when the Rev. H.O. Judd was called, additional expense was incurred by enlarging and improving the church, and the total indebtedness now exceeded $1,100, which became a heavy burden during the panic which began the same year. The Rev. Francis B. Dunham was called to the rectorship in 1877, but the financial strain grew too great and in 1878 the church was closed.

The names of clergy do not match those of Richard Mote's history, and the date of closing actually seems to have been 1882. Nevertheless, the story given here of struggle and apparent defeat is correct. The "frequent changes" in ministers warned about at the 1866 convention do indeed appear to have "resulted in discouragement."

We know, however, that the story of Grace/All Saints does not end in discouragement and death. Instead, it would be a witness, more than once, to the central message of the Gospel—that is, Resurrection.

Although no documents exist to tell us of the life of the struggling parish at St. Joseph and Pennsylvania, Sarah S. Pratt's memories of the Episcopal Church in Indiana during the 19th century can help us imagine something of that life. She tells us, for example, of worship using the American Prayer Book of 1789 (**Episcopal Bishops**, p. 17):

> To a child the ownership of a Prayer Book was a proud thing. Perhaps with her name upon it, she carried it to church, first marking carefully with little purple ribbons the collect and the psalter for the day, and the catechism for Sunday School. And in those small services the congregation took a hearty part. Everybody sang the canticles, everybody read the psalter and said the Creed. In the back of the Prayer Book were one hundred and fifty hymns and versifications of certain psalms. One hymn and one psalm were sung at each service, and every one sang to the accompaniment of a little reed organ and a small choir.

The people of Grace would surely have come to know their bishops well, since the bishop's house was next door to the church. Mrs. Pratt's memories of Bishop Upfold add to our picture of him and of worship in the Church in those days (**Episcopal Bishops**, p 21-23):

> A Bishop was in some way almost like the Apostles, and had received some strange and holy power, part of which he would give to us when we should be confirmed. Bishop Upfold was a rather austere Englishman who was wholly absorbed in the catholicity of his sacred calling. He was plain and dignified in appearance. He was a High Churchman, teaching constantly all Catholic doctrine; but he was not ritualistic except as the Prayer Book rites directed. There was nothing extraneous in his service; he did not exhume discarded practices of the English Church to bewilder his simple flock. There was never a hint of Latin fulsomeness or sensationalism. The plain, forceful teachings of the Church, in a "tongue understanded of the people" was his interpretation of his high calling

Clerical vestments were very simple. The alb and the chasuble had never been heard of and I doubt whether Bishop Upfold wore a rochet. His chimere or surplice was very long, and around his neck were the clerical bands, consisting of a band of lawn covering the collar, from which depended two other bands, stiffly starched. This was probably devised to conceal the ordinary collar, the Roman collar not having yet been adopted by our clergy.

Bishop Upfold did not permit the use of flowers in the chancel. The worship was the adornment.

Here is one of the stories about Bishop Upfold which Mrs. Pratt had heard from Emily Upfold, the bishop's daughter (**Episcopal Bishops**, p. 25):

Bishop Upfold had a gentle humor … . Dr. Pusey was then very prominent in England because of his part in the great Oxford Movement. The movement, which was a renewal of the fundamental tenets of our faith, had sympathizers among Churchmen of this country, among whom was Bishop Upfold. In America Pusey's name was often pronounced "pussy". One day the Bishop went into a closet in which he kept certain books. Opening the door, he was surprised by a plaintive "meow" and looking behind a stack of books he saw the house cat with a litter of new kittens. The Bishop summoned the family to see the novel arrangement, "showing great discrimination," he said, and then gently raising the mother cat, he added, "They call me a Pussyite and I guess I am."

The bishop, of course, would not have always been available to Grace Church. He spent much of his time traveling the state over log-corduroy roads and in all kinds of weather, despite rather fragile health. (In 1863, for example, his doctor prescribed "magnetic electricity" for Upfold's neuralgia.) He recorded in his diary, "I think I shall die of the hog's lard and cold spare-room sheets I endure on my visitations." Whether it was of hog's lard and cold sheets or not, Bishop Upfold did die in 1872, just as Grace was struggling to establish itself.

A part of the struggle for Grace was financial. And a part of the cause was outside the church's control. The depression following the Panic of 1873 brought hard times which lasted ten years. (In the 1880's there were a number of bank failures in Indianapolis.) The city was growing dramatically (from 18,611 in 1860 to 169,164 in 1900); however, much of the growth was among ethnic groups with no natural allegiance to the Episcopal Church.

Upfold's successor was Joseph Cruikshank Talbot, already known to Grace and the rest of the diocese because he had been rector of Christ Church in Indianapolis and then Bishop Coadjutor for seven years previous to Bishop Upfold's death. (Before being elected Coadjutor, Talbot had been Missionary Bishop of the Northwest. Since that jurisdiction included North Dakota, South Dakota, Nebraska, Kansas, Montana, Wyoming, Colorado, New Mexico, Utah, Arizona, and Nevada, he was famous in the Church as the "Bishop of All Outdoors.")

In 1865, for his first Christmas as Coadjutor, Bishop Talbot had come from his home in Terre Haute to Indianapolis. On December 24 he officiated at Christ Church; on Christmas Day he was at Grace, where he administered Holy Communion to Bishop Upfold.

Mrs. Pratt describes Bishop Talbot as a "portly, impressive personage, emanating well-being and enthusiasm; very agreeable, and reflecting in his manner his southern birth and training." She also tells how insistent he was about instruction in the catechism: "Learning of the Catechism was stressed at the opening of classes for confirmation. No slipping into the Church in some easy way! No hearing a few lectures and thus being prepared; the Catechism was the sine qua non" (**Episcopal Bishops**, p. 29)

Bishop Talbot's diary gives us little glimpses into parish events at Grace in the early days. In 1871, for example, the Grace Church picnic was held in June at the new fairgrounds, which the bishop found to be a "poor place." In that same year, a joint Thanksgiving service for the congregations of Christ Church, Grace Church, and Holy Innocents was held at Christ Church. The preacher was The Rev. Warren H. Roberts, rector of Grace Church.

In another memoir of Indianapolis, Charlotte Cathcart's **Indianapolis From Our Old Corner** (Indiana Historical Society, 1965), we learn that Pennsylvania Street had a streetcar line with a "side switch at the

Blind Asylum on North Street" which terminated at St. Joseph with a turntable right in front of the "small, frame Grace Episcopal Church." The author also tells us that

> The first streetcars, which were called "bobtails," had five windows on each side and a small step at the rear. In winter straw was spread on the floor to keep the passenger's feet dry, and the drivers, who rode outside, wore long bearskin coats. Later there were iron stoves in the cars, which passengers who felt cold would sometimes stoke with more coal. The small black mules had a difficult time when the cars would slide off the track, as they often did in icy weather.

Going to church must have sometimes been a real adventure for the people of Grace!

We know the names of a few of those people attending Grace Church from the list of founding families and from vestry lists. Names of prominent Indianapolis families appear in those lists.

*The Indianapolis News* reported, for example, that Mrs. J.O.D. Lilly and Mrs. E.W. Sloane "received" New Year's calls on January 1, 1870. Both were wives of Grace Church vestrymen. Mrs. E.W. Sloane's address was 451 North Tennessee Street; her daughter had recently married Col. Eli Lilly.

The J.O.D. Lilly family was not related to the Eli Lilly family of the pharmaceutical firm. J.O.D. Lilly was the owner of a paint manufacturing business which would later become Lilly Industrial Coatings. J.O.D. Lilly was Senior Warden from 1868 until 1874, when he was replaced by W.H. Thurston. (There was no rotation of vestry in the 19th century, and wardens often served for many years.)

Of the original list of Christ Church families who left to form Grace Church in 1864, many evidently did not stay at Grace Church. We have already noted that David Snyder was heavily involved in starting St. Paul's. James L. Fugate had returned to Christ Church and become Treasurer there by 1878. W.J. Holliday had returned to Christ Church by 1875, when he was appointed to a committee of leading citizens to plan a Centennial Celebration in Indianapolis. Dr. George Mears also returned and was buried from Christ Church on May 20, 1879. Dr. Mears had been a vestryman of Christ Church, a member of the Diocesan Standing Committee, and a Trustee of the Diocese. The pulpit of Christ Church is a memorial to him. He was a member of the Board of Health and was on the staff of the City Hospital in 1867. One wonders if the Mears and Fugate and Holliday families left because of the discouraging and shaky start of Grace—and of the changes in clergy leadership.

Those changes certainly came quickly. In 1868 Bishop Upfold announced to the annual convention that Martin Averill had resigned to become the rector of the newly organized parish of St. John's in Elkhart. His successor was The Rev. Charles B. Davidson, D.D., who quickly left to go to the Diocese of Ohio in 1871. During his tenure the number of communicants increased to 66. The parochial report for 1871 indicated that Holy Communion had been celebrated only four times in the course of the year. (True, there must have been a vacancy for part of that year; however, it is also true that the primary public service during that era in the Episcopal Church was Morning or Evening Prayer.)

The next rector was The Rev. Warren H. Roberts, who came to Indiana from Pittsburgh, and who left Grace to go to St. John's, Lafayette, in 1874. Next came The Rev. Harvey Orrin Judd, a deacon from Maryland who was ordained priest by Bishop Talbot on Trinity Sunday, 1874. In 1875, there were 96 communicants; but the number of Sunday School teachers and students had declined since 1871. Mr. Judd stayed as rector less than four years; nevertheless, his was the second longest tenure in the history of the parish up to that time.

In the spring and summer of 1878, Bishop Talbot organized St. Anna's School for girls. It opened on September 12 with 34 pupils in the house just south of Grace Church on Pennsylvania Street—the house which had been the bishop's residence during Bishop Upfold's episcopate. (Bishop Talbot lived in a house on the Tinker Farm just north of what is now 16th when he first moved to Indianapolis in 1867; in March of 1871 he moved to a house built for him just south of W.H. Morrison's house on the Circle.) The Rev. Jonas B. Clarke, of Iowa, was to be head of the school and rector of Grace Church. Faculty were E.A. Bradley (later rector of Christ Church and candidate for Bishop in 1883) and J.S. Reed. St. Anna's, a "Diocesan Boarding and Day School for girls and young ladies," was the first of several incarnations of a girl's school associated with Grace and All Saints. Bishop Talbot gave an impassioned address to the convention of 1878 about the school: "It will educate the future mothers of the Church, and, through them, train the coming generation in her holy ways—train too, as no other influence can or will." Bishop Talbot was also worried that Episcopalians were sending their children to Roman Catholic schools, "upon the plea that we have no school of our own."

A copy of an advertisement for the school is reprinted in the Mote **History of All Saints**. The address listed is 477 Pennsylvania Street. Bishop Talbot is cited as the "Founder and Visitor." In addition to being headmaster and rector, Clarke was professor of "Moral and Intellectual Science", English literature, ancient literature, and classics. Mr. Bradley lectured on sacred music and church architecture. Mr. Reed, "Rector of the Cathedral Church" (St. Paul's) and member of the Society of Biblical Archeology of London, lectured on archeology. A Professor Jaillet taught French. Miss Louise Bright was "in charge of the School Room." Miss Helen Clarke taught music; Madame Flora Wulschner, conversational German; L.J. McCoy, penmanship; Miss Grace Clarke, mathematics, drawing and painting; Madame Ada Heine, vocal music. Miss Grace Clarke must have been very busy indeed because she was also listed as teacher of the Primary Department. The advertisement assures the reader that "The eight teachers … are thoroughly experienced and competent persons." Furthermore, "The object of this foundation is to establish, maintain and perpetuate on an avowed Christian basis in this Diocese, State and city, a systematic and thorough course on instruction for children and youth in good English, ancient and modern languages … Our new school building, chapel and 'House' are well ordered and located conviently (*sic*!) for the comfort and success of the school." The advertisement shows Grace Church with the former Bishop's House to the side. Behind the church is another building with a small belfry and cross. According to the advertisement, scholarships were available. The Bishop Talbot scholarship was for the education of a person nominated by the Bishop. The Hon. David Macy scholarship was available to a student nominated by the rector of the school, and the Diocesan scholarship was for one nominated by the Standing Committee of the Diocese. Tuition was $275 per year for boarders. Day pupils paid $12-$15 per quarter; primary children, $5-10 per quarter. There were extra fees for music and art. The fee for boarders included board, washing of "1 dozen plain pieces", fuel, lights, Latin, English, and a "seat in church" For a maximum fee of $325 boarders could also have instruction in pipe organ or piano.

By 1882, however, Mr. Clarke had left the parish and the school. The Rev. William Richmond was made Minister in Charge of Grace, but there were only 22 communicants. There is no record to suggest a reason for the decline, but both church and school had fallen on hard times. St. Anna's had closed before Clarke's departure.

Grace had been founded on diocesan property with the blessing of Bishop Upfold. Bishop Talbot had kept an interested eye on the parish and was particularly interested in its school. And now, just when Grace Church needed leadership most, Bishop Talbot was in failing health. He died on January 15, 1883 after a year's illness.

When the new Bishop, David Buell Knickerbacker, arrived, he would find the church closed for worship and rented out for use as a gymnasium. From 1882 until early in 1884, Grace Church existed only as a memory.

In his address made at the annual convention in 1886 and preserved in the Journal, Bishop Knickerbacker said:

> In coming to the diocese of Indiana and looking over its church property in this city, it was to me a sad sight to find this consecrated church desecrated by being rented for a gymnasium to a secular school. I resolved that as soon as the lease expired I would reclaim it for the holy uses to which it had been consecrated and strive to regather its scattered flock and to win others to share its privileges of holy worship ... Accordingly after restoring it to comparative decency and order, on the 1st of October, 1884, I appointed a priest to the work, personally guaranteeing his support. Quietly and unobtrusively for a year and a half the work has gone on.

Services were resumed. Deloss Root (a founder) and William Edmunds were elected wardens; The Rev. Augustine Prentiss was made rector. In the 1885 parochial report, there was an increase to 41 communicants. The Sunday School reported 60 students.

Grace Church was alive again. And Bishop Knickerbacker had plans for it.

Circa 1878-1882

# ST. ANNA'S SCHOOL,

*PROTESTANT EPISCOPAL,*

## A BOARDING AND DAY SCHOOL FOR GIRLS,

477 N. PENNSYLVANIA ST., INDIANAPOLIS, IND.

### FACULTY.

THE RT. REV. JOSEPH C. TALBOT, D. D. LL. D., Founder and Visitor. THE REV. J. B. CLARKE, A. M., Rector and head Master; Moral and Intellectual Science, English Literature, Ancient History and the Classics. THE REV. E. A. BRADLEY, Rector of Christ Church, Lectures on Sacred Music and Church Architecture. THE REV. J. SANDERS REED, Rector of Cathedral Church, Member of Society of Biblical Archæology of London, Lectures on Archæology. PROF. JAILLET, Teacher of French. MISS M. LOUISE BREEN, in charge of the School Room. MISS HELEN G. CLARKE, Instrumental Music. MADAME FLORA WILHÖRNER, Conversational German. L. J. McAVOY, Professor of Penmanship. MISS GRACE B. CLARKE, Mathematics, Drawing and Painting. MADAME ADA HEINE, Vocal Music. MISS GRACE B. CLARKE, Teacher of Primary Department.

The eight teachers under the above head-ship are thoroughly experienced and competent persons in their respective departments. The object of this foundation is to establish, maintain and perpetuate on an avowed Christian basis in this Diocese, State and city, a systematic and thorough course of instruction for our children and youth in good English, ancient and modern languages. In accordance with this view all the departments of a liberal education are provided for in such a way as to secure practical and illustrative knowledge of every branch, from the rudimental to the most advanced, beginning and finishing the school education of girls. **Our New School Building, Chapel and "Home"** are well ordered, and located commonly fine, roomy and and convenient of the school. The Bishop Talbot Scholarship educates a pupil nominated by the Bishop. The Rev. David Macy Scholarship educates a pupil nominated by the Rector of the school. The Diocesan Scholarship educates a pupil nominated by the Standing Committee of the Diocese.

### CALENDAR.

There will be two sessions for the Scholastic year. **Trinity Term** will open the second Monday in September, and end Friday before Christmas. **Easter Term** will open the second Monday after Christmas, and end second Friday in June. Charges payable at the opening of each session. Boarders for Scholastic Year, $375; Day Pupils, $60, $75 and $90 per year; Primary Children, $75 to $90 per year. Music—Instrumental and Vocal—each $75 for 20 lessons; Drawing and Painting—Water Colors, $5 for 20 lessons; Oil Painting, $5 for 20 lessons. Day pupils paying $75 per annum will receive instruction in English, Latin and Music without extra charge. The minimum price for board, washing (1s. the plain pieces), bed, lights, Latin, English, seat in church, $375. The maximum price for the above, with lessons on the pipe organ or piano included, $425. Application for information and admission may be made to the Bishop of the Diocese, or directly to the Rector of the School, 477 North Pennsylvania St., Indianapolis.

Rt. Rev. Cruikshank Talbot, D.D.

# CHAPTER FOUR

## From Gymnasium to Cathedral
## Grace Cathedral: 1884-1899

In 1884, Grace Church was a gymnasium. Thanks to the new bishop, Knickerbacker, it would within two years of re-opening become a cathedral.

Grace was not the original cathedral in Indianapolis. St. Paul's, with its much larger and grander edifice seating 1,000, had previously been used as the official church of the bishop. St. Paul's had become a cathedral at the request of Bishop Talbot. The consecration of St. Paul's as the cathedral of the Diocese of Indiana took place on June 6, 1875. Thus, "Indiana became the first diocese in the United States to inaugurate the cathedral system." (This quotation and the story of St. Paul's as a cathedral are taken from Alice Ashby Roettger and Joseph F. Thompson, M.D., **Blessings on Thee Old St. Paul's**, Carmel, Indiana, 2000.) The rector and dean of St. Paul's, The Rev. John Fulton, said that his primary reason for coming to St. Paul's was to take advantage of the mission possibilities of a cathedral, since its focus would be larger than the parish and would include the entire diocese. The idea of a cathedral evidently had to be explained time and time again. At the Service of Consecration, The Rev. Hugh Miller Thompson of New York preached about the purpose and need for a cathedral. Mr. Fulton would preach on the subject later. He said that a cathedral church does not mean a "selfish, ostentatious parish ... It means no innovation on the doctrine of the church ... It does not mean the fanciful elaboration of cast-off medieval rituals, but quiet comeliness and ... decency." Fulton resigned less than a year later, on June 30, 1876, saying "It is

needless to annoy you with the details of the reasons which compel me
to my present course"
(**Blessings**, p. 30).

Alice Ashby Roettger and Joseph F. Thompson, M.D., in their history
of St. Paul's, attribute one of those reasons to conflict with Senior
Warden, W.H. Morrison. The Senior Warden was not a stranger to
church controversy: he had once sued his neighbor, Christ Church on
the Circle, over placement of the rectory stable.

The beginnings of the story of the dissolution of the cathedral
relationship go back to the election of a successor to Bishop Talbot.

> Following the January 1883 death of Bishop Talbot, a prolonged period
> of contentious political wrangling took place regarding his successor ...
> And although spokesmen stated that the extremes of "high" church-"low"
> church were almost non-existent in Indiana, backroom negotiations belied
> the fact. According to the *Indianapolis Journal*: "It may be depended upon
> that the next bishop will not be a high churchman, the laymen, particularly,
> having a decided objection to any taint of ritualism" ... *The Indianapolis
> Journal* covered the entire selection process in gossipy detail, saying at one
> point: "It is now stated, upon good authority, that Dr. [Isaac] Nicholson [of
> St. Mark's, Philadelphia] had decided to accept the bishopric, but he was
> influenced to decline by a number of letters which he had received, many of
> them anonymous, containing hints that he had better decline, as he could
> never hope to live in harmony with the members of the diocese on account
> of his high church views" ... The St. Paul's laymen present at the convention
> included [Governor and later Vice President of the United States] Thomas
> Hendricks ... Despite Hendrick's efforts [to elect another candidate,
> Nelson Rulison of Cleveland], the Reverend David B. Knickerbacker from
> Minneapolis was elected. (**Blessings**, pp 37-38)

Knickerbacker was consecrated as a bishop at the national General
Convention of the Church instead of in Indianapolis. Perhaps St.
Paul's, the logical site locally, would not have been appropriate under
the circumstances.

Shortly after the election, The Rev. F.M.S. Taylor resigned as rector and
dean of St. Paul's. The issue then became one of control over selection
of his successor. Would the candidate be that of the bishop or of the
vestry? Knickerbacker did not like the first choice of St. Paul's, the

Rev. Dr. Sidney Corbett. In 1884, the parish called The Rev. Joseph S. Jenkes, Jr., "who had seconded Hendricks's nomination of Nelson Rulison." Knickerbacker accepted Jenkes as rector, but "Hendricks had not supported Knickerbacker for bishop and continued to oppose him and/or his own church's continued designation as a cathedral church." In 1885 Hendricks introduced a motion to the Diocesan Convention abrogating the agreement between St. Paul's and the diocese which had made it a cathedral. "The motion carried. It had been introduced and passed without explanation or comment" (**Blessings**, pp 38-39).

At the next convention in 1886, Bishop Knickerbacker's address noted he did not have a "proper home for the celebration of those functions that belong to his office." He went on to praise Grace Church for having "its seats free to all." (In other words, the pews were not rented as a means of supporting the parish, the usual practice. Knickerbacker had introduced the envelope system of giving to replace pew rental in his former diocese.) Grace Church, re-established under the personal direction of the bishop, was not governed by a vestry. There would be no Senior Warden or powerful laity to fight with the bishop for control. Instead Grace had a committee selected from the congregation and a priest appointed by the bishop. Grace Church, despite its modest building, would become the Bishop's Church. Technically, Grace would be a Pro-cathedral—that is, a parish designated as the seat of the bishop.

The year of the congregation's new status as a cathedral was also the year that "Women's Work" was organized at Grace. Miss Emily Upfold, the former bishop's daughter, had introduced a Woman's Auxiliary to the Board of Missions in the Diocese of Indiana in 1884. By 1886 two guilds were already active at Grace. St. Mary's Guild had 11 members and had raised $103.87 for altar expenses. The guild reported that Mrs. J. Schmuck and Mrs. Lina Bario, were its president and secretary. St. Agnes Guild had eight members. Its officers were Mrs. J.O. Cooper and Miss Mattie Madison. The two guilds reported to Miss Upfold in 1886 that they intended to merge into one Grace Church Guild.

The other significant event of 1886 was the reopening of a school for girls. This time the name was The Indianapolis Institute for Young

Ladies. It opened in September, 1886, at 447 North Pennsylvania, next to the church. Professor James Lyon and his wife were in charge of the school. Mr. Lyon's first report, preserved in the Convention Journal for 1886, said, "The house adjoining the school building had been leased by the Principals Lyons in time to receive twenty boarding pupils in September, and an able corps of teachers have been engaged."

Bishop Knickerbacker had yet more plans for his new cathedral. In 1889, a quarter of a square block at what was then known as Tinker Road (later 16th Street) and Central Avenue was purchased by the diocese. In a document dated January 30, 1889, and preserved in the diocesan archives,

> John Wocher, Jr.. and E. Bertha Wocher his wife of Marion County in the State of Indiana convey and warrant to the Trustees of the Protestant Episcopal Church of the Diocese of Indiana in the State of Indiana for the sum of Ten Thousand Seven Hundred and Twenty Five Dollars the following real estate in Marion County in the State of Indiana to wit: Lots One Two Three and Four in John Wocher Junior Second Subdivision of a part of the south east quarter of Section thirty six Township Sixteen North of Range Three East in the City of Indianapolis.

At the 1889 convention, Bishop Knickerbacker would review the transformation of Grace from a closed and partially dismantled building in 1884 into a self-supporting congregation (reporting 135 communicants that year). He also rejoiced in telling the convention that a generous member had deeded 1,200 acres of land in Arkansas to the diocese. Another person had informed him that "he has made his will leaving $5000 for the endowment of the cathedral." The seeds of the resources, and certainly the vision, which would result in the building of All Saints Cathedral were now planted.

There were two flourishing Episcopal churches downtown, Christ Church and St. Paul's. Grace Church, just a few blocks from them, always ran a rather distant third. The northern part of the city was growing. It was time to move.

The new property on Central Avenue was soon occupied. The "new" Grace Cathedral was placed on the property at a cost of $5,000. The building, however, or at least a part of it, was simply the old frame structure which had been on Pennsylvania Street.

In a whimsical volume called **Autobiography of a Cathedral**, by Louis Howland, the author has the cathedral speak for itself to tell its story of joys and sorrows (p.4).

> It was an old and very humble parish church which was moved from one site to another, becoming a cathedral by adoption. Two other qualities, in addition to the ugliness and meanness of my early days, are, or have been mine, though not so often found in other members of my family—youth and unfixedness. The ramshackle wooden structure was moved from one site to another. As a cathedral I was again moved—a short distance this time—and raised sufficiently to permit the construction of a basement under the building.

This description places the frame building at first at a site on the diocesan property other than its eventual resting place facing 16th Street near the alley which parallels Central Avenue.

A new Pilcher organ (whose pipes have been used in a number of re-buildings since) was donated to the renewed Grace Cathedral and valued at $2,500.

The Rev. George E. Swan was the rector during this transition, replacing Mr. Prentiss who resigned in 1887. At this same time, the Indianapolis Institute moved to a building adjoining the church on the 16th and Central property. In 1891, the name of the school was changed to St. Mary's Hall. Mr. Swan resigned as rector to assume the duties of Principal of St. Mary's. His wife was Co-Principal. Mr. and Mrs. Lyons remained as instructors. The next report for the school spoke of 12 boarders and 45 day students.

The Trustees of the Diocese made a schedule of all property owned by the Diocese in 1891 and reported these assets to convention. The Indianapolis properties were listed as the Episcopal Residence on North Pennsylvania St, five houses and lots at St. Joe and Pennsylvania, a lot on North Meridian Street, St. Mary's Hall and Grace Cathedral on Central Avenue. And in Arkansas the church owned 1,200 acres which had been given in 1889 "for the benefit of Grace Church." In 1893,

100 feet of land adjoining St. Mary's Hall was purchased. In 1894, apparently another 60 by 200 feet adjoining St. Mary's was added. This was to provide a home for the homeless to be called the "Tuttle Home and Orphanage."

Sarah Pratt lived across the street from the Central Avenue property for 20 years. According to her memoirs,

> At the same time was started another building intended as a home for aged Churchwomen. This building, I think, was built by donations from Church people, for the Bishop used to present the subject at his visitations and also by means of his little paper, The Church Worker. I remember his coming to Logansport, which was then my home, when he was soliciting for the institution. To swell the fund for the home for aged Churchwomen, Bishop Knickerbacker asked for old stamps, which were then at a premium. They came pouring in by the hundreds. Old war letters, old love letters, old bills were exhumed from attics and strongholds, and the stamps cut off and sent to the Bishop, Mrs. Knickerbacker, who survived her husband for many years, told me that the Bishop showed an almost childish interest in those stamps. He would place a quantity of them in an old dishpan, and after submerging them for a while, would detach and assort the stamps, and send them to dealers or private philatelists. This impresses me as a rather restful diversion from ordinary Episcopal routine. I still have bundles of letters from the envelopes of which the stamps are gone, stamps which went into that building fund. I have a letter from my young son, dated February 20, 1893, which states, "We have 357 stamps for the bishop now. Quite a good many." I lived opposite that home for twenty years. However, the building was never used for its designated purpose, for there were not enough old ladies to be found in the diocese. It was used for a Bishop's residence and then as a boys' school. (**Episcopal Bishops**, pp. 34-35)

The next rector of Grace was Christopher S. Sargent. He is the first priest of Grace/All Saints whom we can call "Father." Sarah S. Pratt tells us in her memoirs that he preferred that title. He had come to the diocese in 1889 and served Grace from 1891 to 1895. At the time of the 1896 convention his address was listed as Leipsic, Germany. By the next year he had transferred to the Diocese of Milwaukee, but in 1898 he returned to Indianapolis as the first rector of a new parish, St. David's. Mrs. Pratt says of St. David's, "It was a small church with a pleasant rectory, on Twenty-first Street, which was then considered very far north. The congregation was composed of Churchmen who desired a more formal service than was used elsewhere. Father Sargent, as he loved to be called was very devout and accomplished. The functions at St. David's were well attended." (**Episcopal Bishops**, p.45)

Fr. Sargent's practice and teaching of fasting is reflected in the following story told by Mrs. Pratt: "We were always glad when the Auxiliary met there [at St. David's]. Once when Mrs. Sargent served breakfast after early service during the Clerical Retreat, on a Friday in Lent, she said, 'Of course, I couldn't serve them meat, so I served asparagus on toast.' I answered, 'You have obeyed the letter of the law but not the sprit. Nobody could fast on asparagus on toast.'" (**Episcopal Bishops**, p 45)

In other words, Grace, the predecessor of All Saints, was not the "high church" of Indianapolis. One wonders if Fr. Sargent had left Grace because Bishop Knickerbacker's liturgical oversight had prevented him from the practices he preferred. By the time of Sargent's return to Indianapolis, a new bishop would be in office. It is also interesting to note that by the turn of the century, Grace had ceased to be the northern outpost of the Episcopal Church in the city. The city's relentless march northward had passed 16<sup>th</sup> Street.

A new **Book of Common Prayer** was issued in 1892—the first revision since the original American Prayer Book of 1789. This was not a radical revision, but rather it was enriched with some additional prayers and canticles, and made slightly more flexible. Two canticles, the *Magnificat* and the *Nunc Dimittis*, were added to Evening Prayer. The texts for the approximately 200 hymns printed in the back of the 1789 book and so loved by Sarah Pratt, were now replaced by the **Hymnal Revised and Enlarged** of 1892. Now there were 679 hymns from which to choose. At the front of the hymnal, the Canon of the Church on Music was reprinted: "The Hymns which are set forth by authority and Anthems in the words of Holy Scripture are allowed to be sung in all Congregations of this Church before and after Morning and Evening Prayer, and also before and after Sermons at the discretion of the Minister whose duty it shall be, by standing directions or from time to time to appoint such authorized Hymns or Anthems as are to be sung." Note that hymns are "allowed" (not necessarily assumed), that only the authorized hymn texts or Scripture could be set to music, that there was no regulation of the music (just the words), and that music at Holy Communion (except at the sermon) is not even mentioned.

Also in 1892, Grace received one of its treasures: a silver chalice and paten still used on special occasions and called the "Apostles' Set" because figures of the apostles appear on the jeweled chalice. These were given by Captain Oskaloosa M. Smith, of the U.S. Army in memory of his parents. A crozier in the same pattern is now kept at Christ Church Cathedral.

Grace Cathedral at its new location was used regularly for Diocesan events. The Special Convention for the purpose of electing a new bishop was held there on February 6, 1895.

Bishop Knickerbacker had died suddenly of pneumonia on December 31, 1894. His last official acts were at Grace. He had celebrated Holy Communion there on Christmas Day and attended the Grace Sunday School Festival on December 27.

*The Indianapolis Journal* reported the bishop's funeral on January 5, 1895. One headline read "Imposing and Solemn Ceremonies at St. Paul's Church." Evidently Grace was not large enough for "all who could possibly crowd into the large St. Paul's Church including 13 ministers of the church holding the rank of bishop." The church was decorated with black and purple streamers "relieved by a strand of cedar." The choir was "surpliced" and "composed in part of boys." Burial was in Crown Hill Cemetery where the *Gloria in Excelsis* was sung. "It was severely cold and many shook with chill during the service."

The delegates from the cathedral to the convention in February, 1895, to elect a successor to Bishop Knickerbacker were Fr. Sargent, A.P. Lewis, E.A. Munson, William Archdeacon, and J.O. Cooper. On February 5, there had been special observances remembering Bishop Knickerbacker at Grace. "Devotions" were led by Bishop Tuttle of Missouri; and, in the evening, Bishop Hugh Miller Thompson of Mississippi had conducted a memorial service for Bishop Knickerbacker. The voting of the clergy for a successor to Bishop Knickerbacker took place in the Guild Room of Grace. The laity voted in the nave. The Rev. John Hazen White of Faribault, Minnesota, who had been nominated by John Hilliard Ranger (rector of Christ Church) and seconded by Louis Howland of Christ Church (but soon to move to Grace), was elected. The *Gloria in Excelsis* was again sung and the Secretary instructed to telegraph White. By resolution, 10 dollars were allowed to the sexton of Grace Cathedral for his extra work in connection with the convention.

In Louis Howland's **Autobiography of a Cathedral,** that convention of 1895 is remembered in some detail. Bishop Hugh Miller Thompson "could not, even if he had tried, have preached a poor sermon." This first electing convention to be held at Grace Cathedral, he says, "was not without heat. There were many candidates, including three priests resident in the diocese, and many ballots, in the neighborhood of forty, as I remember" (p. 12).

According to Sarah Pratt, the Bishop-elect "was engaged in the practical job of putting up a stove" when he received that telegram of election. Mrs. Pratt continues with a description of Bishop White and of his liturgical preferences:

> This seemed an augury of good. Bishop White gave both heat and light to his diocese ... [The Whites] lived for a time in a house on Pennsylvania Street owned by the Diocese and later removed to the Central Avenue residence ... Bishop White will be remembered as a man of strong personality. He had a very sonorous voice and there was no difficulty in hearing him. He was of commanding height, being the tallest in the long procession of Bishops that entered the opening service of the triennial conventions. His height was emphasized because he wore a rochet with a trail at least half-a-yard long ... Bishop White disliked the names "High Church" and "Low Church." "We are all the same Church. It is just the way of doing it and not the thing itself," he would say ... Bishop White did not always enjoy a formal choral service. He said, "I have listened to a Sanctus twenty minutes long when I became so tired that I had to lean against the Altar." He once openly reproved a clergyman at the Pro-Cathedral, Indianapolis, for having candles on the altar at Christmas. However, after his first visit to England, he was so deeply impressed with ritual that thereafter he used it always. Even his pronunciation of certain ecclesiastical terms became anglicized. Once when Mrs. White was asked about the matter she said, "My husband is a thorough Connecticut Churchman and that explains it all" (**Episcopal Bishops**, pp. 42ff).

Perhaps that does not "explain it all," since probably no one but Mrs. White knew what she meant by the term "Connecticut Churchman." The new bishop may have disliked talk of "High Church" and "Low Church", but questions of how much and what kind of ritual would trouble Grace/All Saints for years to come. And one can imagine that the priests of Grace, subject to public reproach (like the unfortunate one who lit candles on Christmas), were not always happy to have the Bishop right next door (after his move to the property on Central Avenue into the building which had been intended for the aged ladies).

Bishop White had not been consecrated at Grace Cathedral. The much larger St. Paul's had been chosen instead. However, White used his cathedral for other purposes. On June 1, 1895, for example, he used it to for both a sad and a happy event. In the morning he read a sentence of deposition there, with Fr. Sargent present, upon The Rev. Joseph S. Jenkes (who had seconded Governor Hendricks's candidate for Bishop at the time of the Knickerbacker election). Jenkes had renounced the worship of the Episcopal Church to join a religious order of another communion. Then in the evening of that first day in June, the Bishop read Evening Prayer, preached the baccalaureate sermon for St. Mary's Hall, and confirmed eight (perhaps students of St. Mary's Hall?).

The regular convention for 1895 was again held at Grace on June 4 and 5. Delegates from Grace were A.P. Lewis, E.A. Munson, William Archdeacon (quite an appropriate name for an Episcopalian), and Albert Michie.

Bishop Knickerbacker had faced a crisis involving Grace Parish after Bishop Talbot's death. Bishop White now faced a crisis involving the school which was Grace's sister agency and neighbor. The Report of Trustees of the Diocese to the convention of 1895 describes the action taken with regard to the situation at St. Mary's Hall,

> By action of Trustees the name of the young ladies school was changed from St. Mary's to Knickerbacker Hall. The school has been conducted by the Rev. Mr. Swan and Mrs. Swan as a private enterprise under Diocesan supervision. This proved a source of embarrassment to the late Bishop and the Trustees as well as to Rev. and Mrs. Swan. The Trustees after carefully looking into the affairs of the school unanimously decided with the full

concurrence and approval of Bishop White to relieve Rev. and Mrs. Swan from its charge and make it a Diocesan school under the charge of the Bishop and Trustees and responsible for its maintenance and support. In arranging with the Rev. and Mrs. Swan, the Trustees conceded an indebtedness due them of $1,937.50 and assumed an indebtedness of $1,300, a part of which will run for one year, without interest, taking a bill of sale of all furniture and effects, amounting to about $1,500 … The Trustees believe … that in a short time Knickerbacker Hall will prove a source of revenue.

Bishop White, in his first Address to convention, outlined his vision for the Cathedral:

I can not refrain from saying to you, dear brethren, that in view of all that Bishop Knickerbacker has done and given to this diocese there should be some lasting and living memorial to him here, that will generously express the appreciation of the Church people of Indiana for his life and service. I can think of none that would with more propriety constitute such a memorial than the upbuilding of a beautiful temple to God in place of the present pro Cathedral, and for which I understand he himself set apart so considerable a provision. Should those who are blessed with large means be moved spontaneously to take up this thought, and prepare the way for carrying out such a plan by generous benefactions to that end, it would then be possible to give humbler Churchmen an opportunity to add their offerings, that all might have a portion in a monument to one who deserves to be honored by those among whom and for whom he labored.

To paraphrase I Corinthians 3:6, Knickerbacker planted, White watered, but God was not to give the growth to the vision of a new cathedral until the tenure of yet another bishop, Joseph Marshall Francis. Evidently "those blessed with large means" did not step forward "spontaneously to take up this thought."

There were other portions of Bishop White's first address which concerned Grace directly: "Let me say that the hope of a diocese or a parish lies in the stability of its rectorships. Let me urge this thought most affectionately upon both clergy and laity. The consequences to both clergymen and parishes is most disastrous from frequent changes in rectorship." Certainly what the bishop was describing applied to Grace, which still had not had a priest stay for more than four years.

The bishop continued:

> In a modest corner of the Diocese and without ostentation there is busy an agency to be much commended, and deserving of great expansion. I mean the little company of Sisters who are at work at the Cathedral. We are all painfully sensible that in some quarters of the Church there is more mental distress over their plain garb, their habits of life, their self-assumed obligations and their modes of service, than is occasioned by the immoderate, unbridled, impenitent irreligion they seek to soften. We do not share that feeling, nor do we fear the Church is in any danger of departing in any degree from her holy faith because she finds it wise to seize upon and use every agency capable of consecration in breaking down the kingdom of wickedness, Satan and sin ... In coming to my duty I am much grieved to find Knickerbacker Hall in great financial perplexity. Too much cannot be said in pride of the patient, persevering service which has been given to it by its leaders, Mr. and Mrs. Swan ... I have felt that this is the most fitting time to re-cast the work of the school and put it on a different, if not a better, basis. After careful consultation with Mr. and Mrs. Swan and the trustees, we have agreed upon a plan for assuming the care of the school, and carrying on its future work.

The order of sisters was named Sisters of Mercy. They had been formed sometime in the 1890's, but they seem not to have been involved with the running of the school. And from the tone of the bishop's remarks, they must have needed all the support they could get in a hostile environment.

The convention reports show that Grace Cathedral's payment to the diocese for all purposes for 1894-1895 was $339.65. For purposes of comparison, that of Christ Church was $725.32 and of St. Paul's, $594.40. The wardens for the year were Albert Michie and A.P. Lewis. E.A. Munson was clerk and William H. Archdeacon, treasurer.

At that convention Miss Emily Upfold's report on the diocesan library was read. If not already located there, the library would also soon be on the Central Avenue property. It had been formed from the bequests of Indiana's three departed bishops. Bishop Knickerbacker, for example, added 924 volumes.

A report to convention also noted that the population of Indianapolis was now 125,000.

The Woman's Auxiliary report for Grace mentions 31 members, who had raised $111.80.

> Regular missionary teas have been held monthly and well attended. The various subdivisions have met weekly. The Diocesan Branch has given $22 for diocesan missions and collected $30 for diocesan assessment. The general society has given $21 for diocesan mission; the domestic branch has spent $34.60 for parish purposes and the foreign branch has given $6.75 for foreign missions. Mrs. F.M. Curtis President; Mrs. Albert Michie, Secretary.

The Woman's Auxiliary to the Board of Missions was a "missionary" work. There was also the "parish work" of the women at Grace. A "parochial branch" with seven members had raised $96.51, a portion of which was to help with the debt incurred in the building of the Guild Room. Mrs. James Ross was president, and Mrs. W.S. Budd secretary. The Altar Guild's five members had raised $13. Their officers were Miss Fanny Carleton and Miss N.W. Babcock. St. Faith's Chapter of Daughters of the King listed 18 active members, 5 associates, and 17 inactive. They had raised $104.65 to be spent for various purposes including a choir camp. Their president and secretary were Mrs. Carl Ellis Franklin and Anna W Curtis. There was also a St. Agnes Guild for Little Girls which had raised $15.75 and spent $15.20. Mrs. Welby Gillitt led this group.

A year later at the June 1896 convention, also held at Grace Cathedral, the situation at 16th and Central and the diocesan financial crisis were very much the focus of the Bishop's annual address:

> The Diocesan property comprises all the Cathedral property, the Episcopal Residence [next to Grace], Knickerbacker Hall, the Church Home and Howe school [in northern Indiana] ... Knickerbacker Hall has been run at a loss every year for the past five or six years until there is an indebtedness standing against it of $9,000. I have taken the position that we should fund our indebtedness until such time as it can be paid, return our borrowed sums to the trust funds of the Diocese so that they may be secured to their proper uses and then apply ourselves to the extinguishing of our debt in a legitimate way. The Church Home and Orphanage is no nearer completion than a year ago, and as the result of my year's consideration of the enterprise I should say there is not enough interest in it within the Diocese to finish it in ten years or to sustain it in a lifetime. The only question is how to dispose

of it ... The Bishop's home is a large and expensive residence, costly to keep up, in which there is invested $25,000. Without any loss to Diocesan dignity or interest we can part with this expensive property, remove our embarrassment to our Cathedral institution, finish the Church Home as a Diocesan house for the residence of the Bishop and such clergy as he may desire to associate with him in missionary work, properly house the Diocesan library in a place accessible to all who desire to use it without inconvenience to any one and convert a sufficient sum into the episcopate fund to provide for the Bishop's maintenance. From this suggestion let me pass on to a consideration of ... our Cathedral work. Last summer I had laid before me a proposition by the rector and vestry of Christ Church to sell the present property, unite with the Cathedral congregation, build a dignified edifice for its work and worship and make it the center of the missionary and educational work of the Diocese. After giving it most careful study I have given it my most enthusiastic commendation for a variety of reasons. First, the Cathedral work as at present carried on is feeble in the extreme and far from able to support its operation with the dignity and power that will attract to it the vast population within the radius of a mile or more to which it should minister. We are losing ground every day by this failure to seize our opportunities. Christ Church, on the other hand can never hope to realize a great future as at present located ... St Paul's parish has equipped itself to do the central work of the city and can provide all the Church facilities which are needed there. The two parishes are too near together for the best development of the life of both in any event ... The death of the rector of Christ Church made the filling of that position very difficult without reference to this (proposed union with Grace) ... The Rev A. J. Graham has been called to the rectorship of Christ Church with the clear stipulation that it carries with it the deanship of the Cathedral when the real estate market will permit of the sale of the present property without sacrifice.

The bishop had clearly stated a mission strategy for Indianapolis: secure a loan on Knickerbacker Hall and pay back the diocesan trust funds used to bail it out; sell the expensive Bishop's Residence; remodel the proposed home for aged ladies (which had little or no support now that Bishop Knickerbacker was no longer alive to collect stamps for it) as a residence plus diocesan library; close Christ Church on the Circle; merge it with Grace and build a new cathedral on 16th Street. His plan was to be only implemented partially. The continuing existence of Christ Church on the Circle witnesses to the defeat of the Bishop's solution for the problem of two parishes too close together and another trying to be a cathedral without sufficient resources.

Eli Lilly provides the outline of the story from the point of view of Christ Church. In June 1895, Christ Church proposed improvements to and redecoration of its building to cost $12,000. Pledges of $4500 were reported, but on June 21 it was proposed instead to merge with Grace Church and build a cathedral in the north of Indianapolis. On July 18, a committee was appointed to sell Christ Church. Then in October, The Rev. Mr. Ranger, rector of Christ Church, died. His replacement was The Rev. Andrew J. Graham, who accepted in February 1896. No sale resulted from the option on the property given to Tuttle and Seguin, a real estate agency. On June 4, 1897, the new rector stated his opposition to the merger and the move and suggested raising $30,000 for improvements to Christ Church instead. The vestry then rescinded its action of July 18, 1895, for sale of the property. This was in opposition to the wishes of the Bishop, in whose home the meeting took place. Resignations from the vestry followed—Meredith Nicholson, Louis Howland, W.A. Van Buren, and W.W. Lowry. All these families transferred to Grace. Nicholson, Howland, and Van Buren had composed the committee charged with dealing with the architects for the proposed new building.

Grace needed these new families. The women's work in the congregation may have been impressive, but Grace was still "feeble," to quote the Bishop. The problem of instability in clergy leadership continued. In 1896 The Rev. Edwin Johnson, formerly of St. James, Vincennes, was priest in charge. By 1897 he would be replaced by Edgar F. Gee. Next would come John H. McKenzie, who for one year was both Dean of the Cathedral and Rector of Howe School in northern Indiana. Robert E. Grubb followed him, again for one year.

Yet, Grace continued to pay its assessments to the diocese. The Daughters of the King chapter at the cathedral even pledged in 1896 an additional $10 for the support of an Archdeacon. In that year also, Mrs. Albert Michie held the diocesan office of recording secretary of the Woman's Auxiliary. Her husband would be secretary of the Standing Committee of the diocese in the coming year.

In 1897 the Convention was, as usual, held at Grace in the first week of June. Bishop White's address for that year gives an update on Knickerbacker Hall and the plan to consolidate Central Avenue property:

> The serious illness of Mrs. McGuffey compelled her retirement, early in the year, from Knickerbacker Hall ... In December an engagement was entered into by the Trustees with the Misses Yerkes, whereby they become the Principals for the future ... The Misses Yerkes are ladies of ripe culture and large and successful experience as teachers ... Acting under your commission the Trustees of the Diocese have carried out the plans submitted to and approved by you for the completion of the Diocesan House. This has involved a great deal of difficulty and much delay, owing to our inability to make the desired loan. After repeated efforts they have succeeded in borrowing eleven thousand dollars with which they have cancelled the outstanding obligations of the Diocese and finished the Diocesan House which will in the future become the residence of the Bishop, the home of the Diocesan Library, and the center of Diocesan work. It remains for us to dispose of the present Episcopal Residence, invest the proceeds profitably in order to meet the interest on our loan and as rapidly as possible pay off the principal.

We hear nothing more about the Sisters of Mercy, but another momentous step for women's vocation to ministry had been taken. The address continues:

> On the 1st of January after most careful consideration and study, and conference with older Bishops, I instituted an order of Deaconesses in the Diocese by admitting and ordaining according to prescribed canon, Mrs. Zuna Potter Jaynes as a Deaconess attached to Grace Cathedral, and working under my personal commission. Mrs. Jaynes is a woman of mature years, and has for some time been actively and efficiently engaged in mission work in the city of Indianapolis.

Bishop White's caution reflected the fact that deaconesses were still controversial. For some time, there had been agitation in the Church for the creation of some way to recognize the ministry of women, though the Church had, in fact, been using their services all along. Gradually the agitation crystallized into a demand for the revival of the primitive order of deaconesses, and of sisterhoods. The latter was too definitely Catholic a measure to win general approval for some time. The canon establishing deaconesses and which the bishop mentions, however, was passed in 1889.

Bishop White's address to the 1897 convention was very upbeat: "There is not a parish or mission vacant and in a period of unparalleled difficulty I have scarcely had a complaint during the year from the clergy concerning their personal distress." According to the bishop's diary of actions reported to the Convention, he officiated at Evening Prayer at the "Illinois Street Mission" (corner of 22$^{nd}$ and Illinois Streets) on December 15, 1896, and January 12, 1897. This mission would later be known as St. Agnes and eventually be incorporated into St. David's parish. The Episcopal Church had marched north past Grace Cathedral.

The Bishop also told the convention:

> I believe it would be most wise for this council to make a determined effort to secure the erection of a missionary jurisdiction in the southern half of the State and to collect such data as would compel the General Convention to listen to its presentation of the facts. There is a vast Diocese really without our having foothold in it. It will never be reclaimed in any other way.

This suggestion would soon turn out to have rather momentous repercussions.

The annual report of the Trustees of the Diocese provides details on financial transactions affecting the work at 16$^{th}$ and Central. A lease of the school to the Yerkes sisters was signed for $10 per year beginning February 1, 1896, "the Misses Yerkes to be at all expenses for the conduct of the school and all expenses for repairs on building, Insurance, etc. and as an inducement for the Misses Yerkes to take said school, the Trustees would appropriate the sum of one thousand and five dollars to defray and cover the expenses of the school until June 1$^{st}$, 1897." Furthermore,

> At a meeting of the Trustees, held on February 29th, the Secretary reported that he had been able to secure a loan of eleven thousand dollars at six per cent on the property known as the Church Home. A resolution was passed instructing the President and Secretary to make such loan for a period of five years; the proceeds of said loan to be used in paying off bank and other indebtedness, and to finish the building known as the Church Home, in a suitable manner for the bishop's residence, and to get contracts for said work. The Secretary was further instructed to borrow one thousand dollars

for a period of one year to pay the street improvements bills against this property

The Trustees approved the idea of selling the Bishop's Residence at 442 North Pennsylvania (near Michigan Street). They also approved contracts for the remodeling of Grace Church in the amount of "five thousand seven hundred dollars, including steam heating." By the time of the June convention, the remodeling had been completed within the contract price, except for a small frame addition needed for structural reasons.

In business sessions, the convention approved a committee of five to follow up on Bishop White's suggestion about a missionary jurisdiction to be formed in the southern third of Indiana and funded through the national church for more intensive missionary effort than could be supported by the diocese alone.

Meredith Nicholson, the registrar of the diocese, moved a resolution that a committee on the state of the church in Indianapolis be formed. It was to be composed of the bishop, the rectors of St. Paul's, Christ Church and Holy Innocents and the dean or priest in charge of the Cathedral, along with the rectors of such other parishes as might be formed later. In addition there were to be two laymen from each of the parishes chosen by their vestries plus two laymen appointed by the bishop. The committee was "charged with the duty of promoting the aggressive development of the Church and mission work in the city of Indianapolis and with counselling and advising the Bishop and Standing Committee with reference to the location of such parishes and missions as may be hereafter established." Nicholson's experience of defeat of the plan for a new and merged cathedral parish surely was in the background of his request for a real strategy for the city and for the placement of its congregations.

The Committee on Christian Education reported to the diocese that the Misses Yerkes had undertaken the "thorough and systematic education of girls and young women ... by the most approved methods now employed by educators ... It is the desire of principals to provide all such influences as will tend to cultivate refined taste, promote unselfish common life, and develop nobility of character."

The families brought to Grace by the failure of the Christ Church merger were prominent both within and outside the church. Eli Lilly, for example, says, "The Howland family, Caroline, Louis, and Hewitt were glowingly prominent in the annals of [Christ Church] before their transfer to Grace Cathedral. Their home, near the big elm tree on Pennsylvania Street south of Thirteenth, was ever a center of culture, forthrightness and erudition" (**Little Church**, p. 236). It did not take some of these prominent church people long to exercise leadership in both the parish and the diocese. By the 1898 convention, Louis Howland was representing Grace as a delegate and Meredith Nicholson was an alternate. Louis Howland was president of the Churchman's League (which was composed of representatives of several parishes in the diocese) in 1905. His professional affiliation was with *The Indianapolis News*. Sarah Pratt remembered Howland as "a scholarly gentleman and a devout Churchman, who for several years went every Sunday to St. John's, Crawfordsville, and gave a most acceptable service" as lay reader (**Episcopal Bishops**, p. 51)

Meredith Nicholson was the author of **House of a Thousand Candles** (the setting of which was a house just south of 16th Street on Delaware). From 1903 until 1925 he wrote an average of one book a year. In 1912 Nicholson published **A Hoosier Chronicle**, a serious work examining Indiana society and politics at the turn of the century. He was a Democrat and later would become American minister to Paraguay (1933-34), Venezuela (1935-38) and Nicaragua (1938-41) under President Franklin D. Roosevelt.

The other committee member to come to Grace after the failure of the merger with Christ Church was W.A. Van Buren. He was a United States Commissioner and had been a member of the committee which had secured the first pledges at Christ Church to enable that parish to have "free seats."

Bishop White's tone at the 1898 convention of the diocese was just the opposite of his optimism of one year before:

> Our coming together this year is with the storm cloud of war just breaking about us. The eager, restless, adventuresome spirit has swept like a contagion over the land. Our youth are hungry to participate in the contest. The evils

that follow in the train of war need not be enumerated to inspire us to earnest prayer that we may speedily be returned to the avocations of peace.

The bishop leaves us no doubt about where he stood on issues of peace and war and on his willingness to face rather than avoid controversy.

His annual address then moved to a discussion of "storm clouds" hovering over the Church in his diocese and over his cathedral, in particular:

> It is to me a matter of deep regret that I cannot this year give you the same joyous report of the state of the Church in the diocese that I did a year ago ... A spirit of unrest and discontent is prevalent; a number of our parishes and missions are, or have been, without ministrations ... Another fruitful source of trouble lies in the persistence with which many clergy and a few laymen continue to indulge their taste for fanciful and questionable ritualism, even to the point of wrecking the work entrusted to them, without any perceptible advantage gained to any one or any cause ... The Church is strong and growing; is peaceful and prosperous where a vigorous Churchmanship, capable of intelligently unfolding the principles of our holy faith, still adjusts its conduct of public worship to a degree of conservative simplicity that is not beyond the taste and comprehension of the people to whom it would minister. I am unable to appreciate the spiritual condition of anyone, be he priest or layman, who exhibits that peculiar form of spiritual selfishness that demands gratification for his individual taste in such matters, even though an entire parish be ruined as a result.

The "unrest" had been named. It would be a struggle directly affecting Grace and All Saints for years to come. As the bishop's comments illustrate, the issue was ritualism, sometimes called "churchmanship" with the extremes being "high church" emphasis on ritual, vestments, etc, and "low church" emphasis on simplicity.

Next, Bishop White gave his version of what had gone wrong with the proposed merger of Grace with Christ Church into one strong cathedral in the north of the city.

> Two years ago I laid before this convention plans for the development of a strong cathedral system, which contemplated the gathering about a strong center for the missionary, educational and charitable interests of the diocese, which would do more than all else to secure a grand future to

the Church in Indiana. These plans were worked out with much careful study and conference with wise laymen and neighboring Bishops whose confidence I enjoy. The hope of my Episcopate hung on them. It is with saddest disappointment that I inform you that through influences of which I was wholly ignorant and whose hostility to this work I had not even suspected, these plans have been effectually overturned. In years to come the magnitude of this loss will be better known than it is now. Nor does the evil seem to aim at anything else than the entire destruction of what little remains of our cathedral system.

Not everyone agreed with Bishop White that the failure of the merger with Christ Church was "evil". At the convention of 1898, the same one which had heard the Bishop use the word "evil", the Committee on Missions reported,

> Christ Church for some time past has had hopes of selling its present property and of relocating farther towards the north. But this plan has now been abandoned and they have determined to unite their efforts to keep this old parish church where it is. This is wise. Christ Church, where it is now situated, with all of its associations of the past, stands for far more than the worship of the Church. It is not sentiment alone which would wish to see it remain where it is.

Who were the "influences" hostile to the bishop's "hope of my Episcopate"? Was it The Rev. Andrew Graham, the rector of Christ Church who was brought to Indianapolis to carry out the merger but seems to have changed his mind and determined that Christ Church should stay on the Circle? Was it the laity of Christ Church who voted down the plan supported by Nicholson and Howland? Was it The Rev. Mr. Gee, who had so rapidly disappeared from the scene that he was gone by the time Bishop White addressed the convention on the hostile "influence"? Whoever it was, the issues were connected to churchmanship:

> To the generous and almost unremunerated help of the Rev. Dr. McKenzie do I owe it that I have been able to administer the cathedral during the past year and to avert the ruin which was threatened in the fall and early winter. I must begin at the bottom and with the loyal help of such laymen as shall stand by me attempt to give this diocese at the Cathedral such an administration as is consistent with the formularies adopted by the Church for the government of the same and the regulation of public worship. A portion of the cathedral congregation, unwilling to submit to the Bishop's

direction of worship at the Cathedral, or deeming itself possessed of superior wisdom in matters of faith and the conduct of public worship, has drawn off and taken steps for the organization of a parish independent of the restraint the Bishop may impose at the cathedral. To this movement I have given my consent, as the canons require, but not my approval. I deem it unnecessary, unwise, self-willed and in every sense of the word schismatic. But I take it the canons provide that a given number of communicants may organize a parish, even if it is unnecessary and unwise, provided the other parishes in any given city consent. All the parishes in Indianapolis have consented and I have deemed it wise to acquiesce … It exists because its leaders have chosen to withdraw from the church as the Bishop is administering it and force my hand to make martyrs of them or permit them to commit suicide. I prefer they should commit suicide if they are determined on that course … We have nothing to do with vague, ambiguous, ingenious modern inventions, whether they spring from Roman ingenuity or Protestant ignorance … I do not feel myself compelled to put in operation every definition or decree made by the college at Rome.

The "schismatics" were in the process of forming St. David's parish. One of them was Albert Michie. Soon the "schismatics" would call Fr. Sargent back as their priest. The ritualistic practices that so roused the Bishop's ire are unnamed. As we have seen, he thought of himself "Catholic" in the Oxford Movement sense of that term, holding a "high" view of the Church as the Body of Christ as it is primarily expressed in the Eucharist, but without the "high church" ritualistic practices which were thought by many to be "Roman Catholic." His journal of official acts reflects his devotion to the daily offices, and he personally increased the number of celebrations of Holy Communion at Grace Cathedral by presiding at the Eucharist. The Sunday schedule at Grace was not the "first Sunday of the month Holy Communion" so prevalent in the church at the turn of the century. There was Holy Communion at 7 a.m. every Sunday. The later morning service (at 10:30) was Morning Prayer, Sermon, *and* Holy Communion. At 4 p.m. there was Evening Prayer. In addition to whatever practices the bishop refused at Grace, it may have been the very fact that the direction of parish life was under his thumb which caused resentment at Grace and led to the formation of St. David's. St. Paul's, just a few years before, had ceased to be the cathedral to escape the thumb of the bishop. And, of course, All Saints would later relinquish its status as a cathedral also.

By 1927, Louis Howland was able to "speak" for the Cathedral about this chapter in its history in the following words:

> I have had my dissensions, and even quarrels, mostly over ritual, and some of them were exceedingly bitter. But as they have been forgotten, and those who were parties to them are now best of friends, it seems profitless and even heartless more than merely to refer to them. They cannot be passed over wholly, for they are a part of my history. I like to believe—I do believe—that even in connection with these, my influence has been on the side of peace, charity and forbearance. Certainly I have endeavored to stand for inclusiveness and comprehensiveness—that is, for true catholicity. Much that calls itself catholicity and passes for it, does not seem to me to be that. Moderation, I know is not highly or generally esteemed, yet I have striven to cultivate it. (**Autobiography**, pp. 29-30)

The "ruin" of the fight over churchmanship began after Bishop White's return from the Lambeth Conference in England on September 1, 1897. Two days after his return he moved into the newly remodeled home next to Grace. On the sixth of the month, he met with the congregation of Grace. For the next two months, his record lists almost daily offices in the Cathedral, celebrations of Holy Communion there on Sundays and Holy Days, and sermons to the remnant of the Cathedral congregation. His trips to other parts of the diocese were rare.

Dr. McKenzie, whom he talked into helping him at Grace during the emergency, was the Rector of Howe School in Northern Indiana, a flourishing institution of the diocese and certainly a full day's travel away from Indianapolis. Bishop White instituted McKenzie as Dean of the Cathedral on October 17. On November 10, there was a reception for the new Dean. And on November 14 there was a special guest preacher at Grace, the Bishop of Delaware.

Diocesan and congregational life went on despite the "schism." On October 10, the Bishop blessed a little chapel or "oratory" in his new home. Thereafter, his journal records daily offices and other private or semi-private services in the oratory. On Holy Saturday he had confirmed at the Cathedral. On Easter Day (April 10, 1898) he celebrated at the 7 a.m. Holy Communion at Grace. At 9:00 a.m., he was at Holy Innocents, where he confirmed and gave the "address." By 10:30 he was back at Grace for Holy Communion and Sermon. At

3:30 he was at St. Paul's and at 7:30 at Christ Church for confirmation and an address. One hopes that he was able to use the same "address" in each place!

Some things at 16th and Central were going well in 1898. The report of the Trustees to convention (and preserved in the Journal) tells us that Knickerbacker Hall is "all that can be desired. The Trustees have no financial interest in its management. It is rapidly growing in numbers and influence; it deserves and should receive your patronage."

Also the women's work at Grace was active and well. The Diocesan Chair of the Woman's Auxiliary was Miss Caroline Howland. Her report tells us that there were 20 members at Grace (and only 17 at Christ Church) who had raised $54.85 for missions. In parish work, the Grace Altar Guild had four members; and the 20 members of what was called the Cathedral Guild had raised $126.50 Miss Howland's narrative itself displays a missionary zeal. She says, "You cannot be auxiliary to the Board of Missions by doing parish work, though your parish may be a mission, and yet two of our branches in flourishing parishes report that they have done only parish work." The Chair of another diocesan project, a group supporting the bishop's periodical titled *Church Worker*, was Mrs. Meredith Nicholson. The local chair at Grace Cathedral for the project was Miss Fanny Carleton. She had collected $13. (The Christ Church chair had managed only $2.50.)

Our picture, then, of Grace Cathedral near the end of the 19th century is of a rather small congregation, housed in an unprepossessing building and struggling with the problem of a lack of stable clergy leadership. It had just suffered through a fight and a split. On the other hand, its assets were faithful people, whose names we find in the lists of its women workers and its vestry and delegates. The cathedral was part of a complex of diocesan buildings housed at 16th and Central—clergy and bishop's residence, office, and library in one building, with a flourishing school for girls in another.

And this is what a new bishop would find waiting for him in 1899.

Bishop Knickerbacker

Bishop White

# CHAPTER FIVE

## Patience in the Midst of Hard-headed Opposition and Warped Religious Partisanship Grace Cathedral: 1899-1910

Much had happened in the year between June of 1898 and June of 1899. Bishop White's suggestion that there be a separate and nationally supported missionary district in southern Indiana snowballed into a split of the Diocese of Indiana which took away the northern one third of the state, not the southern one third. The 1898 diocesan convention resolution had called for a missionary jurisdiction to be co-terminous with what was called the Southern Convocation or the southern third of the state. The action of the national church's General Convention (the legislative body which meets every three years and which has jurisdiction over diocesan boundaries) resulted instead in a locally supported northern diocese (not a missionary district with national support) co-terminous with the former Northern Convocation. Bishop White sent a written report to June 1899 diocesan convention, since he had already vacated the diocese and called the first convention of the new Diocese of Michigan City. His written report narrates the avalanche of developments:

> With this report I must sever my connection with a large portion of the diocese over which I have been privileged to preside for the last four years … In reviewing the work of the past year let me refer in a few words to the movements which have led up to the division of the diocese and the erection of a new diocese out of a portion of our domain. The almost unanimous action of the sixty-first Convention of the Diocese of Indiana led me to the profound conviction that, if it could be safely accomplished, it was the desire of the Diocese that a division of its territory should be affected … In the existing condition of affairs at Michigan City, I thought I

could discern a possibility for accomplishing this ... Possessed of a valuable property, and having received a most generous bequest from its late Senior Warden, it was within the power of that parish to make it a foundation for an Episcopate which could be accomplished in no other way. After my mature consideration of the subject, I laid the project clearly before the authorities of Trinity parish, Michigan City, and to my very great surprise received their most enthusiastic assurance of cooperation ... I subsequently made a canvass of the entire Northern Convocation, and found the plan universally commended by that portion of the diocese which in case of a division would constitute a new diocese. I thereupon laid before the Trustees of the Diocese the facts which I had gathered and the pledges I had received ... All of which were generously commended and approved, and thereupon I prepared the papers for submission to the General Convention and submitted them to the consideration of your delegates, who had been instructed as to your will in connection with the petition for division. This application was signed by all the delegates present at the General Convention and submitted in due order to both houses of the General Convention, by which it was duly considered and acted upon. The petition from the Diocese of Indiana asked for an erection of that portion of the diocese which was the Southern Convocation, into a new diocese. The House of Bishops unanimously acceded to the petition for a missionary jurisdiction in the south, but the House of Deputies withheld its consent. Both houses having consented to an erection of a new diocese in the north, it remained only for me to return home and determine the time at which this should be carried out.

Had the House of Deputies concurred with the bishops of the church there would have been three dioceses in Indiana!

The General Convention which split off northern Indiana instead of southern Indiana and which created the present Diocese of Indianapolis had taken place in October, 1898. Whatever his feelings might have been, Bishop White did not neglect Indianapolis and Grace upon his return from General Convention and in the months he was preparing for the separation. He continued to administer the whole diocese until the 25th of April, 1899, when he summoned the first convention of the new Diocese of Michigan City and left Indianapolis. (The name of the new diocese would later be changed to Northern Indiana.) On November 27, 1898, the Bishop, for example, was at Grace for a full day: Holy Communion at 7; Morning Prayer, Holy Communion and Sermon at 10:30; Sunday School at 3 p.m.; and "Choral Vespers" at

4 p.m. Apparently sung services were not on his list of prohibited ritualistic practices.

As the plans for separating the northern diocese and his own move to Michigan City proceeded, Bishop White must have felt at least some relief in escaping the problems right next door to him at Grace and the "hostile influences" to the plan he had proposed for it and upon which he had hung the "hope of my Episcopate." He would also no longer have to deal with Fr. Christopher Sargent, who was back in town as rector of the new St. David's. (The Bishop had accepted Fr. Sargent back into the diocese on July 18, 1898.)

In addition to electing a new bishop, the diocesan convention of June, 1899, had to decide whether or not to admit the fledgling St. David's into union with the convention, the official act necessary to make it an Episcopal Church. The committee charged with the matter reported as follows:

> That in the matter of the application of St. David's parish, Indianapolis, while the conditions imposed by the Bishop have not been complied with, yet the committee after careful examination of the papers in the case, after consultation with the Chancellor of the Diocese, and after due deliberation recommend the admission of St. David's parish.

The recommendation was adopted.

The delegates of St. David's then took their seats and were able to vote in the election for bishop. In addition to Fr. Sargent, those delegates were Albert Michie, R.N. Merritt and Edward R. Pellet. A new priest from Grace also was able to vote. He was The Rev. Robert E. Grubb, and he was listed as "Rector" of Grace. At 7 a.m. on the first day of the convention he had officiated at the opening Morning Prayer.

Before it got to the business of voting for a new bishop, however, the June convention dealt with a motion to take away one of the "cathedral prerogatives" of Grace. There was a resolution to change the constitution of the diocese by substituting, in the section dealing with date and site of convention, "the first Tuesday in May at such place as shall have been appointed by the previous convention" for "on the evening of the first

Tuesday in June at the Bishop's church, Indianapolis." The resolution was adopted, and Grace was no longer the only possible venue for the diocese's annual legislative gathering.

At the time of the division of the diocese, the Trustees had arranged for an appraisal of diocesan assets, which was included in the Convention Journal. They included:

> Value of the five houses at 123 and 125 E St. Joseph and 927, 931 and 933 North Pennsylvania, $20,000;
> Value of the former Bishop's Residence at 442 North Penn St., $20,750;
> Grace Cathedral and lot valued at $9,000 ($1,500 for the church building);
> Church House (1501 Central Ave) valued at $12,000;
> Knickerbacker Hall, $17,500

There was a loan of $15,000 on the Central Avenue property. The property measured 314 feet 6 inches by 200 feet. The five houses at the former site of Grace Church were rented and produced some income for the diocese. The rent received for the former residence of the bishop was not sufficient to meet the mortgage on it.

Louis Howland had apparently not forgotten that the forming of new parishes and defining parish boundaries in Indianapolis was a source of continuing friction. He moved that "the matter of prescribing parish boundaries be recommitted to the Committee on Canons, with instructions to report a canon, prescribing such boundaries." The motion was adopted, but nothing concrete came of it. Meredith Nicholson's resolution from 1897 for a committee to coordinate the work of the Episcopal Church in the city of Indianapolis work was still on the list of "unfinished business."

Howland had cause for concern. St. David's had taken strength away from the cathedral, which was already weak in comparison to St. Paul's and Christ Church. The parochial reports show that Grace's income had declined from about $1,900 per year to $1,000. St. David's reported $7,750 in income for its first year, evidently including special gifts to start the parish. The cathedral's communicants declined from 141 to 103. (This number was probably generous, according to a note to the report made in the next year and quoted below.) St. David's had 69 communicants at its first report.

A motion was made, but defeated, to postpone the election of a bishop for one year because $2,500 "is the sum maximum that this Diocese can promise or undertake to pay its Bishop." Finally, the delegates got to the business of election. The Rev. Joseph Marshall Francis nominated George Williamson Smith of Trinity College, Hartford, Connecticut. Then R.C. Wilkerson then nominated Francis. Among other nominations, Louis Howland proposed the name of A.W. Knight of Atlanta, Georgia. The second to that came from J.E. Long, another delegate from Grace. The clergy then went to the Guild Room of the cathedral to vote; the lay delegates remained in the nave for their ballots.

On the third ballot, Joseph Marshall Francis (a descendant of Chief Justice John Marshall) was elected by a majority in both the clergy and lay order. A new era had begun for Grace, an era in which the dream of successive bishops for a "real" cathedral instead of a frame "shack" would be fulfilled.

Although the election of Bishop Francis followed so closely the troubles of 1897 and 1898, there seems not to have been as much struggle between different styles of churchmanship or as many ballots as there had been at previous elections. However, Howland's memoirs say that, at none of the elections taking place at Grace,

> did the delegates appear to be conscious of divine guidance, or greatly to rely on it. One delegate, I remember, was deeply interested in the election of a man he had never seen, and of whom he had but the slightest knowledge. His nominating speech went very well till it became necessary to take the convention into his confidence and as to the name of his candidate, when the orator turned to a member of his family sitting beside him, and, in a heavy stage whisper that was heard from narthex to apse, asked: "What's the man's name?" He then proceeded smoothly, and apparently without embarrassment, to his peroration. His candidate was not chosen, though later became bishop in another jurisdiction (**Autobiography**, pp. 14-15).

Sarah Pratt, in her memoirs, also recalls the election of Bishop Francis:

When the Reverend Joseph Marshall Francis came up from Evansville in June, 1899, to be present at the Diocesan Convention, he little thought that he would return as elected Bishop of Indianapolis, but such was the case. The convention was held in the old Pro-Cathedral, long since razed. Several names were proposed without much enthusiasm. Finally a layman from St. Paul's Evansville, in a very earnest speech, nominated his Rector, who was forthwith elected … He was our youngest Bishop, but thirty-seven years of age. He had passed ten years in Tokio (*sic*), Japan, in varied forms of Church activity (**Episcopal Bishops**, p. 50).

Howland's concluding motion at this convention of 1899 was to extend the thanks of the delegates "to the Church women of Indianapolis for the bountiful lunches served to its members."

Bishop Francis was consecrated at his parish in Evansville on September 21, 1899. The new bishop arrived in Indianapolis on September 28 in the evening, and took up his residence in Diocesan House by the cathedral. Fresh from his consecration in the large and attractive stone church of St. Paul's in Evansville, he described his first impression of the wooden structure of Grace this way: "Farm property occupied everything beyond the creek, and the entire aspect of Grace church slightly aspired to 'cathedral' proportions" (Wynne, "All Saints Had Beginings").

The day after his arrival, he celebrated Holy Communion at the Grace altar, opened Knickerbacker Hall for the school year, and said Evening Prayer in the oratory. The next Sunday was October 1, and the bishop presided at both services of Holy Communion, gave the sermon, and officiated at Evening Prayer in the cathedral. On October 2, he met with the Finance Committee of the cathedral. As Bishop White had done, he also presided at the Christmas services of the cathedral. In 1899, we find a first record of a Christmas midnight service, with another Holy Communion at 10:30 on Christmas Day. But the Christmas Eve service was undoubtedly the more memorable; it had been preceded by the installation of Roger Hanson Peters as the cathedral dean.

The 1900 convention was held at both St. Paul's and Grace. On June 5 the evening worship and organizing business took place at St. Paul's. The delegates then came to Grace on June 6. There may have been logistical reasons for this, but it also sounds like a compromise between the sentiment of the constitutional change of 1899 and the tradition of conventions at the Cathedral. Peters, the new dean, celebrated Holy Communion for the convention at 7 a.m. on June 6.

In Bishop Francis' first address to convention (1900), he had much to say about the situation at Grace:

> The Rev R.H. Peters, for four years Rector of St Paul's Church, New Albany, in response to my earnest request has accepted the office of Dean of the Cathedral. With many peculiar difficulties to meet and overcome, he has reason to believe, what is entirely clear to me, that a forward movement has begun at the Cathedral, which with God's blessing, will some day result in the erection of a building worthy of the worship of Almighty God, and meet to be the center of all our diocesan activities ... Knickerbacker Hall, the diocesan school, and our only diocesan institution has closed the most successful year in its history ... During the summer a new brick building will be erected, taking the place of the frame building now standing ... I feel strongly that the convention should meet, as a rule, in the Bishop's Church, both because of the fact that Indianapolis is a more convenient place of meeting for the majority of delegates than any other city in the Diocese, and because the Bishop's church should be the center of all Diocesan work.

Already Bishop Francis was dreaming of what would become the Cathedral of All Saints. And in the meantime, he wanted the present cathedral used as his church and to be the site of convention no matter what the delegates had voted the previous year. The bishop from Evansville had stated that Indianapolis was the most convenient place for the diocese to meet!

In the Christian Education Committee's report of 1900, we learn that Knickerbacker Hall had 22 boarding pupils and 60 day pupils. Boarding pupils were required to attend Morning Prayer each Sunday at the Cathedral, but many attended the other services voluntarily. The Trustees of the diocese had spent much time and energy during the year in resolving the financial arrangements with the new northern diocese. On October 31, 1899, they had deeded 442 N. Pennsylvania to the Diocese of Michigan City. The only matter still outstanding was division of the Knickerbacker estate.

The Trustees also reported that on March 13, 1900, the "Misses Yerkes" had proposed to rent Knickerbacker Hall for 5 years at $1,200 per year if improvements were made. The plan was approved, and a contract was let for a three-story brick building and laboratory in the amount of $8,955. The contractors were "to give a good and sufficient bond that the new steam heating plant will fully warm the school building with the thermometer below zero."

Dean Peters attached a note to his Parochial Report for the year:

> This report dates only from December, 1899, when I assumed charge. Before that time services were held with more or less regularity by the bishop and such assistance as he could get. I found the parish records very defective, which may make this report, as compared with the last, somewhat puzzling, e.g. we have a gain of twenty-eight communicants, but with a total gain over last year of but two.

In the Woman's Auxiliary report, Miss Caroline H. Howland (of 1221 N. Pennsylvania Street) is listed as corresponding secretary. The president was Mrs. W.D. (Sarah) Pratt (the neighbor of Grace Cathedral who lived at 1504 Central Avenue). Miss Fanny Carleton (1329 N. Pennsylvania) was a member of the diocesan committee. Grace Cathedral Branch reported 22 members and had raised $50 for missions. The Cathedral Guild had contributed $115.62 from its 24 members; Daughters of the King at Grace had 12 members who collected $40.50; the Altar Guild had three members and had contributed $20.32. There was a Junior Auxiliary with seven members; they had earned $11. Miss Howland added a personal touch to her report: "Your Secretary has written 114 letters, 42 postals and has sent out 58 packages of reports, an average of 9 ½ messages to each branch."

The diocesan convention for 1901 was held at Grace on June 4, 5, and 6. Louis Howland was elected to the Standing Committee of the diocese. Dean Peters was named registrar and examining chaplain. Fr. Sargent of St. David's evidently had some support in the diocese for his "high church" position because he was elected an Alternate Deputy to General Convention. Lay delegates to diocesan convention from Grace in 1901 were E.A. Munson, Louis Howland, H.W. Buttolph; alternate delegates present were J.B. Whitehead and A.B. Coffy.

The dean celebrated Holy Communion on Wednesday June 5 at 7:30 a.m. For those who wanted to sleep in a bit, the bishop celebrated at 9 a.m. "The Rev. R.H. Peters, in behalf of the clergy and certain of the laity presented the bishop an Episcopal ring, which the bishop accepted." We are fortunate to have a description of this ring. Sarah Pratt tells us,

> Very well I knew that ring, for it had been privately shown me the day before it was presented in June, 1901. The gem is a large and perfect amethyst, on which is engraved the Diocesan Seal. This seal has been pronounced by Ralph Adams Cram to be one of the several really good Diocesan seals. The inscription states: "Rt. Rev. J.M. Francis, D.D. From certain of the clergy and laity of the Diocese of Indianapolis, 5th June, 1901" (**Episcopal Bishops**, P. 51).

The diocesan convention amended its constitution and canons in 1901. Article IX of that revised constitution defined the office of registrar, to which Dean Peters had been named and which had previously been held by Meredith Nicholson: "A registrar shall be elected every three years … . He shall hold in his custody the archives of the diocese and shall act as historiographer of the same … . It shall be the duty of the registrar to collect in detailed form, and as fully as practicable, and to record in a book to be provided for that purpose, an account of the origin and progress of each parish and mission."

Dean Peters, in his report as registrar, said,

> The attention of the registrar for the past year has been given chiefly to the task of receiving, assorting and arranging in order the Convention Journals of the several Dioceses and Missionary Jurisdictions … The duplicates still remaining on hand are safely stored away awaiting the erection of a third diocese within the borders of the State of Indiana … Also I have received from Mr. Meredith Nicholson, one time registrar, much data referring to the history of the several parishes and missions in the diocese … If this office is to become serviceable, either to the diocese or individuals, it is imperative that we have proper shelving room. I therefore recommend that the convention appropriate from its funds $25 or $30 for this purpose.

Evidently hope of splitting off the southern third of Indiana into a separate jurisdiction had not died with the failure of the previous attempt. A resolution was passed instructing the Deputies to General

Convention to request it again with a change in the name of the diocese—from Diocese of Indiana to Diocese of Indianapolis. The convention journal does not record whether or not the dean got his new shelves.

The Rev. Lewis Brown, rector of St. Paul's, reported for the Board of Missions. He began with a description of the difficulties of establishing the Episcopal Church in Indiana: "Indiana is peculiarly a missionary jurisdiction. There are no thrilling, hair-breadth escapes by land or water or encounters with savages to record, but for downright hard work and the cultivation of unremitting patience in the midst of hard-headed opposition and warped religious partisanship few places can produce a parallel."

As usual, the bishop's address gives us an update on the progress of Grace as an outpost in a land of "hard-headed opposition and warped religious partisanship."

> The cathedral has a little more than held its own. A Cathedral Building Fund has been started which amounts now to two hundred dollars. A church in this part of Indianapolis is of the utmost importance not only to the city, but to the diocese, and a cathedral which shall be a reality and not a name is an institution in which every member of the Diocese should feel a personal interest … It is almost superfluous for me to speak of Knickerbacker Hall, which is so well known to you all, and yet no statement of the condition of the Diocese would be complete without a statement of the work of our one Diocesan institution. With the enlarged facilities provided by the new wing that was built during the summer, the school has increased in numbers and efficiency, so that we may well feel proud of it.

Once again the bishop was trying to keep alive his and his predecessor's dream of a "cathedral which shall be a reality" and not just one in "name" like humble Grace. A fund of only $200, however, was not much of a start, even in 1901. In contrast, St. David's had reduced debt on its building by $2,000 in the year between 1900 and 1901.

The Bishop's log of official functions for 1900-1901 indicates that when he was not out of town, he celebrated Holy Communion at the cathedral on weekdays and holy days. In addition he used Grace for diocesan functions—for example, meetings of the Woman's Auxiliary. He also celebrated Christmas and Easter at his cathedral.

The Woman's Auxiliary report for 1901 documents the continuing work of the women of Grace. In 1901 they reported 29 members who had raised $122.05 for missions. That was in addition to the women's parish work. The Cathedral Guild's 14 members had raised $235.75 for local needs, and the two members of the Altar Guild had raised $15.93. The Daughters of the King chapter had 13 members and had contributed $136.15.

Bishop Francis had begun his episcopate saying that he wanted the diocese to meet annually at the cathedral for its convention. But in 1902 that did not happen. The convention used both Christ Church and St. Paul's. Perhaps the reason was that Grace was once again without a priest. Dean Peters had left to go to Kalamazoo in the Diocese of Western Michigan. The bishop had issued his transfer in January. The report of the Indianapolis Convocation to the convention of 1902 speaks of the dean's departure: "It was with regret that we parted with Dean Peters, who took up work in Kalamazoo. He had endeared himself to the whole diocese, and his place at the cathedral had been most admirably filled … Rev. Mr. Granniss has resigned Richmond, but his acceptance of the deanship of Grace Cathedral is hailed with deep satisfaction, and the future can not but be bright under his charge."

Bishop Francis once again made clear in his address that "frequent removals" of clergy were a major factor in the weakness of parishes. One suspects he was thinking very much about Grace as he spoke: "Of the thirty-three clergy on our list today only seven have been continuously connected with the Diocese for more than five years … . Our congregations, as a rule, require a great deal of their clergy, and if they do not fulfill all that is expected of them, criticism is not withheld nor is any effort made to help them in their work … . The Rev F.O. Granniss, who has resigned the rectorship of St. Paul's Church, Richmond, has accepted a call to the Pro-Cathedral and will enter on his duties at the beginning of September."

The Committee on the State of the Church was also concerned about "frequent removals": "Your committee would emphasize the short term of service of many clergy who come to our midst, and which, in your committee's opinion, is to be deprecated as the cause, above all others, to which is to be attributed the existing undeveloped condition of much of the work of the Diocese."

Dean-elect Granniss, however, offered a ray of hope for both stability and leadership. In the list of 33 clergy in the diocese, he was second in seniority, having come from Southern Ohio in 1892. He served on the Board of Missions, and he was president of the Standing Committee.

The annual address of Bishop Francis for 1902 brags about another ray of hope emanating from 16th and Central and proposes another building project to use the diocesan property more efficiently.

> Knickerbacker Hall has had a most successful year, hampered only by the lack of accommodations necessary to meet the demands of its increasing patronage. The house now used as the Bishop's residence, which was planned and built for a diocesan institution, adjoins Knickerbacker Hall and is well adapted for school purposes. The Trustees have leased this building to the Misses Yerkes for a term of years and have determined to build a Bishop's Residence on the corner of Central Avenue and 16th Street, applying the rent received from the present house on the payments for the new and permanent residence. To supplement this sum and to pay for the house as soon as possible, I have organized "The Bishop's Guild" and have put forth an appeal to the Diocese for individual subscriptions for this purpose. Annual pledges, which may be withdrawn at any time by the pledgor, are asked in sums ranging from fifty dollars to one dollar. The advantage to the Diocese of owning a Bishop's residence and having the income to be derived from the School property for diocesan support cannot be overestimated. It will relieve every parish and mission of part of the burden which they are now carrying ... This is the first important undertaking of a material kind that I have attempted during my Episcopate, and I appeal to the Diocese and to every individual in it for cordial and sympathetic support.

The Trustees had already dealt with this plan. The lease agreement with the Yerkes for 1501 N. Central was for a rent of $600 for one year and of $700 per year for the next four years. Bids for construction of a bishop's residence at the corner of Central Ave. and 16th St. had been received for $10,908. Construction had been approved with expenditure limited to

$11,000. The location of and expense of a bishop's residence had been a concern of the diocese for years. The house built under this plan, with the old Grace to its east, and the lot where All Saints would later rise to its south, would stand on the corner of 16th and Central for about 50 years. We have an eye witness account of the blessing of this residence from Sarah Pratt:

> The bishop built a residence on the corner of Central Avenue and Sixteenth Street. This is a pleasant and commodious building with a private chapel ... Bishop Dudley of Kentucky was invited to the opening of the bishop's new home, and the laity and clergy crowded the ample rooms. Bishop Dudley pronounced an appropriate dedication of blessing. He was a man of impressive stature and great earnestness as he appeared standing on the stairway in the central hall. He was seemingly pleased with the new house, saying that he hoped it might move the people of his own diocese sometime to give him such a residence (**Episcopal Bishops**, pp. 53-54).

Tracing the history of the buildings on the diocesan property becomes confusing. Evidently the building originally intended for the "aged Churchwomen" became a bishop's residence plus library. Then it was used (with addition and improvements) for Knickerbacker Hall. After a further incarnation as a "Home for Working Girls", Bishop Francis "for various reasons ... in later years removed his residence [from the house on the corner] back to his former house," says Sarah Pratt. She continues, "That house, revised and improved is now called the Cathedral Apartments. The other house is very useful for parish purposes and is the residence of the Dean of All Saints' Cathedral" (**Episcopal Bishops**, p. 54). The house on the corner would later be known as Cathedral House and then the Parish House, and parts of it would sometimes be used as a clergy residence. The building which had been the major portion of Knickerbacker Hall was torn done in the early 1940's. (The last event held there was an Apache Ball sponsored by the Young People's Fellowship.) The lot on which an annex to Knickerbacker Hall had stood would later be repurchased and the building used as St. Francis House during the 1960's and 1970's; the lot between St. Francis House and the Church was used to build the building known at various times as Diocesan Hall, the Parish House, Episcopal Urban Center, and Dayspring Center.

The bishop's report included in Convention Journal of 1902 indicates that he was not at Grace for Christmas in 1901, but at Grace Church, Muncie. After Dean Peters left, however, Bishop Francis officiated at many services of the cathedral, including Sundays. He "gave a reception to the members of the Pro-Cathedral congregation" on January 28, 1902.

Two deacons are listed as resident at Grace in 1902, Willis D. Engle and John Mitchell Harper. It is unclear how much of the parish responsibility they undertook in the absence of a priest. Engle worked in the missions in Indianapolis. Harper had been recently ordained. One mission not under The Rev. Mr. Engle, but rather under Dr. Brown of St. Paul's, is mentioned in the 1902 Journal of Convention as "St. Philip's (Colored)."

The delegates from the laity of Grace in 1902 included the familiar names of Howland, Buttolph, and Nicholson. A new name appears as an alternate, Dr. O.N. Torian. Louis Howland still served on the Standing Committee. Meredith Nicholson had, once again, stepped in as registrar after the departure of Dean Peters; he would serve as registrar until 1913. Nicholson had also been appointed a lay reader. Perhaps he was officiating at Morning Prayer at Grace on Sundays when the Bishop had to be away on parish visitations.

The women of Grace continued their work, evidently undaunted by the clergy vacancy. The 30 members of the missionary branch raised $142.00. "Grace Cathedral Guild" listed 12 members and contributions of $178.70 for parish purposes. The Daughters of the King had a new name. They were "St. Faith Catholic Daughters of the King," with 12 members who had raised $43.87. This guild would certainly have intended the new name as a strong statement. No other parish, even St. David's, used the word "Catholic" in organizational titles.

The hopes for the leadership of Dean Granniss were not disappointed. However, his tenure was to be no more than four years. Richard Mote sums up the years 1902-1906 this way: "The Cathedral was doing well in all respects ... The communicant strength rose rapidly as did the Sunday School. The Woman's Auxiliary played its role in missionary work, and Knickerbacker Hall continued sending the church's daughters out into the world. Unfortunately, Fr. Granniss resigned to leave the diocese" (**History of All Saints**, p. 7).

Perhaps the (temporary) stability at the cathedral encouraged the diocese to think once again about a mission north of 16$^{th}$ Street. In 1907 the diocese purchased land at 30$^{th}$ and Pennsylvania.

The next priest after Dean Granniss was The Rev. George Huntington, who also stayed for only four years. During that time a new organization was formed—the Churchman's Club of the Pro-Cathedral. It was for male communicants only (shamed into action by the Woman's Auxiliary?). Its purpose was to advance "the interests of the Church in Grace Pro-Cathedral parish and to help the rector in every possible way" (**History of All Saints**, p. 7). Perhaps the men had taken to heart the appeal of Bishop Francis for the laity to support their clergy so that they would not be so interested in moving.

In 1908 there were 4,401 communicants in the diocese; 283 were at Grace. For purposes of comparison, Christ Church reported 545; St. Paul's had 522. Grace was the fifth largest congregation. Terre Haute had the most communicants (562). St. Paul's Evansville, the parish from which Bishop Francis had come, was just ahead of Grace with 305.

But another exciting development was on the horizon. The "cathedral as a reality" was becoming a reality. In 1910 the cornerstone was laid for the new brick Cathedral of All Saints.

The Rt. Rev. Joseph Marshall Francis

# CHAPTER SIX

## No Liking for the Boudoir Style of Church
## All Saints Cathedral: 1911-1939

Where had the money come from to swell the Cathedral Building Fund from the $200 mentioned by Bishop Francis in 1910 into a sum big enough to start construction? Two names already familiar to our story turned the dream into reality. A bequest from the estate of Bishop Knickerbacker for the purpose of constructing a cathedral became available in 1904, "which together with another bequest of 1200 acres of western land [in Arkansas] from Deloss Root, made a handsome building fund" (Wynne, "All Saints Had Beginnings"). It was, however, not handsome enough. A loan of $14,000 at 6% interest was obtained from the American Church Building Fund Commission of the national church, with a first payment due on February 1, 1913.

In Bishop Knickerbacker's estate there was property in Sioux Falls, South Dakota. Buyers were obtained for the lots, but the title was not clear. Apparently, the church was a residuary beneficiary, mentioned in Paragraph 8 of the bishop's will as recipient of property remaining after the first 7 paragraphs were disposed of. The Indiana Trust Company was executor of the will and believed, in error, that there would be property left to be considered under Paragraph 8. In that belief the Trust Company had obtained a deed conveying the property to itself as trustee for Sarah M. Knickerbacker (the bishop's widow) and the Trustees of the diocese. When the error was discovered, it was necessary to sue to quiet the title. As a result, buyers of property "sold" in 1911 did not receive deeds until January, 1914. And in the meantime, some had not paid taxes. One of the lawyers wrote to Bishop Francis, "When this result [quieting of title] is accomplished, we, as well as you, will feel a great relief from the delays and vexations which have been experienced in this matter."

The "Arkansas lands" were to involve the church in even more complicated legal matters. The lands were deeded to the trustees of the diocese by Deloss and Anna E. Root on June 7, 1888. The deed says they are "to be held in trust for the benefit of Grace Church or Cathedral in Indianapolis, Indiana as follows—Whenever in the judgment of the bishop and finance committee of said church said land ought to be sold, the said trustees are to sell the same on such terms as the authorities may direct." Another deed with the same wording and involving the same property is dated March 5, 1889. It seems to have been the original intention of the Roots that the proceeds of sale were to be re-invested in Indianapolis property with the proceeds going to support and maintain Grace Church. The quitclaim deed for the property mentions two portions—one containing 560 acres (in sections 3 and 10); and the other, 640 acres (in sections 20 and 21).

Deloss Root had been born in New York state in 1819 and had come to Indianapolis in 1850. According to **Representative Men of Indiana**, "He was then engaged in the manufacture of stoves, being the only man in that business in Indiana." He was a stockholder in "the first mill for the manufacture of merchant iron" and two banks (including the First National Bank of Indianapolis, of which he was an organizer). But he was most well known for "the present excellent system of water works." He owned several buildings, including "Root's Block at the corner of South and Pennsylvania Streets." He had married Kay Howard in Trinity Church, New York City, in 1861. He was for many years a vestryman at Grace (and Senior Warden in 1885 and 1886). One of the stone baptismal fonts in All Saints is inscribed "In memory of Robert Howard Root Entered into life January 8 AD 1866." The article in **Representative Men** says that of the five sons of Deloss and Kay Howard Root, all but one died at the age of five or six. In the Root plot at Crown Hill Cemetery, there are four small identical grave stones with the names too faded to read. There also is a stone for Harry Root, died January 25, 1885 at age 15. The stone for Kay gives a death date of March 14, 1885 at "age 50." A large pillar in the middle of the plot lists the death date of Deloss as 1891.

Throughout the year 1909, Bishop Francis was involved in correspondence (preserved in the diocesan archives) with a number of real estate agents and lawyers about the "Arkansas lands" because, when the decision was made to sell them, it was discovered that the church did not have title! A lawyer was sent to examine both the courthouse records and the lands. The property was described as "hilly" and "near the north line of the county [Cross County] and is eight or ten miles from the Iron Mountain R.R.", the nearest stations being "Cherry Valley or Hydrick." The tract amounted to 538 ½ acres "according to the Government Plat." A certain William M. Bloch had been acting as agent for the diocese in Arkansas. He had written to Bishop Francis in both 1900 and 1901 that he had paid taxes on the land. Bloch later claimed that the land in sections 20 and 21 were sold to R. Bloch in 1897. A search of the diocesan records was undertaken. It revealed only that "on August 5th, 1896, proposition was presented by one William M. Block, offering three hundred and twenty dollars for the standing timber on three hundred and eighteen acres near the bay of St. Francis." When an abstract was run, the land in sections 3 and 10 was found to have a competing claim in a record entitled "Swamp Land Patents"; a deed had been issued to the Iron Mountain and Helena Railroad, assignee Thomas P. Hare. The land had then been sold for taxes in 1903. Therefore, the matter had to be taken to court, and a quitclaim had to be obtained from the "holder under tax title." Also current taxes had to be paid. This action recovered the tract in sections 3 and 10. The remaining timber was sold off the land (for $1,077) to help defray the legal fees. The Indianapolis attorneys then tried to get the Arkansas attorneys to lower their fee. Bishop Francis was informed on March 19, 1909, that title had finally been established. Another flurry of correspondence followed when a real estate agent wrote the bishop that he had an offer to purchase the land at $5 an acre. Bishop Francis replied that $5 would be "considered" with a 25% commission for anything over that price. The agent replied, "referring to a former letter of yours we sold this land to Mr. Stacy and he deposited with us $100, which is actually an acceptance of your offer." The bishop wrote back, "I am more surprised by your letter than you could possibly have been by mine, for, on looking over our correspondence, I find nothing whatever which could have given you an idea that we authorized you to sell our lands."

One of the lawyers involved in the "Arkansas lands" wrote Bishop Francis in a letter of receipt for payment of fees, that he was "trusting that the church will make its fortune out of this land at some future day." Finally on October 31, 1910, Bishop Francis received a note that the land had been sold for $8 per acre (533.67 acres).

Not the church's fortune, but at least a part of its cathedral had been obtained. Bishop Francis called together a Cathedral Building Committee. Its first meeting was on December 13, 1909. Representing diocesan clergy were The Rev. Messrs. J.D. Stanley, Lewis Brown, J.E. Sulger, and W.R. Cross. The Board of Trustees was represented by Aquila Jones. W.H. Armstrong was from the Standing Committee; H.H. Bassett, from the Board of Missions. From the Grace congregation, the bishop appointed Louis Howland, D.C. Walmsley, J.M. McIntosh and H.W. Buttolph. At that time the resources consisted of $12,000 from the Knickerbacker estate, $383 from the Women of Grace Cathedral, $3,712 in other funds, and $3,853.84 in "subscriptions." making a total of $19,948.90, without considering the 538 acres of the land in Arkansas, which was thought at that date to be worth at least $5,000. A motion was passed that $40,000 be named "as the maximum cost of the proposed building." Another motion selected Alfred Grindle as architect and asked him "to submit plans for a building to be made of brick with stone copings, the interior to be furnished in brick, the general style of architecture to be Gothic and of a severe type."

The women of Grace, meeting at "the house of Miss Howland," had pledged $2,000, "payable from within two years from October 1ˢᵗ next—1910—provided work on the building is begun." There was also a men's club at this period. Minutes of the June 7, 1909, meeting of this group, preserved in the diocesan archives indicate that they met in the home of Mr. Brook. Other names on the attendance list are Webster, Wilkinson, Adams, Hubbard, Cassady, Sumwaldt, Torian, Walmsley (two persons with that name), Chrisler, Huntington, Quitel, and Grindle. "The ladies guild kindly favored the members of the club with an opportunity to assist them in the disposition of some 750 tickets for the Old English Fair ... The club was favored by an Aeolian recital of some very beautiful compositions, Mr. Chrisler operating." (Apparently, the music was provided by a mechanical reproduction apparatus.) The number of tickets taken to sell was noted for each person in attendance. Alfred Grindle took the highest number, 36. Evidently the meeting was not totally absorbing because the handwritten minutes are decorated with a doodle.

On January 24, 1910, Grindle presented two sets of plans to the Building Committee. One of them was adopted "omitting only the tower, at a cost of $40,000." (Copies of Alfred Grindle's original plan with tower have been reprinted by the parish and distributed on several occasions.) The architect was asked to prepare plans and specifications and seek bids.

By May 26, Grindle had the plans and bids ready, but no action was taken on them at the meeting of the Building Committee. Instead there was direction to convert all possible assets to cash in order to be able to enter into contracts.

One such action was authorized on May 12, 1911, when the Finance Committee of the Cathedral Chapter resolved to "sell the land belonging to Grace Cathedral, and situated in Cross County, Arkansas on such terms as may seem to be desirable." One wonders if this means that the sale of 1910 was not concluded or if negotiations had continued until this time.

A "Statement of the Cost of Building the Cathedral and the Sources of Income" was prepared. To the cost of $40,000, architects fees of $1,264 and interest payments of $2,416.94 were added, making a total cost of $43,680.94. The sources of income were as follows:

| | |
|---|---|
| Bishop Knickerbacker Estate | $13,211.04 |
| Rev. H.B. Stuart-Martin Estate | 1,378.30 |
| Diocesan contributions | 5,000.00 |
| Gifts from outside the diocese | 3,300.00 |
| Sale of Arkansas Lands | 4,864.71 |
| Cathedral Building Association | 5,000.00 |
| Cathedral Easter Offerings | 2,204.72 |
| Dean's salary while the Bishop was Acting Dean | 1,923.23 |
| Subscriptions from congregation, etc. | 6,799.94 |

The new cathedral absorbed the congregation of the old Grace Church. The original copy of the enabling resolution from Grace Church exists in the parish archives. It is the earliest document in those archives to have been produced on a typewriter. It reads as follows:

Whereas, by reason of the erection of All Saints Cathedral in the City of Indianapolis, Indiana, and its close proximity to the Church heretofore known as Grace Pro-Cathedral, it is expedient and necessary to discontinue the worship and services of said Grace Pro-Cathedral, and

Whereas, it is deemed wise to combine the congregation of Grace Pro-Cathedral with that of All Saints Cathedral,

Therefor (*sic*) Resolved: That the congregation of Grace Pro-Cathedral affiliate and worship with the congregation of All Saints Cathedral and be and become in all respects a portion of the congregation of said last named Cathedral.

Resolved further that any and all property heretofore belonging to said Grace Pro-Cathedral which can in any way be used in connection with the maintenance of the services of All Saints Cathedral be, and the same is hereby ordered and directed to be delivered to such last name Cathedral.

Resolved further that it is the sense and desire of the Vestry that the members of the congregation of said Grace Pro-Cathedral ally themselves in all respects as church members in connection with said All Saints Cathedral: and that they are earnestly and prayerfully requested to support and maintain the services and work necessary and proper for the enlargement and prosperity of said All Saints Cathedral.

Resolved further, that a copy of these Resolutions be furnished the Bishop of the Diocese as evidence of the desire of the Vestry and members of Grace Pre-Cathedral to become a part of the congregation of All Saints Cathedral.

I hereby certify that at a duly called meeting of the Vestry of Grace Pro-Cathedral, Friday evening, October 20th, 1911, the above resolutions were presented and unanimously adopted by said Vestry.
(signed) Frank Walmsley Clerk of the Vestry

I hereby certify that at a meeting of the congregation of Grace Pro-Cathedral, held after service Sunday evening Ocbober 22nd, 1911, the action of the Vestry in adopting the above resolutions, was ratified by the unanimous vote of the congregations. The same to take effect November 1st, 1911.
(signed) Frank Walmsley Clerk of Meeting

A deconsecration service was held in the old building and the structure was used as a parish hall; but after fires partly destroyed it, the building was torn down. (Louis Howland says in his **Autobiography of a Cathedral** that after one fire in the building's history, "There were expressions of regret that my home had not been completely destroyed, and of belief that no such good luck could be expected by the congregation" (p. 70).

The new All Saints was praised for its austere beauty. The Building Committee's request for a "severe" brick Gothic structure had been fulfilled. Howland, using the device of the building speaking for itself, describes this beauty as "austere."

> Those who know me best find me somewhat austere in my outward seeming, as I am, and was designed to be. I have no liking for the boudoir style of church—soft, cushioned, padded and luxurious … . In my concrete, uncarpeted floor, uncushioned pews, plain brick walls, wooden roof, stone pulpit and brass lectern, I cannot help taking a modest and chastened pride. My feeling is that a church ought not to inspire one entering it to say "how comfortable," but "how worship-inspiring it is!" It should not appeal merely to the aesthetic sense, but to the sense of mystery as well. The worshiper should see in his church, not a triumph of the art of the upholsterer or interior decorator, but an offering to Almighty God, and a place indwelt by Him (**Autobiography**, p. 70).

Howland also describes a time when "on a glittering winter afternoon … my bishop, accompanied by a stranger … entered my west door. When the stranger's eyes fell on my brass altar cross, bathed in the brilliant sunlight which it seemed to absorb into itself, he murmured, with a reverence that could not be mistaken: 'How beautiful!'"

Here is another description of the building by an outsider, Ethel A. Wynne, who wrote a series of newspaper articles on Indianapolis churches in the 1930's, including one entitled "All Saints Had Beginnings in Civil War:"

> Although the All Saints Cathedral at Central Avenue and Sixteenth street has not been entirely completed, the structure, patterned after a cathedral in Scotland, presents the noble and striking features of pure English Gothic architecture. Constructed of red brick trimmed in white Bedford stone, the edifice of majestic height will when complete be topped by a splendid

tower. Over the main entrance on Central Avenue, the gable bears a stone cross. Within the porch is hung a stone tablet designating the cathedral and its dedication, which reads, "as a perpetual witness to the faith of Our Lord Jesus Christ This Cathedral Church of All Saints' is Erected to the Glory of God and in Loving Memory of the Bishops, Clergy and Laity of the Diocese who Having Finished Their Course in the Faith do now Rest from Their Labors." Double doors lead into the interior and just inside the auditorium is the baptismal font placed to symbolize baptism as the entrance into the church. The stone font is octagonal in shape, eight-sided to symbolize perfection, with a copper ewer. The auditorium with walls of uncovered red brick reaching to majestic heights is built to resemble a cruciform (*sic*). The nave with a rear gallery, in its severe substantiality and austerity, symbolizes the ruggedness and simplicity of the Christian faith. It is said that the whole aspect of the nave, with high straight walls and ceiling of open-roofed construction with exposed beams, resembles a boat turned upside down. According to tradition the fishermen of Bible days camped under their boats at night, and the word nave from the Latin "navis" meaning ship, exemplifies the symbolism. The floors of concrete, and the pews are unadorned except for a cross carved at the end of each … . In the South transept is the pulpit constructed of stone to symbolize the strength of the preached word. Wrought iron steps lead to the pulpit and a wide canopy and sounding board cover it. At the crossing of the north transept is the brass lectern depicting an eagle, the symbol of St. John the Divine. Before the chancel is the litany desk used for the litany service. The chancel, a temporary structure, includes the choir and sanctuary. On the altar are the Eucharistic candles, the seven-branched candelabra, and the glorified cross which is placed on three steps to symbolize the Christian concepts, faith, hope and love. The altar, a temporary piece, is of oak simply carved. Within the sanctuary are the clergy seats, the Epistle on the south and the Gospel on the north. Outside the sanctuary is the bishop's throne, carved from walnut with a high pointed canopy and back of it the organ. Behind the chancel are the choir and vestry rooms, the ambulatory and the sacristy rooms.

The permanent chancel will be built of red brick, but it is to be as beautifully and artistically ornamented as possible to contrast with the severity of the nave. The pointed arched windows of the chancel are temporarily of opalescent glass. Another feature of interest are the Holy Communion vessels. Those ordinarily used were made from family silver of Bishop Francis and given as a memorial for the bishop who ordained him.

As the article indicates, the bequest of Bishop Knickerbacker and the generosity of Deloss Root were not sufficient to complete the building as planned. The architect, Alfred Grindle, had drawn plans for a building nearly twice as long as the one constructed in 1910-1911. Instead of the sanctuary and choir proposed, a temporary wooden sanctuary was attached to the crossing, where the brick construction stopped. Grindle, a member of All Saints, also intended the completion of a square bell tower over the crossing. There is an apocryphal story, which has circulated for some time, that the building was unfinished because part of the funds were given away to help earthquake victims in South America. Unfortunately, there is no trace of supporting evidence in the archives.

*The Indianapolis Star* announced on November 1, 1911 that

> The new All Saints Cathedral, Central Avenue and Sixteenth Street, which is to cost $55,000 when all interior decorations are completed and furnishings installed, will be dedicated with impressive services, beginning at 11 o'clock this morning ... At 8 o'clock this evening the Rev. Roger Hanson Peters of Louisville, Ky., former dean of the Indianapolis diocese will preach. The fall meeting of the Woman's Auxiliary will be held tomorrow afternoon in the diocesan house. A missionary service, with various addresses, will be held Friday evening. At 2 o'clock Saturday afternoon there will be a general meeting of the Junior Auxiliary in the diocesan house. The feature of the services on Sunday will be sermon in the morning by the Rt. Rev. William Andrew Leonard, bishop of Ohio. The style of the architecture of the building is early English Gothic. It is built of brick and trimmed with Bedford limestone, and the inside walls are of plain brick, unplastered. The building is heated with steam radiators set in the side walls. It has a seating capacity of about 500.

The next day's article was titled "Solemnity Marks Cathedral Benediction." According to the *Star*, the sermon by former Dean Peters was on "The Grace of God," in which he said, "the ultimate purpose of Christianity is to produce such character among men and women that a mere glance at them will testify that they are consecrated to God." Other clergy participants named, in addition to Bishop Francis, were George G. Burbank, A.W. Lefflingwell (of New Albany), Fr. Sargent, and the new dean of All Saints, Charles S. Lewis. "Bishop Joseph M. Francis and the clergy proceeded from the diocesan house to the Central Avenue entrance. Upon reaching the door, the bishop knocked three times and Alfred Grindle, the architect, opened ... The clergy walked to the altar chanting three psalms where the architect delivered the keys to the Rev. Charles S. Lewis, the dean."

Here is another first-hand account, from Sarah Pratt, of the new cathedral:

> The building of the cathedral followed. Plans were submitted by Mr. Alfred Grindle, an English architect, and his achievement is a stately and dignified temple. It was dedicated with the traditional ceremony of cathedrals, on November 1, 1911. It is a brick edifice, surmounted by a large, beautiful stone cross. Its interior is dark and rich; its eagle lectern and stone pulpit are impressive. During the World War a large service flag was displayed over the chancel from the roof, making a colorful note against the somber interior (**Episcopal Bishops**, p. 54).

A new cathedral needed a new Dean. Four days after the dedication, on November 5, Bishop Francis installed The Very Rev. Charles Smith Lewis with these words (the Letter of Installation is preserved in the diocesan archives):

> To you as Dean of the Cathedral Church of All Saints and as Pastor of the Congregation worshipping herein, we herby commit the pastoral care of this portion of the Flock of Christ and the direction of the affairs of the Congregation subject only to the regulations which you shall receive from us regarding the conduct of the services and the general plan and scope of the work to be undertaken and performed by the Cathedral Church.

There was no doubt but that the bishop was in charge——and especially in all matters liturgical!

Grace Church had officially been a pro-cathedral—that is, a parish used by the bishop. All Saints was to be a true cathedral, governed by a bishop and chapter rather than a vestry elected by the congregation. A Constitution and Statutes for the Cathedral of the Diocese of Indianapolis were drawn up for the diocesan convention of 1912. Section I of the diocesan canon called "Of the Cathedral" said,

> The Church in the Diocese of Indianapolis, hereby acknowledges All Saints' Cathedral, Indianapolis, as the Cathedral Church of the Diocese; with such ecclesiastical jurisdiction, rights, privileges and obligations as pertain to any Parish organization in unison with the Council; and with all the jurisdiction, rights and privileges and obligations, that are assigned to the Bishop's Church in the Constitution and Canons of the Diocese.

Bishop Talbot had wanted a cathedral and been frustrated in the attempt to make St. Paul's into one. Bishop Knickerbacker had left a bequest to make one possible. Bishop White had kept the vision alive and made Grace Church his own church, even if it meant conflict with some of the congregation. Bishop Francis now had a cathedral, governed as such even if it was only half finished. The statutes of governance which were proposed to the convention in 1912 contained a preface which outlines the mission and function of the new cathedral.

> The Cathedral Church of All Saints, in the city and Diocese of Indianapolis, erected as a perpetual witness to the Faith of our Lord Jesus Christ, and to the glory of God; and in loving memory of the bishops, clergy and laity of the Diocese, who having finished their course in faith, do now rest from their labors; stands for the following purposes:
>
> I.  It shall ever be a House of Prayer, where all persons, of whatever race or nation, may have opportunity to worship God, the Father, Son and Holy Spirit; to draw near to Him in prayer and praise, and to hear the good tidings of the Gospel of Jesus Christ;
>
> II. It is the Bishop's Church; and, as such, shall be his official seat and spiritual home, wherein he shall be free to exercise the responsibilities of his sacred office without let or hindrance or division of his apostolic authority;
>
> III. It is the Diocesan Church, representing the whole Diocese in its Chapter, in the spirit of its administration, and in the catholicity of its teaching; and as such, it shall serve as the center of Diocesan work and worship.

Note that, as early as 1912, one aspect of the mission of the cathedral was to be open to all races.

Statute I vested the government of the cathedral in the bishop and chapter. Statute II listed the persons and offices which were to form the chapter. Another statute outlined the prerogatives of the bishop: he was to "preside, if present, in choir" at meetings of the chapter; he was to have unrestricted use of the cathedral; he was to officiate at any time he desired, giving the dean twenty four hours notice; he was to "determine the ceremonial to be used, which when established, shall not be changed without his written instructions"; he was to approve all special services and preachers; he was to install the dean and canons and to receive their promise to obey the statutes. The dean was to be elected by the chapter upon nomination by the bishop. The dean was the pastor of the congregation worshipping at the cathedral and its "executive head", with jurisdiction over organizations and other clergy of the cathedral; he was also to "have the care of the treasures of the cathedral", its buildings, grounds, and employees. The statutes envisioned two canons, priests jointly nominated by bishop and dean, to help in the "worship, preaching, and work". One of these two could be named Canon Precentor and have charge of the music. In addition honorary canons and other clergy could also be attached to the cathedral. A chancellor, "a layman learned in the law", was to be elected by the chapter. The chapter was also to elect a treasurer. A Finance Committee was to be composed of bishop, dean and the lay members of the chapter elected by the congregation; it was to "have the care and expenditure of the moneys pertaining to the support of the congregation." The annual meeting of the chapter was to be on All Saints Day, with another meeting in conjunction with the diocesan convention. The members of the cathedral congregation were to consist of all members of Grace Pro-Cathedral, communicants later added to the rolls, and "all persons who regularly worship at the cathedral and contribute systematically to its support." Any amendments to the statutes were to be ratified by diocesan convention.

The new mode of governance was implemented by a "provisional chapter" since the official chapter could not be formed until after elections at diocesan convention. On May 20, 1912, Bishop Francis reported that the Cathedral Building Fund had received and disbursed $33,333.93 and was now dissolved. The provisional chapter had received an additional $4,205.54 and disbursed $4,167.62, leaving a balance of $37.12! Still owed was a mortgage of $14,000 with American Church Building Fund Commission. There were estimated assets of $10,000 including the balance of the Knickerbacker estate, the presumed value of the "Arkansas lands," and pledges. All Saints was beginning its career in debt and operating on faith.

The parochial report for 1912 recorded in the journal of diocesan convention showed evidence of encouraging progress under the new arrangement. The Very Rev. Charles S. Lewis was functioning as dean.

He had an assistant in Willis Engle. Eighty-nine families were in the congregation. Communicants now numbered 233. The Sunday School had grown from 50 (1899) to 78 (1912).

The treasurer of the cathedral chapter reported that for the period November 1, 1913, to November 1, 1914, $7,434.56 had been received for the Cathedral Building Fund. Of this amount $2,849.56 was the final settlement of the Knickerbacker estate and $1,500 had been received as a payment for the "Arkansas lands." A disbursement of $6,863.04 paid for taxes on the Arkansas properties, drainage work on the Cathedral grounds, interest, payments on the note, and legal expenses.

Evidently the bishop personally followed up on "subscriptions" to the Cathedral Building Fund which remained unpaid. In the diocesan archives, there is a letter dated March 7, 1913, which begins,

> Dear Bishop,
>
> Your notice rec'd and needless to say how grieved I am that you were obliged to remind me again of my pledge.

Another letter is dated February 5, 1914, to a "subscriber" from Bishop Francis. It leaves no doubt about the bishop's investment in the cathedral project and his sense of responsibility for it: "Within the next few weeks it is necessary for me to pay the interest on the cathedral mortgage and a note of fourteen hundred dollars … I must, in some way or other, endeavor to meet the payment. Last year I was unable to pay what was due at the time when it was due, and I cannot afford to do that again."

Dean Lewis resigned effective July 1, 1914, to accept a call to St. Mary's, Burlington, New Jersey. In his note informing the bishop, he said, "I wish to place on record with this resignation my appreciation of the cooperation I have had in the work here, and how deeply I value all you have done to help make it a success."

The bishop responded on June 11, 1914,

> In accepting your resignation I desire not only on my own behalf but in
> the name of the Cathedral Chapter and of the Cathedral congregation to
> express deep appreciation of your ministry in the Cathedral, and to thank
> you for what you have done and even more for what you have tried to do.
> I cannot but regret that you feel compelled to surrender your work at the
> Cathedral at this time, as I had hoped that you would be able to remain for
> many years and to continue, in a difficult position, the accomplishment
> which has marked your three years' service.

Meanwhile, the "Arkansas lands" transactions were not yet complete.
A real estate agent in Memphis, Tennessee, wrote Bishop Francis that
the person who had a contract on the land had failed to act on it by the
expiration date of June 30, 1914. The agent then obtained a tentative
offer from another potential buyer. When the original buyer heard
about it, he increased his bid $1.50 more per acre to a price of $7.50.
So a new contract was drawn up for $4,846, with $1,500 to be paid
in cash and the remainder in "good first mortgage real estate notes on
improved Memphis real estate, with the definite agreement that the
deal will be closed upon delivery of a new deed with slight changes." In
return for such diligent work, the agent thought that $500 would be
"not unreasonable" as a fee for his service.

The bishop, however, thought otherwise. He explained that the original
agreement was for a fee of 5%. A fee of $500 would have been "more
than 5½% on the combined transaction or more than 10% on the
actual sale … I should have gladly consented to an additional sum of
$100 or a total commission of $350." On the other hand, Francis said
he would not dispute the charge if legal counsel said it was "reasonable."
The lawyer from Tennessee replied and said that it was "reasonable,"
given the extra effort that the agent had made to complete the sale. The
amounts Bishop Francis actually paid on July 21 were $450 to the real
estate agent and $100 to the lawyer.

But the deal still was not finalized. The lawyer in Memphis had
to negotiate about a survey and taxes. He also had to do "constant
jogging" to collect payments on the notes the buyer of the land had
handed over.

At Easter, 1916, the Finance Committee of All Saints made the following appeal to the congregation (in a letter dated April 17, 1916, found in the parish archives):

> Easter is at hand. At the beginning of Lent it was decided that our Easter offerings should be asked for two objects: a) Missions, b) The Cathedral Building Fund.
>
> However, it was also stated at that time that in order to make it possible for the Easter offering to be devoted to these purposes it would be necessary that our pledges be paid up, and kept paid up. It is with gratification that we can now advise you this has been done in the majority of cases, so that we can carry out the announced intentions as to the Easter offering. We thank you for this, if you are among the majority who have thus paid your pledges; and if you are among the minority, will you not join the majority?
>
> As a result of your efforts, all our bills are paid up to date, but it will be necessary that our efforts continue so that we may not fall behind during the summer.
>
> You will find enclosed herewith two envelopes for each member of the family, one marked "Missions" and the other "Cathedral Building Fund." Will you kindly use these for your Easter Offering?
>
> The debt on the Cathedral is Seven Thousand Dollars. Half of this sum must be paid at the next interest-paying period—April, 1917—and the balance a year later. The interest for the next year will be Three Hundred Fifty Dollars; and in June of this year One Hundred Eighty Dollars must be paid for insurance.
>
> We thank you again for your support in the past, and rely on it in the future; and we most earnestly ask you to give all you can at Easter for Missions and for the Cathedral Building Fund.
>
> Sincerely your representatives,
> The Finance Committee:
> Louis Howland
> U.G. Cassady
> O.J. Parrish
> James F.T. Sargent
> G.B. Schley, Secretary
> Austin C. Sigelen, Treasurer

The next treasurer's report for the cathedral chapter was for November 1, 1914, to May 15, 1916 (indicating the infrequency of cathedral chapter meetings). During that time $2,576.64 had been received, including further payments on the "Arkansas lands", "rent of old church" ($50), and gifts of the cathedral congregation ($302.29 from the Easter appeal of the Finance Committee).

For the next report, covering the period to May 1, 1917, receipts of $3,118.26 included the final payment on the "Arkansas lands." Bishop Francis, as the treasurer, also reported that as of May 14, 1917, $4,500 was still owed on the mortgage. $1,000 was due on April 1, 1918, and the balance on April 1, 1919. The minutes of the 1917 meeting (in the diocesan archives) include the following:

> The bishop presented his report to the chapter. In this report he told of the resignation of the Rev. R.R. Sloane, canon and vicar of the cathedral, to accept an election as assistant minister at Trinity Church, Buffalo; and of the nomination and unanimous election as dean of the cathedral of the Rev. John White of Zion Church, Oconomowoc, Wis., who was inducted into his office on the first Sunday in January, 1917. The bishop also recommended that an amendment which will be reported to the council by the committee on the revision of the constitution and canons providing for only one stated meeting of the chapter yearly, to be held on the first day of the annual council ... The dean reported that at the annual meeting of All Saints Cathedral congregation held May 1, 1917, Messrs. C. B. Schley and C.A. Trask were duly elected members of the chapter to serve for three years.

(Diocesan convention was known as the "annual council" at that time.)

In the past Knickerbacker Hall had prospered even when the parish was languishing. Now the tables were turned. The last of the Yerkes sisters left in 1907. Miss Julia Landers had replaced her, but evidently had been unable to attract enough students. "In the summer of 1912 Bishop Francis reported that he had ordered the fitting up of Knickerbacker Hall to be a 'Home for Working Girls'. He appointed an able committee of five laywomen—Mrs. Benjamin Harrison [wife of the President], Mrs. Alexander Holliday, Miss Julia Harrison, Mrs. E.G. Peck, and Mrs. J.H. Ranger, to assist this operation. By Christmas of 1912 Knickerbacker Home for Working Girls opened its doors"

(**History of All Saints**, pp. 8-9).. Although the name of the institution now sounds quaint, it represents a response to the changing social situation—the increasing number of single, working women drawn or pushed to cities for employment.

More social change came with the First World War, and All Saints was not immune to the effects of the war. The bishop himself would go to the front!

As we have seen, Bishop Francis installed The Very Rev. John White from the Diocese of Milwaukee as the second dean of All Saints in January, 1917. Then, within a matter of months, the bishop requested permission from the diocese to become an army chaplain. His assignment was to a hospital that had very close Indianapolis connections. Charlotte Cathcart was another Indianapolis resident who volunteered to serve at that same Base Hospital No. 32, not far behind the lines in France in 1917 and 1918. Organized on April 6, 1917, by several Indianapolis physicians, J.K. Lilly had equipped it by a gift of $25,000, and requested that it be named after Col. Eli Lilly, his father, who had served in the Civil War. Miss Cathcart says, "Everyone was talking of the Lilly Base Hospital and everyone in Indianapolis seemed to want to help in any way possible" (**Our Old Corner**, p. 82). Thus it was that, from a battlefield near Contrexeville in the Vosges mountains of France, Bishop Francis wrote his annual address to be read at the 1918 Convention.

Francis "returned to the United States on leave in August 1918, and was engaged until the end of the war in speaking for Liberty Loan drives. He received the Crown of Belgium Medal, given for outstanding civil activities in an order dated June 17, 1925, by Albert, King of Belgium" (Biography of Bishop Francis at www.indianapolis.anglican.org)

We have a detailed glimpse into the life of the cathedral during the year 1917 in the form of a report of the new dean, John White, to the cathedral chapter:

> I beg to make the following report as Dean of All Saints Cathedral. I took up the duties of my office on January 1st, 1917; but the report covers the year's work.

During the past year the total receipts have amounted to $3,555.69. The disbursements have been as follows: for Current Expenses not including Communion Alms $2,696.29, for Diocesan Purposes $329.56, and for General Missions $427.25, making a total of $3,538.88 and leaving a balance of $16.81. At the time this report was compiled there was a deficit of $200 in the General Fund. This amount has since been reduced to $100.

In addition to the above the cathedral congregation raised $1,056 for the Clergy Pension Fund.

The budget for the coming year provides for the expenditure of $3,800. We have a dependable income of $2,850 thus leaving a balance of $950 to be raised, plans for which are already under way.

As a fair idea of the condition of the cathedral work can be gained from the annual report which will appear in the Diocesan Journal details will be omitted here. It may interest the chapter, however, to know that the past year has seen an increase of 25% in the list of communicants.

A mission is conducted under the auspices of the cathedral at Arsenal Avenue and Seventeenth Street. A Sunday School is conducted regularly and has an enrollment of forty six children. A Bible class is held by Mrs. Francis twice a month. During Lent preaching services were held each Sunday. This work is very important, has a splendid beginning and we hope to go on and develop the work there.

Perhaps the most important work which the cathedral should develop is that among the various state, county and city institutions within the city. The Woman's Prison more and more turns to the Church for religious services. Occasional services have been given on request on Sunday afternoons and the dean has just been requested to conduct religious services on Wednesday evenings during the coming two months. We were very glad to use this opportunity.

Regular meetings of the Finance Committee have been held and the services maintained as usual (Report dated May 14, 1917, in the parish archives).

This will not be the last time we hear of a connection between All Saints and outreach to the Women's Prison.

On November 7, 1917, the American Church Building Fund Commission, which held the note on the cathedral, granted a one year extension for the final payment of $3,500, saying, "We trust that this will be found satisfactory and will give you such time as you need." This extension must have been a relief. Bishop Francis' report as treasurer of the Chapter stated that at the end of 1919, only $501.81 was on hand. His report as of December 31, 1920, says that instead of paying off the remaining mortgage, an additional $2,000 had been lent by the American Church Building Fund. The reason for this additional note was the wrecking of the old church building. On December 16, 1919, $127.50 had been paid for choir vestments "to replace those destroyed by fire." This was apparently one of the fires in the old frame Grace Church building. In August and September of 1920, various amounts were received for sale of material from the old building. On December 31, 1920, $2,606.08 was paid to a contractor for demolition of the old building. In April, 1921, there was a payment for "ploughing and cultivating church lot." Perhaps this was the lot upon which the old building had stood. These treasurer's reports also demonstrate the bishop's commitment to the cathedral. Every month he gave over a portion of his salary to the Cathedral Fund.

Meanwhile, the Home for Working Girls was not doing well. Its finances were precarious. It was close to closing the doors during the winter of 1917-1918, saved only by the efforts of the prominent people on the governing board. But by the convention report of 1918, things were looking better. It was filled to capacity and expected to pay $800 in rent to the diocese.

Following the war, Bishop Francis returned to Indianapolis and to a nation caught up in controversy over the League of Nations. At the diocesan convention of 1920 held at All Saints, Louis Howland introduced a resolution referring to the fact that the diocese was already (since 1919) on record as supporting the League and urging the Senate to ratify the treaty and conclude peace with Germany.

Howland's book on the Cathedral leaves no doubt of his and All Saints' passion for peace:

> Fear and hate are widespread, and they usually go together. Such, it seems to me, is the least part of the harvest of war, and, as I see it, it is a crop of tares, and tares only … I am against war—though I do not suppose the fact is important—not only because it is senseless and horrible, but also because of its debasing effects on the minds and consciences of the people, effects

which operate long after peace is declared. When peace does come, it should be a real peace, and not one hedged about with provisos and limitations, the peace of a people unafraid rather than of a people cowering in panic, eager to throw away or murder their liberties in return for a protection they do not need, and which they should scorn. "Neither shall they learn war any more"—has not the time come for the fulfillment of that noble prophecy? (**Autobiography**, pp. 130-131).

One of the casualties of the war appears to have been St. David's parish, which closed at this time "because of financial difficulties" (Georgianne Strange, **Trinity Episcopal Church: 1919-1969**, Indianapolis, 1969, p.2). St. David's had been located at 21st Street and Talbot Avenue. A new parish, at first called Church of the Advent and later Trinity Church, held its first service on April 6, 1919 for "the area north of Fall Creek" which had "become a rapidly growing residential district" by the end of the war (**Trinity**, p. 1). One of Fr. Sargent's sons, J. F. T. Sargent, was instrumental in donating the altar and furnishings of St. David's to the new parish. The altar had been carved by Fr. Sargent and his three sons. The new parish would flourish, reporting 148 communicants in its first year.

At the 1920 convention, Henry W. Buttolph of the cathedral was completing his tenth year as diocesan treasurer. While All Saints did not report financial trouble that year, the communicant strength had declined from 233 (in 1912) to 196. The Sunday School now had only 20 pupils. Perhaps this decline discouraged Dean White and led to his departure, which took place in 1920.

Bishop Francis did not look for a replacement but put himself in the position of acting dean. Herbert Denslow was made sub-dean, but was replaced within a year by A. Lindsay Skerry, who was titled vicar. In the midst of the rapid succession of priests, communicant strength continued to decline, with a loss of 50 more in two years.

Knickerbacker Hall was in even worse condition. In 1923 it closed its doors permanently. The building was converted into apartments (as was also the upstairs portion of the diocesan headquarters building to the south, which was also known later as St. Francis House). The financing of this project was through a loan against the Central Avenue property for $20,000, at an interest rate not to exceed 6%, "said loan being for the purpose of refunding a loan of $4,000 from the Crown Hill Cemetery Association, and to provide the necessary funds for the remodeling of the building at 1535 Central Avenue, Indianapolis."

The Rev. Mr. Skerry served at the cathedral in 1923-1924. A clergyman named McKnight was also there in the year 1925-1926. The Rev. Henry A. Hanson was curate for the cathedral from 1925 to 1929. And the bishop, of course, was a constant presence.

During the 1920's, the cathedral may have been lacking in stable clergy direction (other than that of the bishop); but there was no lack of stable, lay leadership. George B. Schley served as a member of the bishop's cabinet which had been organized in 1921. Henry Buttolph continued as diocesan treasurer. Louis Howland was a trustee of the diocese.

In the summer of 1927, Christ Church was vacated so that ground could be excavated underneath it for the construction of a parish hall. "All Saints' Cathedral provided hospitality" to the Christ Church congregation until their building could be re-opened on November 6 (**Little Church**, p 283).

At the end of the decade All Saints finally obtained a priest who would stay for a significant time. His name was Robert C. Alexander. He was ordained deacon on June 30, 1929, and priest on December 22 of that year. The bishop gave him the title of resident canon and vicar.

1929 was also the year that All Saints and the Church adapted to a new **Book of Common Prayer**. Louis Howland gives his impressions of one of the revisions:

> My burial service has recently been revised, the idea being to make it less "gloomy," and to free it of its mediaeval spirit. Yet generations of men have been deeply impressed by its power and majesty—and solemnity. Happily it has not been seriously marred. I am now thinking of the spirit that seems to have prompted the changes, the same spirit that was shocked by the last clause—which has been eliminated—in the prayer for the sick: "Or else give him grace to take thy visitation that after this painful life ended, he may dwell with thee in life everlasting; through Jesus Christ our Lord." To me that has always seemed the most important part of the prayer. I never

have been able to understand the objection to it unless it is that it suggests a doubt of God's willingness to heal. But surely there should be a doubt, for it is quite possible that healing may not always be the best.

But Howland's reflections continue in a most Anglican tone:

> Though I reverence the past, would maintain unbroken my connection with it, and draw all the power that undoubtedly flows from it, I would live in the present, and serve to the best of my ability the men and women of my own day, and the children too. I would be a contemporary of them as well as a neighbor to them. Nor does there seem to me to be any inconsistency between the two attitudes and points of view (**Autobiography**, pp. 42-44).

Howland's memoirs give other glimpses into the life of the Cathedral congregation. These anecdotes are undated, but probably occurred during the Bishop Francis years. A young girl was coached by the bishop to hold up her finger when she thought the sermon was too long. "Docilely, she followed the Episcopal counsel, but, as I recall, quite without effect, since the preacher had not been instructed in the meaning of the signal … I should add that the bishop told the child that on no account should the monition be given when he was the preacher" (**Autobiography**, pp. 61-62).

Another vignette is of a wedding:

> It took place immediately after the Sunday morning service, such members of the congregation as cared to, remaining in their seats. The bride and groom took their place at the chancel-rail—and were married. That was all there was to it. There were no attendants—except the brother of the bride who gave her away—no flowers, no elaborate gowns, no paradings of young men and women to places carefully fixed for them at a "rehearsal," no painful approach to the altar with precisely measured steps and dragging feet—but there was a marriage that was a real and reverential church service, led up to by the beautiful service that had preceded it (**Autobiography**, pp. 74-75).

In 1930, a parish newsletter called the *Parish Record* began publication, probably at the instigation of Fr. Alexander. Although it contained some syndicated articles, it claimed that "a certain portion will be of local interest." It told, for example, of the activities of the Woman's

Auxiliary and the Mother's Club. This latter organization had chosen to equip the Cathedral House as its project. The newsletter also gives us first notice of a group that would play a prominent role in the life of All Saints for the next 20 years—the Young People's Fellowship, which the newsletter called "an active enthusiastic, devoted body of Christian Young People" (**History of All Saints**. p. 11). The September 1931 issue reported that in the Church School there were 47 pupils and teachers, with an average attendance of 23. Ages ranged from kindergarten through high school.

Philip Smith has vivid memories of All Saints while Fr. Alexander was the priest and Bishop Francis was very much a presence in congregational life. The Smith family first came to All Saints in 1936. Philip Smith remembered that his father had met Bishop Francis because they were both "fond of railroads". The Smiths had been attending Third Christian Church but started to go to All Saints because of the connection with the bishop. Philip and his brother Ralph were baptized there on Holy Innocents' Day, 1936. At that time, Fr. Alexander was living in the parish house (Interview with Philip and Jean Smith conducted by The Rev. Mary Lockwood Campbell, 2001).

The parish house was frequently used as a residence for clergy working on diocesan projects. In October, 1932, for example, The Rev. Francis H. Tetu (or perhaps Jetu) took up residence as missionary canon. His assignment was St. George's Mission (on the near south side of Indianapolis) and working with the poor of the community. Philip Smith recalled that Fr. Tetu took the street car to get to St. George's. This priest's awareness of social issues is apparent in a letter he wrote to President Franklin D. Roosevelt in October, 1935, (and preserved in the FDR Library):

> In answer to your letter regarding conditions in my city … there seems to be a great deal of unemployment despite the fact that many have returned to work. Numbers of young men and women are desirous of securing employment but are unable to do so … . It is to be expected that youth is deteriorating morally and mentally as a result of idleness. The city is also faced with the problem of transient men. Many of them are begging on the streets because of the closing of the transient shelter houses. The abolition of the NRA has brought about a lengthening of hours of labor reduction of wages, worse laboring conditions, and the discharge of many employees.

In the depression years, "apparently All Saint's Cathedral was not greatly affected … although it did suffer a slight drop in communicant strength during the early 1930's" (**History of All Saints**, p. 11). Also during the depression (1935), almost 100 years after Bishop Kemper first came to Indiana, the diocese ceased to be "aided" by the national church and became self-supporting.

As the nation and the church emerged from the depression, All Saints launched a pledge campaign in 1939. A little brochure was prepared for that campaign and kept in diocesan archives. It is entitled "The Churchman's Imperative: OUGHT?" Ten questions are asked, beginning with the word "Ought." Questions six and seven, for instance, are "Ought the regular dignified Prayer Book Services of Worship at the Cathedral be adequately supported?" and "Ought the Cathedral congregation support the whole program of the Church cooperatively?" The answers given are, of course, in the affirmative. Each parishioner was asked to study a chart of the "Amounts of Weekly Pledges for 1938" and try to move into the next higher category. The smallest weekly pledge in 1938 was $1.10; the largest was $10.55.

Giving us another facet of All Saints life during the Alexander and Francis era, there is also in the archives of the Diocese of Indianapolis a collection of materials in an envelope upon which the name Rev. Robt. Alexander is hand-written. In the envelope are proposals (with drawings) for cloths to ornament the altar—a frontal and super-frontal, a dossal and curtains with wings (with a carved triptych as an alternative). The proposal for the super-frontal states confidently: "It is incorrect to hang it over the narrow edge of the alter (*sic*) and still more incorrect to design it so that the corners hang in cones as a table cloth might do." There is also a drawing of a crucifix with the note that "The crucifix is occasionally used instead of X." It is unclear what portion, if any, of this proposal was actually put in place, but it illustrates very definite opinions about liturgical space.

In 1933, Bishop Francis was

> the third oldest prelate, in years of service, still in active work in the Protestant Episcopal Church in America. He was a devoted worker in the missionary field throughout his long ministry. For many years he served in

the executive board of missions and the National Council of the National Episcopal Church. He was chairman of the Indianapolis branch of the United States Society that issued a weekly publication called "Uncle Sam's Diary", giving an impartial view of governmental activities and distributed free to high schools. He was also a member of the Columbia Club.

However, by 1934 the dynamic Bishop Francis was in poor health.

> Falling into ill health in 1934, he gave up his national church responsibilities on the National Council, a position he had held since 1904. In April of 1938 he asked for the election of a bishop coadjutor. On Wednesday February 8th, [1939] the day of Bishop Kirchoffer's consecration, Bishop Francis, being severely ill, sent him a notice giving over full ecclesiastical authority. Five days later, Bishop Joseph Marshall Francis died. He was seventy-six years old, the oldest Bishop in active Diocesan service in the Church. His total time of ordained service was fifty-two years, almost forty of which was as the Bishop of the Episcopal Diocese of Indianapolis (www.indianapolis. anglican.org)

An era ended for All Saints in 1939. In June Fr. Alexander left to take a position in Kansas, after the longest continuous service of any priest in the history of either Grace or All Saints. And also, of course, Bishop Francis, the builder of All Saints and the first bishop of the separate Diocese of Indianapolis, was gone. Bishop Francis had been the youngest bishop in the Church when he was elected in 1899. He was the senior bishop by the time of his death. By 1939, he had attended two Lambeth Conferences and had confirmed more than 9,000 persons.

Sarah Pratt was the friend and neighbor of Bishop Francis for many years. She tells us that

> Bishop Francis began at once [after his consecration] to preach missions. In some parishes the message was not warmly received. I have heard him say within the last few years that he had been criticized for preaching missions too much, but that inasmuch as his interpretation of Christianity was the mission teachings of Jesus, he expected to continue … Once in later years, a woman told me of a sermon which she had heard at a General Convention. She did not know who the preacher was. "He was the most earnest of anyone I ever heard," she said and added, "and he had the biggest ring." I laughed. "That was my Bishop—Bishop Francis" (**Episcopal Bishops**, p. 51)

The ring she refers to was the one presented by Dean Peters in June 1901. Her remark about sermons illustrates the appropriateness of the dedication of the pulpit of All Saints as a memorial to Bishop Francis.

Mrs. Pratt also describes the liturgical style of Bishop Francis and gives us additional insight into the bishop's love for All Saints:

> The service instituted by the Bishop was plain and impressive. Under all of its Deans this service has remained unchanged, unhurried, the congregation given its full mede (*sic*) of worship, and sermons presenting some phase of Christian teaching. It is what I designate as a "Prayer Book service." The most comprehensible sermon I ever heard on the mysterious nature of the Atonement was preached from the Cathedral pulpit ... Once when All Saints' and its adjacent trees and bushes were covered with snow, a young clergyman, the Reverend Rush Sloane, who was staying at the Bishop's, came over to our lawn opposite, and took a picture. This very beautiful picture the Bishop had made into a Christmas card, which he sent to Bishop Lloyd, of New York, and to the Mission House. The Spirit of Missions reproduced it on its cover. Unfortunately the name of the church was omitted, and the Indianapolis Diocese did not receive credit (**Episcopal Bishops**, p. 51).

Mrs. Pratt used this photograph as the frontispiece of her own memoirs. One of the Christmas cards, with the bishop's handwriting, has been framed and preserved at All Saints. Rush R. Sloane was vicar and canon of All Saints from 1914-1916 so we can date the photograph to around 1915.

Gloria Kemper was a member of All Saints for more than 75 years and was the last active parishioner to have known Bishop Francis. She remembered his almost frightening, but certainly awe-inspiring presence. She also recalled how grand ladies drove to the cathedral in their electric motor cars. And she also remembered that her own mother could not receive Holy Communion at the bishop's church because she was divorced.

The Bishop evidently made an impression on many people. Georgianne Strange in her history of Trinity Parish tells us that he was a

> commanding figure, stately and dignified ... He is described as a man of "splendid presence with a marvelous voice. He presided with great dignity, force, and fairness." The bishop's gleaming black Cadillac and chauffeur

were a familiar sight in Indianapolis. In the back seat with the bishop could be seen the dogs who always accompanied him. Raising Airedales was his hobby. His dinner guests were said to have been joined by the big dogs, with their heads bowed, when the bishop spoke the grace before a meal. Bishop Francis enjoyed following the news of baseball and he had, in addition, a consuming interest in doctors and medicine. A canon of the Cathedral was quoted in *The Indianapolis Times* as saying, "Many a struggling young doctor has been helped to success through the bishop's counseling" (**Trinity**, p. 5).

Mrs. Francis appears to have been as memorable a person as the bishop. Here is Sarah Pratt's reminiscence of her:

> It was my fortune to live opposite Mrs. Francis for a number of years. She had many pleasant, helpful plans. She was very hospitable. Bishop Graves's and Bishop McKim's children made long visits there, where they were mothered by Mrs. Francis. Just as she had done in Evansville, she interested herself in the Junior Auxiliary. Having been educated at Kemper Hall, she was able to give the members much churchly training and furnish them with pleasant diversions. Once she arranged the reproduction of a Japanese tea. She had all the fittings and made the occasion very pretty. Mrs. Francis occasionally had a tea on Sunday for girls who worked during the week. Sometimes she would read one of her own stories, vivid pictures of Japan, or someone would read an article from a church paper. When the Auxiliary began to hold Lenten classes, she was always helpful. The first year, the classes were held in the basement of her home, where the diocesan library was then housed (**Episcopal Bishops**, pp. 56-57).

Bishop Francis, the primary mover of the vision of All Saints Cathedral, was gone. The Cathedral Building Fund was in debt (with a deficit of $408.63 on March 25, 1938). The world was again preparing for war, and All Saints was about to face some very difficult years.

*All Saints' Cathedral*

Circa 1915

All Saints Altar (November, 1911)

All Saints Looking East (November, 1911)

All Saints from the north showing wooden extension for altar area
and the bishop's/parish house (November, 1911)

St. Michael's Chapel (November, 1911)

All Saints showing St. Michael's Chapel and Pilcher organ
in the sanctuary

All Saints looking west, showing litany desk, pulpit, eagle lectern, and choir pews, 1911

# CHAPTER SEVEN

## From Cathedral to Parish with
## Shocking Revelations
## All Saints: 1939-1955

Bishop Francis had built All Saints Cathedral. He had lived next door to it and marked it with his personal stamp. He died five days after Bishop Kirchhoffer's consecration and would indeed be missed in the years to come.

The trustees of the diocese adopted the following statement at their first meeting after Bishop Francis' death:

> Joseph Marshall Francis has laid down his burden. He carried it faithfully as Bishop of the Diocese for nearly forty years. He carried it health and in sickness. He carried it to the very brink of the grave; for he relinquished it only five days before his death, and even then only when his successor had taken it. In all things he put the Diocese and the Church ahead of himself and his own advantage. His life was a life of service, and the results of that service and his example will long be felt. So with full realization that nothing we can say can add to his stature as a man and a Bishop, because he stands always in memory for all that was right and that was honest and all that was true, we who in life have served with him through the years now render him homage at his death. Peace be with him.

The trustees, of which The Rev. Robert C. Alexander was secretary, also adopted a resolution creating a memorial fund for the erection of a monument to Bishop Francis in Crown Hill Cemetery and "also one, if possible, in All Saints' Cathedral." A portion of a Bishop Francis Memorial Fund is still retained in the Special Funds of the Diocese for the use of All Saints. And a brass commemorative plaque was placed on the pulpit that had been his. In another action, the trustees resolved that the bishop's widow, Kate S. Francis, would have the use of the Episcopal residence at 1537 for the rest of her life "with heat provided."

The successor, Richard Ainslie Kirchhoffer, was elected bishop coadjutor at a special diocesan convention on October 25, 1938. As a foreshadowing of the decline of the influence of All Saints, the election was held not at the cathedral, but at the recently re-decorated Church of the Advent. And Bishop Kirchhoffer's consecration was not held at All Saints either. It took place on February 8, 1939, at St. Paul's. "The service was broadcast on radio so that Bishop Francis, too ill to attend, might hear it" (**Trinity**, p. 26).

If Mrs. Francis was living in the Episcopal Residence, obviously the new bishop was not. No longer would a bishop be an almost daily presence at 16th and Central. Upon the new bishop's arrival in Indianapolis, the Kirchhoffer family stayed with the rector of the Church of the Advent; "in the years following" the Kirchhoffer family "made Advent their church home" (**Trinity**, p. 26). Here was another sign that All Saints was not to play the same role in the bishop's attention or affection that it had under Bishop Francis. The new bishop, the former rector of Christ Church, Mobile, Alabama, was a self-identified "low churchman." During the episcopate of Bishop Kirchhoffer, however, All Saints would become more and more identified as "high church." For years a legend circulated that the Young People's Fellowship of All Saints and a focus of "high church" enthusiasm had, in protest against Kirchhoffer, detached a mitre from the top of the bishop's official chair in the cathedral. Mary Lockwood Campbell, a member of the Young People's Fellowship, declared this rumor to be pure fiction.

Before his consecration and even before the permission for Mrs. Francis to occupy it for life, Kirchhoffer had indicated that he had no desire to live in the house on Central Avenue. R.H Sherwood had written him on November 10, 1938:

> Those present at the meeting [of the trustees] appreciate why you and Mrs. Kirchhoffer deem the present Bishop's House unsuitable for the needs of your family. Certain lay sources outside of the trustees have also realized

this, and from these sources an additional sum of $1000 per year has been pledged for three years ... for the purpose of insuring a suitable residence for you.

Another letter in the diocesan archives was written on September 21, 1939, by F.G. Phillips of the cathedral congregation (and vice president of Engineering Metal Products Corporation) to the American Church Building Fund Committee requesting a loan.

All Saints Cathedral must be made to seem like a Cathedral ... To meet our own urgent needs and most certainly for a future example of growth and welfare, the Cathedral at Indianapolis should have a new parish house embodying therein facilities for Parish and Sunday School Assembly Room, Sunday School Class Rooms, Parish Dining and Kitchen, Parish and Diocesan Offices. In other words a modern plant in step with the times and as progressive as other militant churches.

The plan proposed tearing down the old Cathedral House on the corner, which was "inadequate" for any residential or parish purposes. In addition to inadequacy, the Cathedral House "obscured" the cathedral church on one side; and Knickerbacker Hall did the same on the other side so "that many people passing there daily are not aware of the cathedral's existence." Therefore, Mr. Phillips proposed tearing down both of "these obsolete buildings." (Knickerbacker Hall was "in such ill state that its rehabilitation for even nominal use is out of the question.") Then landscaping would be done on either side of the cathedral in order "to make everyone realize the diocese of Indianapolis really has a cathedral." In the area vacated, the plan called for the building of apartments,

owned and controlled by the Board of Trustees of the Diocese of Indianapolis. This building would be set well back from the front property line and well to the south from the Cathedral itself. At the rear it would extend in an L shape at the north and back of the Cathedral out to 16th Street. This portion of the building would be the Parish House as previously referred to ... The architect has estimated proposed Parish Hall plant will cost from twenty five to thirty thousand dollars.

Although not fully realized, this plan would ultimately result in the presence of the Cathedral Apartments on the property.

In December, 1939, R.H. Sherwood, Chair of the Finance Committee of the cathedral and president of Central Indiana Coal Company, wrote Bishop Kirchhoffer a letter that gives a reason for the bishop's absence from Cathedral life in 1939, gives a hint of a future significant step in the life of All Saints, and describes how the replacement for Fr. Alexander was called to be vicar:

> You will remember that just before your illness, the congregation of All Saints' Cathedral was considering the advisability of changing their status from that of a Cathedral to a parish. This to be done through the cooperation of the Trustees as to use of the property, with your consent, and whatever confirming action might be necessary canonically by the Convention. It was understood by the congregation that if this was done All Saints would be designated by you as a Pro-Cathedral. It was decided at the congregational meeting at which you spoke shortly before you left, and before any of us knew of your impending illness, to discuss the matter more thoroughly at a subsequent congregational meeting and reach some decision. When you learned that it would be necessary for you to be away from the Diocese for several months, you asked the Finance Committee by letter to assume the responsibility for the welfare of the Cathedral. At a meeting of the Finance Committee held Tuesday, December 12th, the Finance Committee reached the unanimous conclusion that due to your absence it would not be advisable nor proper at this time to ask the congregation to take definite action on the question of maintaining existing status or organizing a parish. While holding this point of view, the Committee felt, however, that inasmuch as the congregation had been without a regular minister since June that further uncertainty as to the program of the Cathedral congregation would have some unfortunate aspects, and possibly tend to some withdrawals to other parishes ... With these thoughts in mind the Finance Committee extended a call to Mr. Linsley.

Already the congregation and the bishop were considering changes in the cathedral status of All Saints.

Richard Mote describes Linsley, the new vicar, as a

> dynamic young priest from Manila, Philippines. Fr. Linsley found no trouble in rallying the congregation around him, but was particularly successful with the young people. His warm personality, added to a natural ability at the piano, was in no small measure responsible for the rapid growth of that group which had been active for the greater part of a decade. Evensong, formerly known as Compline, was continued as the devotional service preceding the social hour in the Cathedral or Parish House, on Sunday

nights. As the war approached, and during its course, the Young People's Fellowship, as it was now called took upon itself such varied activities as entertaining servicemen, holding Evensong at Ft. Harrison and Veteran's Hospital, and visiting other youth groups in Indianapolis parishes (**History of All Saints**, p. 12).

A "Pledge for Support of Vicar" was signed on February 20, 1942, by R.H. Sherwood, chair, and L.E. Gettins, clerk of the Finance Committee of the cathedral, and by Bishop Kirchhoffer. Linsley's salary was to be $2,000 annually, "with living quarters in the Cathedral Apartments, a Pension Premium at the rate of $175 and allowance for transportation in line of local Church duty, not to exceed $25.00 per month."

Philip Smith remembered that Fr. Linsley was married, but had no children. And it was he who introduced the used of plainsong to All Saints.

These, of course, were the years of World War II, which "drained eligible male communicants into the armed forces." By 1944-1945, "the Young People's Fellowship numbered only four, three of them girls" (**History of All Saints**, p. 12).

Fr. Linsley, who had been in the army reserves, was called to active military service as chaplain at Ft. Eustis, Virginia. A deacon named Forest Vaughn was placed in charge of All Saints; and then in March 1941, The Rev. John M. Nelson, the executive secretary and general missioner of the diocese, was given the responsibility for what was supposed to be a short interim. Mr. Nelson was a "low churchman." according to Philip Smith. After two years, Nelson left to go to another diocese, and Fr. James Willard Yoder became the vicar of All Saints. His institution was on August 1, 1943.

All Saints was on the decline statistically. In 1942 there were 117 pledges totaling $5,445.99. The cash balance on January 1, 1942, was $155.53. A year later it was $91.10. The number of pledges in 1943 had slipped to 102 and the pledged amount to $5,241.40. The cathedral was, however, continuing to support ministry beyond the parish. During the calendar year 1942, the total payments for diocesan, national church, and community programs were $1,088.37. This included $157.94 for

"Army, Navy, and British Mission" and $12.36 for "War Sufferers", according to a paper kept in the diocesan archives and entitled "*What the Figures Show.*" In 1944-1945, communicants numbered 195. There were 46 Sunday School students and 5 teachers. Richard Mote lists the names of Smith, Phillips, Lutes, Hull, Robbins, and Bradford as "stalwarts" who stayed with the cathedral during this time.

One other development during these years must be noted. In the spring of 1941, the status of All Saints was changed to that of a parish. The step contemplated a few years earlier was finalized. In other words, the congregation was now to be governed by a vestry elected by the congregation. It was still called a cathedral, but was actually a pro-cathedral, as Grace had been.

Fr. Linsley had written to Bishop Kirchhhoffer on January 9, 1941, requesting a change in the canons of the diocese and the statutes of the cathedral to expand the number of persons on the Finance Committee of All Saints from six to nine, with three classes of rotating terms as is common for vestries. In his letter, Fr. Linsley noted that the chapter

> consists now (according to Canon 30) of the Bishop; the Dean (we assume the vicar takes his place); 3 presbyters elected by the Convention—Rev. Messrs. Thornton, R.F. Keicher, and Yoder; 3 laymen elected by the Convention—Messrs. Knight, Bliss, Trotman; and 6 laymen elected by the congregation—Messrs. W.H. Jordan, C.W. Holmes, L.E. Gettins, J.L. Rainey, Howard Taylor and Dr. C.F. Thompson. We assume that Rev. Francis Tetu is an "honorary canon" as allowed under Statute V, and not an elected Canon member of the Chapter; and we assume that there is no Archdeacon of the Diocese nor Chancellor of the Cathedral. This totals 14 members ... It would likely cause a sensation if it should be possible to have a Chapter meeting ... I explained to the congregational meeting last night that certain formalities would have to be observed before either the "regulation" passed by the congregation in 1939 recommending rotation of membership; or the recommendation passed last night and also previously by the finance committee, concerning enlarging the membership from six to nine.

This letter illustrates more than a little frustration with the bishop and chapter system. So, with the dominating presence of Bishop Francis no longer a factor, All Saints was declared a parish with its own elected vestry. The priest, however, was still titled "vicar;" and it was still the "bishop's church" or pro-cathedral.

A comparison of the Canons of the diocese from the year 1935 to the year 1942 shows how the change was effected. According to Convention Journals, in 1935, Canon 32 read as follows:

> Section 1. The Church in the Diocese of Indianapolis hereby acknowledges All Saints' Cathedral, Indianapolis, as the Cathedral Church of the Diocese; with such Ecclesiastical jurisdiction, rights and privileges and obligations as pertain to any parish organization in union with the Convention.

> Section 2. The Cathedral shall be governed by the Bishop and Chapter. The Chapter shall consist of the following persons: The Bishop of the Diocese, who shall be ex-officio, chairman; The Bishop Coadjutor, should there be one; The Dean of the Cathedral; Two Canons, when such shall be appointed; The Archdeacons of the Diocese; if there be such; The Chancellor of the Cathedral; Three Presbyters, elected by the Diocesan Convention; Three Laymen, elected by the Diocesan Convention; Six Laymen, members of the Cathedral Congregation and elected by it.

> Section 3. The Convention, at each annual meeting, shall elect one presbyter, who has been canonically resident in the Diocese for at least one year; and one layman, a communicant in good standing in some congregation in the Diocese; to serve for three years as members of the Cathedral Chapter.

> Section 4. The Cathedral Congregation shall elect, at each annual meeting, as prescribed by the Canon for electing Wardens and Vestrymen, two laymen, communicants of the Congregation in good standing, to serve for three years as members of the Cathedral Chapter.

> Section 5. Delegates to the Convention, representing the Cathedral Congregation, shall be elected by the Finance Committee of the Chapter in the same way that delegates are elected by a Vestry of a Parish; and their election shall be certified to by the Bishop, the Dean, or the Clerk of that Committee.

> Section 6. The Convention may adopt statutes to govern the Cathedral Chapter, and shall approve all amendments, or repeals thereof.

The 1942 canon was much simpler, allowing more local congregational control.

Section 1. The Church in the Diocese of Indianapolis hereby acknowledges All Saints' Cathedral, Indianapolis, as the Cathedral Church of the Diocese; with such Ecclesiastical jurisdiction, rights and privileges and obligations as pertain to any parish organization in union with the Convention, with the exception that the Bishop of the Diocese shall be Rector of the Cathedral Parish with the privilege of nominating the Vicar, who shall be elected by the Vestry.

Section 2. The Cathedral shall be governed by the Bishop and by the Canon entitled "Of the Vestry" insofar as applicable.

Right before America's entry into World War II, the Cathedral was insured for $40,000 from fire and $10,000 from windstorm. Contents were insured for $500, and the organ for $1,500, from fire. Cathedral House was insured for $8,000 from both fire and windstorm. A report dated February 19, 1941, (and perhaps prepared in anticipation of the switch from cathedral to parish) recommended that insurance on contents be doubled and that property owned by the congregation (and not the trustees of the diocese) be specified as such. After becoming a parish, the diocese retained title to the land and building.

Before his departure, Fr. Linsley had written a three-page memo (retained in the diocesan archives) to the vestry about the financial situation (a hand written note on the document reads, "The things outlined in this memorandum were adopted by the Vestry as a financial plan for the parish"):

By and large the suggestions which I have made have been adopted ... but my principal complaint down through the years has been in regard to a tendency on the part of the old finance committee and now the vestry, to drift on financial affairs and then when they do take them up to shift from one position to another rather than to follow a clear-cut policy.

The vicar's suggestions were to make a budget well before the November Every Member Canvass through a process of meetings with every organization, to include interest and principal repayment in the budget, to organize the canvass as a "sales procedure" (with director, chairman, vice chair who was to be a woman, publicity committee, team captains, and special pledges division), and to establish a promotion chairman who would gather names of persons attending church for purposes of solicitation during the canvass.

Fr. Linsley's successor, Fr. Nelson, followed through on the suggestions. We know this because materials relating to the 1941 canvass are in the diocesan archives. He began his Every Member Canvass letter to the parish with strong words:

> A church must have money with which to carry on its activities and the Cathedral is no exception to this rule. I make this blunt statement at the beginning of a letter to you regarding the Every Member Canvass because it seems a great many people have the attitude "the Church will get along somehow."

The proposed budget for 1942 called for $8,412. It asked for an increase in the vicar's salary from $2,000 to $2,500; in the sexton's salary, from $360 to $480. Other "improvements" requested were $400 for organizing a boy's choir, and $220 for advertising (a neon lighted sign in front of the building and advertising in the Saturday newspapers). But as we have seen, the actual pledges fell far short of the goal and eliminated the possibility of the "improvements."

Letters were written by the vicar to the "special" group asking for leadership gifts to announce at the start of the official canvass. A 14-page packet of materials prepared for the canvass included an introductory letter, a schedule (beginning with a free dinner for all workers on October 30, at which Bishop Kirchhoffer was the speaker), an organization list containing 33 names of leaders and teams for the canvass, an "Outline for conducting a canvass" with suggested approaches for canvass calls, an "Answer to Excuses and Objections," an excerpt from a statement by the bishop that to be a member of the diocese a person had to have a parochial connection through transfer or confirmation, a sample post card announcing to parishioners that a canvasser would be calling, a sample pledge card, a sample canvasser's record for each call, and a sample team captain's tally sheet. (The excerpt from the Bishop's statement and the plan for a "promotion" chair to allow canvassing of all those attending All Saints suggest that some people may have taken advantage of the "cathedral status" of All Saints to avoid making the commitment of transfer and enrollment as a member.)

Furthermore, the canvass was supported by a printed book titled **Forward in Service with All Saints Cathedral.** The frontispiece was a photograph of Bishop Kirchhoffer. On the reverse was a photo of the vestry: J.L. Rainey (Junior Warden), H.G. Taylor, F.G. Phillips, L.W. Danner, M.J. Vidal, C.W. Holmes (Senior Warden). Members not pictured were listed as Dr. C.F. Thompson and D.C. Walmsley. The "Cathedral Program" was introduced by Fr. Nelson (who was also pictured). The four sections of the program were given as <u>Worship</u> ("As Episcopalians we use the **Book of Common Prayer**. Our Services on Sundays, Holy Days and Week days afford regular and frequent opportunities for our members to worship God, receive the Sacrament, and engage in other acts and exercises of devotion for our soul's good, as set forth in that book"), <u>Education</u> ("aims to lead our children and older members in Christian Knowledge, the Ways and Work of our Church, in knowledge of Christian Morals and Duties, and in the development of initiative in Churchmanship and Christian Discipleship"), <u>Service</u> (in parish, community, diocese, nation, and world), and <u>Finance.</u> A map of the parish shows isolated dots for households in Ben Davis, Trader's Point, Southport, Greenwood, Beech Grove, and University Heights. Four to six dots each are located in Irvington, Brightwood and Broad Ripple. The great cluster of dots is on a north-south axis along the Illinois Street to Central Avenue corridors and from the Circle to White River (becoming more scattered north of Fall Creek). Under the heading of Worship, the service schedule is given as follows

Sundays
7:30 A.M        Holy Communion
9:30 A.M.       Church School
10:45 A.M.      Morning Prayer and Sermon
                Holy Communion first Sunday of each month
6:00 P.M.       Choral Evensong—Sponsored by Young Peoples Fellowship

Weekly
5:30 P.M.       Evening Prayer, each Thursday

Holy Days
10:00 A.M.      Holy Communion

Fr. Nelson is pictured wearing a white vestment that appears to be in the shape of a chasuble, but without ornamentation. Another photo shows communicants kneeling at the altar rail (with all the women wearing hats). The cathedral choir, directed by Mr. Spencer, is pictured. There are ten men in the choir, vested in cassock and cotta. Ten women are vested in Canterbury caps and gowns with white collars. Eleven choirgirls are vested in cottas only. The acolyte photograph shows ten boys; crucifers are wearing albs, while torchbearers wear cassock and cottas. There is also a photo of nine ushers (in suit and tie). Another photograph is of the chapel in the south transept (now known as St. Michael's Chapel). A wooden altar is against the east wall. A brass altar cross and two candlesticks (now used at the baptismal font) are on the altar.

Under the heading of Education, the book lists church school classes for Kindergarten, Primary, Junior, Junior High, and Adult (separate classes for men, women, and young people). A Children's Chapel was used for kindergarten and primary children. Also forming part of the Christian Education program were Acolytes, Choir, Confirmation Classes, Young People's Fellowship and Cathedral Women.

Listed first under Service in the Parish is the Young People's Fellowship (also pictured with 20 young people, the girls in dresses and boys in suit and tie).

> Sponsoring Evening Prayer each Sunday evening in the Cathedral provides the Young People's Fellowship with a real opportunity to serve the church. Through its fellowship activities young people without church affiliations are attracted. By joining with similar groups throughout the city it has done much to bring together the young Episcopalians of Indianapolis.

The photo of the Cathedral Women includes 18 women (mostly in hats). Six chapters or guilds are mentioned. They met monthly for worship, study, service, and fellowship. The Men's Club (13 in the picture, all in suits) had a monthly dinner meeting, except during the summer. Its goals were fellowship, increasing attendance of men in church, and helping with the Every Member Canvass.

The section on Service in the Community tells of a survey conducted in the neighborhood (12th Street to 20th Street and Alabama Street to College Avenue) by The Rev. Francis, Tetu, chair of the Diocesan

Department of Christian Social Relations and "an accredited social worker."

> This survey shows that the area is becoming more and more an area of multiple dwellings with absentee ownership. This leads to crowding and attendant problems such as lack of privacy, deprivation of recreational facilities and isolation of families. From one-third to one-half of the mothers in this area are employed. This situation offers the Cathedral an opportunity to sponsor recreational, social, educational and religious activities specifically planned to serve this community, particularly recreation for children after school hours and fellowship for adults.

This quotation from 1941 is indeed prophetic, in several senses of that word. After World War II, the trends toward crowding in multi-family housing and toward mothers employed outside the home would become more than trends; they would help define this increasingly "urban" neighborhood. And the programs outlined in 1941 would become the backbone of the "Altar Centered Social Concern" of the rectorate of Frank V.H. Carthy, also (as Francis Tetu had been) the diocesan Director of Christian Social Relations.

The Diocesan Service section of the 1941 book describes in detail a cathedral garden being developed behind a brick wall enclosing a space where the present columbarium garden is located (although the 1941 garden appears in the photograph to have been larger).

> Under the supervision of Mrs. R.H. Sherwood, the Bishop's Garden is in the process of creation. The rear half is to be used for out-door gatherings, the Men's Club of the Cathedral being responsible for the construction of an outdoor grille. The Diocesan or city-wide young people will be able to use this for their meetings, as well as the Cathedral young people. The center strip opposite the gate will be used for services where an altar and pulpit are to be built, sheltered by the big chestnut tree. The front portion is to be laid out in flower beds, from which flowers for the altar may be furnished. The building of the garden is strictly a cooperative enterprise and the aid of any Episcopalian throughout the Diocese will be welcome. Already an offer to pay for the labor to build the altar has been received from a member of the Cathedral. Other offers of any type are solicited.

(The Sherwood family was a prominent one in the diocese. R. H. Sherwood worked on the canvass of 1941. In later years, the Sherwoods would donate their home at 28th and Meridian to the diocese for use as its headquarters and offices.)

Also noted under Diocesan Service is the fact that the cathedral's contributions helped finance a community house at Charlestown, Indiana, and a Miss Gillespie, the Diocesan Field Worker.

And under Finance, a budget of $9,012 was proposed.

The Every Member Canvass of 1941 may well have been the best-organized campaign in the history of the congregation. Yet it was not to be successful. The final report on the canvass was for only 112 pledges and a total of $5,819.30.

The war years were difficult for all parishes in Indianapolis. In 1942, The Rev. George S. Southworth (with whom the bishop had stayed upon his arrival in Indianapolis) resigned as rector of Advent. In July a plan for the merger of Advent and St. Paul's was proposed,

> at least for the duration of the war. Parishioners of St. Paul's would attend the Church of the Advent, and the Rev. William Burrows, rector of St. Paul's, would become rector of the combined parishes. Property at Sixty-first and Meridian Streets, purchased some months before by St. Paul's, would be the site of a new church to be built after the war by the combined congregations (**Trinity**, p. 35).

Bishop Kirchhoffer was not in favor of the plan, fearing that Advent would be "submerged." The Advent congregation agreed, voting 161 against, 92 for merger, and 67 willing to accept either course.

A new version of a merger plan was proposed in the summer of 1945. This time it was to join Advent and All Saints (which evidently would not "submerge" Advent), and again the occasion was a clergy vacancy.

> Since the vicar of All Saints [Fr. Yoder] planned to leave in August, it was suggested that Mr. Thrasher [new rector of Advent] be made rector of the new parish, to be located at Thirty-third and Meridian Streets. Following a joint vestry meeting at Cathedral House during which Advent representatives accepted the proposal as submitted and those of All Saints' agreed to it with modifications, the unification plan was printed and mailed to members of

both parishes. Parishioners voted on the proposal at meetings in September, and as before, the suggestion was rejected (**Trinity**, p. 38).

An "Official Ballot" was prepared. (A blank sample ballot is preserved in the diocesan archives.) Each voter was asked to state his or her name and to declare whether or not she or he was in favor of "a joinder (sic) between All Saints' Cathedral and the Church of the Advent, thus creating a single parish under a new name." And then the voter was also asked, "If the joinder is consummated will you become a communicant of the new parish?" The ballot was to be returned to the Clerk of the Vestry by September 29, 1945, "excepting those from the Armed Forces."

Despite the chronic financial distress of All Saints, the "joinder" was rejected. As might be expected from such a significant development, some All Saints parishioners disagreed with the decision and transferred out of the parish just when it could ill afford any losses.

The rejection of the proposal determined the geography and character of the Indianapolis parishes for the rest of the twentieth century. Christ Church had long ago decided to stay on the circle instead of joining Grace Cathedral. Before that St. Paul's and Christ Church had rejected a merger. But after the war, Indianapolis would no longer have the problem of two Episcopal Churches almost literally within sight of each other. St. Paul's would build on its lot at 61$^{st}$ and Meridian, capitalizing upon the post-war building boom on the north side of the city. And Advent, renamed as Trinity, would build a new building at 33$^{rd}$ and Meridian. All Saints would stay where it was to face the challenge of a neighborhood becoming increasingly poor and increasingly black in the post-war years of "white flight" to the suburbs.

Fr. J. Willard Yoder resigned from All Saints in 1945 to go to Hammond in the Diocese of Northern Indiana after just over a year of service. He left a very visible mark upon the parish, however, because he introduced the use of full eucharistic vestments. The ground was being prepared for the development of All Saints as an Anglo-Catholic parish. "Many felt that it was unfortunate that Fr. Yoder could not have remained at the cathedral, but the very fact that he was a 'Catholic-minded priest in a predominately evangelical diocese' did not give him any incentive to remain" (**History of All Saints**, p. 13). Fr. Yoder had been ordained at All Saints, had served St. Matthew's parish, and had wanted to come to All Saints, but was at first "not allowed to." According to Philip Smith, after he did become the rector, "he used every holiday as a reason to celebrate the Eucharist. He established a chapter of the Order of St. Vincent's for the acolytes. The first set of mass vestments was white and purchased through the Sisters of the Poor."

The Rev. Charles S. Heckingbottom was curate at Christ Church at this time. He and Fr. Yoder sponsored a diocesan-wide young people's convention at All Saints.

In 1945, Bishop Kirckhoffer was asked for and gave permission to the Cathedral Boy Scout Troop to "use the area south of the Cathedral as a playground area", with the stipulation that a fence be constructed and that the windows be protected. The "adequate fence" was to be erected "on the south boundary between the present lattice work and the brick wall to the west, to avoid trampling the garden on the Cathedral Apts. Side." The bishop stated that, "it must be understood by the cathedral congregation that it is subject to change, if the Diocese should ever make any permanent plans which would involve the use of this property." Prior to use by the Boy Scouts, this portion of the yard had been planted as a Victory Garden during World War II.

As difficult as the war years were, All Saints survived. The Rev. John Thomas Payne replaced Fr. Yoder.

> Fr. Payne was a Canadian, and had come via the Diocese of Michigan. His background was scholarly, but his Canadian reserve and (to some) dry sense of humor were rather strange and confusing. However, under Fr. Payne's rectorship the membership rose slightly, and the Young People's Fellowship was once again its old self, engaging in many spiritual and social activities. The guilds, the choir, the Sunday School all seemed to be in a healthy, active state (**History of All Saints**, p. 13)

Bishop Kirchhoffer instituted Fr. Payne as vicar of All Saints Cathedral parish on December 23, 1945, with the solemn words "you are faithfully to feed that portion of the flock of Christ which is now intrusted to you; not as a man-pleaser, but as continually bearing in mind that you are accountable to us here, and to the Chief Bishop and Sovereign Judge of all, hereafter."

Fr. Payne, originally from Newfoundland, lived in the apartment above the parish hall.
It was now the turn of St. Paul's to worship at 16<sup>th</sup> and Central during a period of construction. Immediately after the war, St. Paul's began to act upon its plan to tear down its building and move north to 61<sup>st</sup> and Meridian Street.

> Both All Saints Cathedral and Church of the Advent invited the downtown St. Paul's Congregation to worship with them during the construction phase, although the Advent invitation came after the vestry already had accepted the All Saints offer. The final service in the old [St. Paul's] church occurred on Whitsunday 1946 (**Blessings,** p. 120).

Since the first service in the new St. Paul's was not held until September 21, 1947, the two congregations shared All Saints for well over a year.

At the invitation of Mary Frances Jones (who was the daughter of Fr. Jones of St. Philip's), Mary Lockwood (later The Rev. Mary Lockwood Campbell) first attended the Young People's Fellowship in 1948. She recalled that the group was a "collection of characters". The ages ranged from 14-25, and participants came from most of the Indianapolis parishes. There were two groups in reality, the "junior high and high school crowd" and the "vets and college kids." However,

> at the time, it seemed natural. The older kids—young adults—read or sang Evening Prayer. Of course only the males did the offices. Attendance at Evening Prayer was required or you couldn't attend the social event later. Our sponsor, Mrs. Harry (Estelle) Lee, was always there. She didn't talk much, but stayed in the background and helped when she was asked for it. The group took turns buying refreshments, set up for, and cleaned up after meetings. Often there was no organized activity. There was table tennis equipment. There was music and dancing—some singing and sharing of stories in small groups. There was a lot of church talk. "Each one teach one" was a United Movement of the Church's Youth slogan one year. Another year the slogan was "To know the Christ and to make Him known." The older kids had a long discussion about that one and pledged themselves to bring at least one other person to the Church sometime in their lifetime. There was love and fun and laughter, but there was also a serious note of

dedication to the Lord and to His Church. Most of us were neither ashamed or afraid to act upon it. I suspect we were a large sized "pain" to our friends on the "outside." I know my focus changed—even my dreams and hopes.

Another member, William Fehr, also remembered the group, but with some differences:

> The YPF at that time (1948-1951) had about 100 members. Many were Episcopalians from other parishes where activities for high school and college age youth were lacking. Many more were non-Episcopalians both from the neighborhood and from churches of other denominations. We met every Sunday evening starting with Evensong (which most of us did not attend) followed by dessert and a business meeting and then dancing to a record player until about 10:00 p.m.

Almost 50 years later, Mr. Fehr still had photographs of two activities which took place during his years of association with the group—a dinner for students of Canterbury College and a Halloween party. The photographs show the young men dressed in suits. He also remembered that the group chartered a bus for a trip to Brown County State Park for a picnic, hikes in the woods, and a touch football game.

In 1948, Fr. Payne "left abruptly with no announcement or warning" to take a position in Maine (**History of All Saints**, p. 13). On October 16, 1948 the *Indianapolis Times* announced that

> Rev. William Edward Ashburn, formerly of St. Peter's Parish, Ellicott City, Maryland, was installed as rector of All Saint's Episcopal Church by the Rt. Rev. R.A. Kirchhoffer ... This marks the beginning of a new epoch for All Saints' for at the request of the membership, the cathedral status was changed to that of a parish church by the diocesan convention.

All Saints ceased to be a pro-cathedral at the diocesan convention in May 1948. As we have seen, the clergy and people of cathedrals sometimes became restive under episcopal control. Desire for more independence at All Saints had been voiced since 1939, the year of transition to the Kirchhoffer episcopate. Richard Mote describes the effects of the change in status this way:

> The relinquishment of cathedral status had little effect on All Saints' either inwardly or outwardly. Indeed, the prevalent feeling among the vestry and

congregation was that since All Saints' had never really been a consecrated cathedral, it could now more normally pursue its spiritual and parochial goals (**History**, p. 14).

The next chapter in the life of All Saints, the rectorate of Fr.Ashburn, would be both short and tragic. Fr. Ashburn was also "high church." He made

> no effort to hide the fact that he intended to bring the full catholic faith, including ritual, of the church to All Saints. The changes which he made brought converts, and made better catholics out of those who had been merely "catholic-minded" before his arrival. Not a few transfers to other city parishes were recorded, however, among them the nucleus of the "old guard" who resented deeply the conversion of the parish" (**History,** p. 14).

Fr. Ashburn's strategy for this "conversion" consisted of a lecture series on Friday nights on doctrine and discipline, of the introduction of incense, of scheduled hours for confession, and of Benediction of the Blessed Sacrament following Evensong on Sundays.

A letter of petition with 70 signatures was sent to the Vestry stating that

> We, the undersigned members of All Saints' Church, are taking this method of conveying to you our desires concerning our Church services. First, we desire a "middle-of-the-road" Prayer Book service with no Anglo-Catholic practices incorporated therein or added thereto. We wish no attempt made to convert us to Anglo-Catholicism. Next, we ask, that, as was our former custom, we have Holy Communion at the eleven o'clock service on the first Sunday of the month only, and that the office of Morning Prayer be read on the remaining Sundays at the late service.

Attached to the copy of the petition in a copy sent to Bishop Kirchoffer (posted on October 12, 1949 and retained in diocesan archives) was an "Explanation":

The so-called "Anglo-Catholic" practices referred to are:
Public announcement of hours of confession.
Establishment of a confessional booth.
Incense.
The use of "Hail Mary" prayers.
Doffing and donning of the chasuble at the altar.
Frequent and ostentatious kissing of the altar by the priest.

Unnecessary and distracting activities of acolytes.
Clearing chancel of choir stalls, thereby giving it a "Romanish" appearance.
In short, the emphasizing of religiosity rather than religion.

Time did not permit of the procurement of additional names—probably twenty more. The Holmes and Holly families (four adults, two children) agree most heartily with the enclosed statement concerning church services; but declined to sign anything being sent to the vestry whose members treated them so shabbily.

Some of the names on the petition and explanation are of persons known to have transferred to other parishes—several to join the congregation of St. Paul's and friends who so recently had been fellow worshippers at All Saints. A few, including Gloria Kemper, continued at All Saints.

Despite the disaffection of many in the parish, Fr. Ashburn put together a booklet (preserved in the diocesan archives) with a very optimistic introduction for the Every Member Canvass to support the 1949 budget: "Many new things are happening at All Saints' Church … We are able to go <u>forward</u> and make plans for the future—Giving <u>new life</u> and vigor for its growth and development, and becoming a <u>more vital force</u> in the lives of the Community and our people." The booklet speaks of plans in Pastoral Work and Religious Education. Pastoral calls, for example, were to "result in increased attendance by both old and new members." Furthermore, Fr. Ashburn stated that "two-thirds of all diseases are brought on by Emotional Conflict"; therefore, "Pastoral work will supplement the Doctor's visit." The goal was to double the "nearly 100 active families" through "constant calling." Religious education was important because Christianity had been "barred from Public Schools." The parish was to "<u>be a worshiping center</u> and a <u>teaching center</u>. The work of Christian Education begins with Children. But also instructs the Parents in the Faith." (Fr. Ashburn was obviously fond of both underlining and capitalization.) The pledge goal to support these plans for 1949 was $12,000 ($2,436 to the diocese and national program; $9,564 for local expense). That goal was extremely ambitious since the 101 current pledges amounted only to $6,186. They ranged from 10 cents per week to $5.77 per week. A breakdown of the amounts contributed by the bottom third, middle third, and upper third: "33 people pledged $651.60, 33 pledged $1,625 and 35 pledged $3,909.40."

The loss of some of the "old guard" was somewhat offset by steadfast support of the rector by the vestry and by the continuing devotion of the young people's group. Nevertheless, within a year the congregation was in the midst of a larger, almost devastating crisis. Richard Mote tells the story, which he knew at first hand, this way:

> Various aspects of Fr. Ashburn's leadership and personal conduct began to draw sharp criticism. An imminent crisis became one in reality with the sudden and shocking revelation of certain acts which he had committed. The subsequent deposition and departure of Fr. Ashburn rocked the whole diocese and plunged All Saints into a crisis the like of which it had never known (**History of All Saints**, p. 14).

Secrecy about the "shocking" revelations, such as found in the Mote quotation, became a kind of hallmark of All Saints history. Gloria Kemper, one of the last parishioners who could have spoken of living through the events, refused to do so.

On June 25, 1949, Bishop Kirchhoffer issued his letter of deposition upon the William E. Ashburn, depriving him "of right to exercise the gifts and spiritual authority as a Minister of God's Word and Sacraments conferred on him at his ordination." The solemn act of deposition took place at All Saints in the presence of The Rev. William Burrows and The Rev. Chester G. Minton. There had been depositions before in the old Grace Cathedral, but this time the priest involved was the congregation's own pastor.

Fr. Ashburn evidently left Indianapolis in haste. In 1958, his mother, Mrs. Ann Ashburn, wrote to Bishop Craine about some of Ashburn's possessions which he had left behind—including his "credentials" of ordination. In this sad correspondence she says, "The separation of my son and his Church has left a dreadful scar, but I try to keep up with God's help and my Church is all I have."

Years later during the rectorate of Fr. Wayne Hanson, the parish would receive a request for information about the deposition:

> I am preparing a parish history of St. Peter's Episcopal Church in Ellicott City, Maryland … and I am looking for information concerning the Rev. William Ashburn … Ashburn served as rector of St. Peter's and left

thereafter to go to Indianapolis. According to information available through the Diocese of Maryland, he was formally deposed as an Episcopal priest by the Diocese of Indianapolis on June 25, 1949. His time in our parish was tumultuous, and he seems to have been quite divisive; after his 1948 departure the parish almost closed. An elderly parishioner who remembers him told me he was "a crook" ... Ashburn was married and had at least one child.

## Fr. Hanson responded,

One current parishioner here at All Saints remembers the scandal, but she was not privy to the details. Another parishioner, who has done historical research about our parish, informs me that there were several newspaper accounts of the incidents leading to William Ashburn's deposition. These parishioners agree that the charges against William Ashburn centered around shoplifting (perhaps even cleptomania) with the clear implication that there may have been some irregularities in the parish's funds.

Mary Lockwood Campbell remembered that the shoplifting had taken place at the local (Roman) Catholic book and supply store. She also remembered that there had been rumors of inappropriate conduct with women in the parish and that, on the other hand, some in the Young People's Fellowship defended Fr. Ashburn as a victim of "low church" attacks.

As a result of the deposition and departure of Fr. Ashburn and

with the unity, if not the very life of the parish threatened, the vestry sought desperately for another priest. Their search was marked by understandable caution. After careful and deliberate consideration, the Rev. Felix L. Cirlot, Th.D., was chosen and installed as rector, December 7, 1949. Fr. Cirlot came from Nashotah House, where he had been an instructor with the distinction of being one of two priests in the American Church with an earned doctorate (**History of All Saints**, p. 14).

On November 2, 1949, Fr. Cirlot accepted the vestry's call with an enthusiasm that was tempered by awareness of the parish's difficulties. In his letter to the vestry (kept in the diocesan archives), he said,

I am sure that by this time I have given the matter of your call to the Rectorship of All Saints' Church adequate consideration. My original intention to accept the call has not in any way been shaken by further thought and prayer … I ask the earnest and wholehearted support of all of you, and of all the members of the parish, in the solution of the many and complicated problems which confront us here in our parish.

The choice of Felix Cirlot as rector reflected the vestry's commitment to continuing an Anglo-Catholic emphasis for the parish. The scandal of Fr. Ashburn did not cause All Saints to swerve from the direction it had so recently chosen at a very high cost. Fr. Cirlot emphasized Holy Communion as the primary service of worship and the practice of auricular confession for all.

More transfers from All Saints' followed, but Fr. Cirlot was careful to impress upon both friends and foes of his program, his belief in and adherence to, the **Book of Common Prayer** as the only guide for the type of religious services and practices that he would allow. Almost on the eve of his installation, Fr. Cirlot began his careful and deliberate policy of drawing dissatisfied persons more closely into the life of the parish. His sermons were deep and scholarly. His participation in the various parish organizations was constant, yet restrained. Newly confirmed persons who had received instruction at his hands, definitely knew what the Episcopal Church was. Perhaps his most commendable habit was his tireless and faithful calling upon the sick and invalid. This was undoubtedly responsible for many converts coming into All Saints' Parish (**History of All Saints**, p. 14).

Richard Mote, in describing the Cirlot years, speaks of

the painful ordeals which invariably befall a parish when it undergoes the transformation from Protestant to Catholic. Voices of complaint would frequently arise, protesting against overly scholarly sermons, the length of the mass, the temperament of the rector, the use of incense, and other items too numerous to mention. This is not to imply that the parish had not moved forward since Fr. Cirlot's arrival, for an amazing degree of unity was achieved and progress was being made. The most critical problem, that of finances, remained to defy the best efforts of priest and laity. Fr. Cirlot constantly preached on this subject, and made special exhortations in order to get out badly needed Christmas and Easter offerings. In 1951, The Diocesan Convention at New Albany reported that "all congregations with the exception of All Saints and St. James, Vincennes, had paid their assessment in full." (**History of All Saints**, p. 14).

Several letters in the archives of the Diocese of Indianapolis from Cirlot requesting the bishop's permission to admit divorced and remarried persons to communion illustrate the pastoral aspect of Fr. Cirlot's ministry. One, for example, says of a parishioner, "I know no reason to think that she is entitled to an annulment in both of her former marriages. But she is not asking to be married in the Church, but only to be readmitted to Communion." The bishop responded favorably "in the interest of justice and mercy and her assurance of making her present marriage a truly Christian one."

Of course, not all marriages presented such pastoral problems. William Fehr and Martha Robinson were married by Fr. Cirlot at All Saints on September 5, 1953. Mr. Fehr remembered that their marriage certificate was filled out in the rector's handwriting because "he had no office help and he had to do everything himself."

A very curious letter in the diocesan archives was sent by the bishop to Fr. Cirlot on March 7, 1952:

It has been brought to my attention that occasionally rumors arise concerning the Church property at 16th and Central Avenue, to the effect that the Trustees contemplate selling it. At the present time my understanding is that the Vestry and Wardens of All Saints' Church have a lease on this property, entered into by mutual agreement, and that the possibility of disposing of the property has never been mentioned or discussed by the Trustees of the Diocese. This is to assure you that any such rumors are without foundation.

Evidently there was enough discomfort about the relationship of All Saints to the diocese to feed such a rumor. And the parish's precarious finances did nothing to dispel the discomfort. The bishop wrote a letter to the vestry on November 23, 1953, about the parish's failure to pay its quota towards the Church's program. (An "assessment" was made upon each parish for the support of the episcopate; in addition, the diocesan Program Fund was supported by "quotas" asked of each parish.) All Saints had paid only $621.90 of its 1952 quota, and by November 1953 had paid only $260 toward its quota of $1,523. The bishop was polite, but clear: "We are hoping that All Saints', being aware of these facts, will make an earnest effort to see that all possible payments are made before the end of the year."

In 1954, the number of communicants was 156. The choir, the Sunday School, and the Young People's Fellowship had all declined. The Sunday School's weakness was apparently related to the post war "baby boom"; there was a "tremendous age gap between babies and older children, and the once young 'young people' had outgrown their tender years ... The regular Sunday Evensong which the Young People had held ... was discontinued sometime during 1953" (**History of All Saints**, p.15). The loss of the Evensong marked the passing of an era, but some of the now no longer "young people" would continue to serve the parish and the larger church for years to come.

One of the members of the young people's group, William Fehr, shared the following reminiscence of Fr. Cirlot:

> My memory is that he was a tall, well built man about 6 ft., soft spoken and very pleasant. He had a wonderful way with young people and I'm sure most of them felt the same as I did, that we could tell him anything and rely on his advice and counsel. I never saw him lose his temper even though some of us, especially me, gave him good reason to do so. Keep in mind, I was eighteen to early twenties when I knew Fr. Cirlot and while we had many long and personal discussions, and I even served as an acolyte, I can't recall his sermons ... I don't recall using anything but the Prayer Book. I was living in California when Fr. Cirlot got sick but I always worried about him living alone over the parish house because of his diabetes.

Other memories of Fr. Cirlot were submitted to the parish by The Rev. Robert Carroll Walters, a member of Trinity Parish who used to serve Fr. Cirlot at the Wednesday morning Mass:

> Breakfasts after Mass were very simple. Father Cirlot would invite me to his room. On one occasion a jar of peanut butter was on his kitchen table. He offered it to me; I must have looked perplexed because he said, "Oh are you one of those who like peanut butter with bread?" He would proceed to tell me about the lives and teaching of the Church Fathers. Two of these sessions of necessity I happened to 'time.' Each had lasted *three* hours. In hindsight what Father Cirlot was doing over those many weeks was giving a course in Patristics to a single student ... He must have recognized the shallowness of his only pupil, but remained driven by his vocation to teach. I came away from Father Cirlot with two indelible gifts: *Awareness of the mystery of the sacramental life* and *The weight and tradition of scholarship behind the Church's teaching and practice ...*

The second remembrance of Fr. Cirlot is of a certain *austerity* in his life. Coming to his room, one saw two chairs, a small table and a *cot* in the midst of his books. It was here that these 'lectures' were given. His teaching style was one which neither dazzled nor overwhelmed but he share gently what he loved.

To honor the rector's twenty-fifth anniversary of ordination, a testimonial dinner was given for him in June, 1953. This was a "bright, brief interlude" for the parish in an otherwise sad time. In 1954, Fr. Cirlot announced that he had begun to have, in addition to diabetes, occasional heart attacks which he described as "not serious, but annoying" (**History of All Saints**, p. 15).

Despite the rector's health problems, the parish embarked upon some major projects. The first was a Preaching Mission conducted by a monk of the Order of the Holy Cross, Fr. Lincoln Taylor. Bishop Kirchhoffer wrote a letter commending this effort on September 11, 1954. According to the bishop, "A Preaching Mission should help us to do two things: to look in upon ourselves—to re-examine the basis of our faith and, secondly, to look out with clearer vision upon the world of men for whom our Lord died, and to identify ourselves with them as perhaps we have never done before."

To improve the parish finances, a professional fund-raising organization (Thomas White Associates) directed the canvass for 1955.

> Mr. Madison Jeffries, of the White Associates, was sent to All Saints' to assume charge of this important effort. The official name designated for the drive was The Budget Expansion Canvass of All Saints' Church. Teams of canvassers were organized, a Loyalty Dinner was held at the Riviera Club, and in February, 1955, the campaign began. Although it started on a note of skepticism (on the part of the canvassers), when it was over the whole parish rejoiced. The quota of approximately $15,000 for the fiscal year had been met, and an atmosphere of genuine optimism seemed to have infected priest and laymen alike (**History of All Saints**, p. 15).

The "Loyalty Dinner" was remembered by Gloria Kemper for another significant reason—it integrated the Riviera Club! She recalled, "At a loyalty dinner held at a private club, precedence was broken as black members attended. (This same club was not to open its swimming privileges to blacks until thirty years later and that after long litigation.)" (Gloria Kemper, "All Saints," **A History of The Episcopal Diocese of Indianapolis, 1838-1988**).

But the optimism of the canvass did not last. A week after Easter in 1955, Fr. Cirlot was hospitalized. When a long rest was prescribed, he moved to Washington, D.C., where he could be cared for by his brother, who was a surgeon. For the first six months, the congregation fully expected him to return; but by the fall of 1955,

> The vestry was now faced with the three-fold problem of seeking a priest to come as assistant rector (assuming that Fr. Cirlot would return), attempting to check defections among loyal pledgees, and securing supply priests for divine services. Except for the irreproachable loyalty of the vast majority of All Saints' parishioners, it conceivably could have closed its doors early after Fr. Cirlot's untimely departure. Unstinting thanks should go to such priests as Frs. Bernhard, Minton, Weldon, and Thornton, who acted as supply. In spite of their kindness, there were many Sundays, especially in the Summer of 1955, when none could be supplied and the congregation had to go to another parish for Holy Communion (**History of All Saints**, p. 15).

Early in October, The Rev. Robert Seaman responded to an ad for a priest placed in *The Living Church* periodical. Fr. Seaman was a retired priest from Maryland. He originally agreed to serve for only one month, but actually stayed until May 1956. Mary Lockwood Campbell remembers that her mother once asked Fr. Seaman, "When are we going to get a priest?" He answered, "What am I, a ballet dancer?"

Fr. Seaman had been persuaded to extend his service to All Saints because the rector's brother had notified the vestry that Fr. Cirlot would never be able to function as a priest again. But in the meantime,

> Fr. Seaman served All Saints' as faithfully as any priest ever had. Holy days of obligation were remembered, sick communions were carried to those in need, Sunday Masses were regularly scheduled—in no category of the priestly life could Fr. Seaman have been reproached. Who can forget his sweet smile and gentle manner? (**History of All Saints**, p. 15.)

On March 30, 1956, *The Indianapolis Star* carried the obituary for Fr. Cirlot, noting that a Solemn Mass was to be celebrated for him at All Saints on the following Saturday. "He was recognized as one of the world's foremost New Testament scholars in the Anglican Communion, and was the author of 10 books and countless magazine articles which were published in this country and in England." Fr. Cirlot was 53 at the time of his death.

One of Fr. Cirlot's books was a defense of the legitimacy of Anglican orders in Apostolic Succession. About 50 years later, a copy of his book would find its way into the parish library. On March 16, 1993, The Rev. Richard W. Daniels, Rector of St. Dunstan's in Tulsa, Oklahoma, wrote to the then rector, Wayne Hanson.

> This is probably completely off the wall. Under separate cover I'm sending you a copy of a very old book by Fr. Felix Cirlot which I came across today in a collection one of my brother priests is unloading—in retirement.
>
> Why I seem to think Fr. Cirlot has a connection with All Saints I can't verify. When I was newly ordained in Indianapolis, eons ago now, I think I recall Fr. Frank V.H. Carthy (we used to say the VH stood for Very High, but it was more like Van Hise), then priest of All Saints regaling everyone with tales of Fr. Cirlot. I thought he was speaking of him as one of his predecessors at All Saints.
>
> So I nabbed the book and whipped it off to you, thinking it might—if any of this recollecting is true—have some minimal interest to visitors to your parish library—if you have one. Silly, isn't it? Obviously you are under no constraint to do anything with it other than put it in the dumpster. It's one of those old, now quaint defenses of Anglican orders vs. the Holy Roman Church.
>
> … My fellow ordinand, now Bp of Michigan, Stewart Wood, is another of your predecessors. Doubtless things are very different at All Saints.

Fr. Hanson answered with pleasure.

> Thank you for your delightful letter and for the book which arrived in the same mail delivery. Your recollection about Fr. Cirlot (and, I might add, about Fr. Carthy's tales pertaining to Cirlot) is absolutely accurate. Carthy has told me that following Cirlot, he felt as though he had inherited an Anglo-Catholic museum.
>
> Cirlot's departure from All Saints is a tale in and of itself. The Rev. Dr. Cirlot became ill and left town (seeking recovery or cure or escape is not entirely clear to me), leaving All Saints in the lurch for rectorial leadership. Finally,

Bishop Kirkhhoffer's representative, The Rev. Canon Earl Conner, had to travel to discuss this situation with Fr. Cirlot. The deal was struck: Cirlot would retire if, and only if, Conner pledged that another Anglo-Catholic priest would be named as his successor. Thus, the ascendancy of Carthy.

Although Cirlot's tenure here was relatively short (that has, interestingly, been true of many of the rectors of this place), it was obviously colorful. There are not many folks left who have any direct recollection of Fr. Cirlot, but his catholic liturgical style and theological perspective (quite reformed at this point, I am relieved to say) both set the tone and established the reputation of this parish. Fr. Cirlot was memorialized here at All Saints with a lovely statue of the Blessed Virgin Mary (Mary, Queen of All Saints). To my knowledge it is still the only statue of Mary in this diocese. She resides in the north transept (with votive lights)—a quiet prayer chapel.

The statue of Our Lady Queen of All Saints in memory of Fr. Cirlot was dedicated on September 29, 1957. According to an *Indianapolis News* article,

> It is the work of Robert Robbins, distinguished New York sculptor, who is known here for his outstanding work on the interior of the new Trinity Episcopal Church ... It is a statue of the infant Jesus in the arms of His mother. The statue is about 5 feet high and stands on a pedestal, surmounted by a tall canopy. The mother is shown standing and wearing a crown representative of her title as Queen of All Saints ... Blessing of the shrine will take place during the solemn procession that follows solemn evensong ... The Very Rev. Malcolm deP. Maynard, dean of Milwaukee will preach. Dean Maynard was a friend of Fr. Cirlot.

The *News* article says that Cirlot was one of three (not two) priests with an earned doctorate in theology in the Episcopal Church at the time of his death on Good Friday, 1956. The degree was from The General Seminary in New York.

> A leading New Testament scholar, he was author of several books, dealing with the holy eucharist, apostolic succession and holy matrimony. In New York and Pennsylvania, Father Cirlot served as a parish priest. At General Seminary, he was a tutor and twice was a member of the faculty at Nashotah House Seminary, Nashotah, Wis. He was also chaplain to convents in New York, New Jersey and Kentucky. It was while he was in Indianapolis that he observed the 25th anniversary of his ordination to the priesthood. He was at his family home at El Paso, Tex., when he died.

By 1956, All Saints was firmly established as the catholic parish in the Diocese of Indianapolis. Bishop White, before the turn of the century, had brought "Puseyite" ideas to his cathedral, but had drawn the line at ritualism. Fr. Sargent had perhaps come close to crossing that line, and his founding of St. David's Church had taken away the parishioners from Grace Cathedral most inclined to "high church" practices. That episode had been the first, but not the last, crisis in the congregation's life centered around churchmanship. Fr. Linsley introduced plain chant. Fr. Yoder bought the first set of mass vestments. Fr. Ashburn's commitment to catholic doctrine and practice led to another exodus of those who objected to his churchmanship. Despite the problems with Ashburn, the vestry called Fr. Cirlot, another priest well known to be "catholic." The next era in the congregation's history would build upon this catholic emphasis, but would also show that God was doing a new thing at 16th and Central.

The Right Reverend RICHARD AINSLEE KIRCHHOFFEER. D.D.
Bishop of Indianapolis

# THE CATHEDRAL PROGRAM

## Rev. JOHN M. NELSON, Vicar.

This book presents the Program of All Saints' Parish, the Cathedral Church of the Diocese. During the past year the whole Church has responded to the call of our Presiding Bishop to engage in a Ten Year Forward in Service Movement.

The Cathedral entered at once, loyally into that Movement, and has followed its plan, step by step.

All Saints' was made a parish last spring, and is continuing its program.

**WORSHIP**

● As Episcopalians we use the Book of Common Prayer. Our Services on Sundays, Holy Days and Week Days afford regular and frequent opportunities for our members to worship God, receive the Sacrament, and engage in other acts and exercises of devotion for our soul's good, as set forth in that Book.

**EDUCATION**

● Our Program of Christian Education aims to lead our Children and older members in Christian Knowledge, the Ways and Work of our Church, in knowledge of Christian Morals and Duties, and in the development of initiative in Churchmanship and Christian Discipleship.

● Here, as portrayed in later pages, the members of All Saints' express thru a number of organizations, their efforts to obey the Gospel Command of love and mutual helpfulness, in these fields:

**SERVICE**

In the Parish
In the Community
In the Diocese
In the Nation and World

**FINANCE**

● In order that the Cathedral may carry on its work effectively, it is necessary to have an adequate budget and provide a means of meeting it. A system of proportionate giving generally adopted by our church gives each individual an opportunity to demonstrate, in a practical way, his responsibility to the Cathedral.

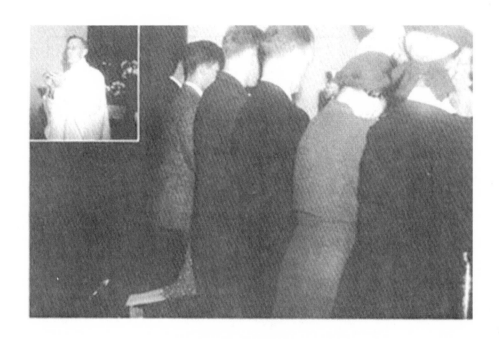

WORSHIP AT ALL SAINTS' CATHEDRAL

CATHEDRAL SERVICES

Sundays

7:30 A.M.  Holy Communion
9:30 A.M.  Church School
10:45 A.M.  Morning Prayer and Sermon
           Holy Communion first Sunday  of  each month
6:00 P.M.  Choral Evensong - Sponsored by
           Young Peoples Fellowship

Weekly

5:30 P.M.  Evening Prayer, each Thursday

Holy Days

10:00 A.M.  Holy Communion

The Cathedral is open daily, 8 a.m.to 4 p.m.,for Prayer
and Meditation.

The Vestry

Left to Right:  J. L. Rainey, Junior Warden;
H. G. Taylor,  F. G. Phillips,  L. W.  Danner,
M. J. Vidal.  C. W. Holmes,  Senior  Warden;
Absentees: Dr. C. Y. Thompson, D. C. Walmsley.

The Cathedral Choir.  Inset:  Mr. Spencer, Director.

The Acolytes                    The Ushers

# All Saints' Church
## Indianapolis, Indiana

### REV. WILLIAM E. ASHBURN
#### RECTOR

# CHAPTER EIGHT

## Stay in the Neighborhood and Slug It Out
## All Saints Parish: 1956-1970

With the call of the next rector, The Rev. Frank V.H. Carthy, a new era would begin for All Saints. A sign that Father Carthy erected in front of the church describes that era in one phrase: *Altar Centered Social Concern.* As far back as Bishop White, the Anglo-Catholic movement in its theological form had influenced the congregation's life. According to the **Oxford Dictionary of the Christian Church,** "Anglo-Catholics emphasize the dogmatic and sacramental aspects of the Christian Creed and life, and the historic continuity of the existing Church of England with that of the Middle Ages." Anglo-Catholicism is often confused with the "high church liturgy" that had become the parish norm by the tenure of Fr. Cirlot. Historically, however, there was another mark of the Anglo-Catholic movement: intentional service to the poor. Beginning with the era of Canon Frank Van Hise Carthy, ministry to the marginalized poor of the neighborhood would distinguish All Saints

The process of the call to Fr. Carthy, however, was not smooth. Richard Mote's **History** tells us that

> The first vestry meeting held in 1956 was truly a historic one. Genuinely concerned over the lack of permanent priestly guidance, Bishop Kirchhoffer met with Dr. Jamieson, Dean Craine and the vestry to discuss various courses of action that lay open. Although parish finances and membership were carefully analyzed, the primary concern remained that of getting a rector. During the course of this meeting the bishop suggested writing to a Rev. Frank Carthy, of the Diocese of New Jersey, as a possible candidate.

> The clerk acted without delay, but apparently from his reply Fr. Carthy was not interested.

Dr. Jamieson was a layman and Treasurer of the Diocese. Dean Craine was John Pares Craine of Christ Church Cathedral, who would soon be consecrated Bishop Coadjutor of the diocese (on St. Mark's Day, 1957).

A consultant from the national church headquarters in New York was invited to come to Indianapolis in April 1956 and make recommendations for both All Saints and St. George's (on the near south side). The consultant, Fr. Musselman, was the Executive Secretary of the Division of Urban Industrial Church Work. His recommendation to the bishop was that St. George's should move further south to capitalize on suburban growth in that area, retaining the present St. George's as a chapel of the Cathedral to spearhead a "really experimental program" reaching out to all races. (That recommendation would eventually lead to Cathedral House, to St. Timothy's parish on the far south side, to the call of The Rev. Malcolm Boyd to lead the outreach at St. George's, and to an Urban Mission Council for coordination of the outreach work of all the urban congregations in Indianapolis.)

The Musselman analysis of the All Saints situation was that the parish was not relating to its neighborhood. As early as 1941, it had been known that the neighborhood was changing to multi-family dwellings. An area that had once been home to prominent and affluent families "moving north", had become almost entirely poor and black after World War II. The GI bill and FHA and VA mortgages had encouraged the building of new homes in suburbs even farther north, had enabled veterans to move to those new suburbs, and had discouraged development in urban cores. "Redlining" by lending institutions and "white flight" had led to the segregation of African-Americans in areas like the one surrounding 16th and Central. Poverty and segregation only intensified in such areas when expressways were built (as a result of The Defense Highway System Act of 1956) to speed commuters away from the city on daily commutes and as urban renewal pushed the displaced poor into the cheapest available housing. All Saints had once again been caught up in great events and developments.

According to Fr. Musselman, however, the parish was not responding to the situation.

> This parish is in a state of near crisis. The obvious element of need is that of an adequate parish house, which is badly in need of repair. The most serious element of crisis, however, is that of the weakness of the congregation in the immediate normal service area of the church ... Unless a parish has a considerable body of communicant strength in the immediate area of the neighborhood, it is inevitably headed for decline. In this parish, the vestry lives, as I understand it, from two to ten miles away from the parish church ... Another obvious weakness of this parish is in its Sunday School, which I understand is made up practically wholly of children of the parishioners ... . Unless the Sunday School becomes an evangelizing agency and includes a large proportion of children from the immediate neighborhood and from families other than the normal parochial constituency, the parish is not actually reproducing itself. We are also emphatically convinced that unless a parish extends certain service facilities to the people of the immediate neighborhood, it will become increasingly irrelevant to the neighborhood and will, therefore, go into serious decline rapidly. It would appear that in the parish program, as far as I have been able to observe it, there is practically no program which is aimed at meeting the recreational, the health, the social and other needs of the immediate neighborhood, let alone the overwhelmingly important spiritual needs.

That diagnosis of a congregation in decline as its "normal parochial constituency" moved away was certainly not unique to All Saints. Unlike many other congregations, however, the parish would not join the "white flight" north, but, with the help its new rector, begin to respond to its neighborhood.

According to the Musselman report there were three options available to All Saints. The first was to move, as St. Paul's had done.

> This is all too often done. It is indeed a very attractive alternative. However, it is apparent that there would be some difficulties in disposing of the present church building, and it would indeed seem to be tragic to allow the present church building to go into other hands in that neighborhood. As I said to the vestry, it would seem to me that unless the Episcopal Church can stay in the neighborhood like that surrounding All Saints' and slug it out, then we really haven't much of a message for American cities. I just think there is a serious moral question about the church retreating from a missionary opportunity such as obviously presents itself in the neighborhood of All Saints'.

Option two was "to continue the program more or less as it has existed. This would mean that they would call some man for the salary that Father Cirlot was getting, which was $325 a month, plus pension and various allowances." The report continued,

> I would not in any way want to discount the effectiveness of Father Cirlot's work. He was a deeply committed man and built a devout congregation. However, if the foundations which he laid are to be built upon and a strong parish come into being, then I doubt very much whether this could be accomplished short of getting a man with more skills than those which are usually obtainable at the salary level mentioned.

(For purposes of comparison, the diocesan minimum salary just a few years later in 1962 was $3,600 per year.)

Fr. Musselman suggested that if All Saints were to call someone at the salary of Father Cirlot, there should still be an attempt to get someone with skills in neighborhood work and his job description should include a neighborhood program. However, the consultant was not hopeful that this idea would work: "My own judgment is that it is already rather late" to try such an approach.

Instead, option three was recommended:

> For a five-year period, to carry on a neighborhood evangelizing ministry coordinated with a Diocesan program of Christian Social Relations. As I pointed out to the vestry, this would require a well trained clergyman with a vocation for social relations and such a clergyman would have to be paid, at the very minimum, $5000 plus suitable housing, plus utilities and car allowance, and pension fund. It is quite probable that to get the right kind of man you need to have to go to $6000. I would think that this rector could be appointed Director of Christian Social Relations for your Diocese ... I would like to see an arrangement whereby the parish would pay at least the amount Father Cirlot was getting and hopefully more while the Diocese paid the balance to the man as Director of Christian Social Relations and the Diocese give some added funds for the proper operation of a Department of Christian Social Relations. Under this plan, the parish of All Saints would undertake a vigorous campaign of evangelism in the neighborhood, trying to do something about the various needs which are apparent in that neighborhood, ministering especially to the high mobility population. At the same time, the parish would become the center of the

Department of Christian Social Relations for the Diocese and thus assume a much greater measure of civic significance than it now has.

This option was indeed followed. After the call was finally negotiated, Fr. Carthy would be made Director of Christian Social Relations and honorary Canon Almoner of the diocese. The suggestions for a neighborhood program as an evangelism tool were precisely what would be implemented during Carthy's tenure. Bishop Kirchhoffer replied to Fr. Musselman:

> My only reaction is that Plan No. 3 is the only feasible one—getting the right man there and having him head up the Department of Christian Social Relations, working out from there and possibly through the Cathedral. What the reaction of the present Vestry to that would be, there is no telling. I was much disappointed that they continue to be bargain hunters.

That reference to "bargain hunters" is explained in a separate letter to Bishop Kirchhoffer written by Fr. Musselman on the same day that he had submitted his recommendations:

> Informally, I want to say that you may or may not know that the vestry approached the Rev. Mr. Carthy on the basis of not the $5000 plus about which I spoke to them but the $325 per month. The letter was misdirected and only reached him the day after Easter. He, of course, has a parish of 700 communicants and his interest in All Saints' could only be enlisted on the basis of proposition #3.

Fr. Carthy was "not interested" (to quote Richard Mote) unless the parish was interested in the vision of "Plan No. 3" and willing to support such a plan with cooperative arrangements and financial commitments. The Mote history says that "several months passed" and the vestry again met with Dr. Jamieson, the Dean, and the Bishop.

> It was agreed that from the tone of his letter Fr. Carthy had misunderstood the nature and urgency of All Saints' Call, and another letter was quickly dispatched. This one was of more than ordinary importance, for the parish had received the shocking news that Fr. Cirlot had died on Good Friday. From this point on there could be no question of looking back.

In the meantime, Ian Douglas Mitchell, a member of the parish, was helping Fr. Seaman in parish work (without pay) and filling a "desperate void" with a "wide-range of non-sacramental duties." Ian would later be married at All Saints, ordained a priest, and would become one of the parish's more famous sons as a musician priest. He was the composer of the American Folk Song Mass and the Morning Glory Mass. In 1995 he published an autobiography, which contained this description of All Saints:

> In 1947 my mother, father, and sister moved to Indianapolis, where my father began working for the Stewart-Warner Corporation. All Saints Church became our Episcopal home in the late 1940s and 1950s It had a distinctive high church presence in the Diocese of Indianapolis where a dynamic young people's group in their twenties practiced their religion with uncommon zeal. Father Felix L. Cirlot, a former professor of theology at General Seminary in New York, and rector during that period was a compelling figure who directed us in the strict orthodoxy of the faith with a dedicated devotion to the priestly life. As a result All Saints sent five men to seminary in the early 1950s.

Ian was one of those five seminarians. Before going to Nashotah House seminary, he had gone to Canterbury College, a college in Danville affiliated with the two Episcopal dioceses in Indiana from 1949-1953. The college's demise was not unlike the crisis which had almost brought about the death of All Saints just a few years before—a scandal involving a priest against a background of high-church versus low-church bitterness. In its short history, however, Canterbury made a remarkable contribution to the church. In his book, Ian Mitchell counted 61 priests of the church who had attended Canterbury. Mary Lockwood Campbell, who would become a Priest Affiliate of All Saints after her retirement, was another one of those priests educated at Canterbury.

Ian Mitchell also wrote a musical called *The Red Lizard*. In it Jesus is one of the characters. He sings (as Fr. Mitchell sang and preached) about the church:

> You can't escape the horrors by coming
> Here to hide.
> There is no sanctuary from the tragedies
> Outside. Run for the doors!
> Run for the doors and listen;
> Listen for the cries you cannot hear

For they make no sound.
Run for the doors and protest;
Protest from the rooftops,
I'm mad as hell, and I won't take it anymore.
Run for the doors. Run for the doors.

The Jesus proclaimed by "Altar Centered Social Concern" was a Lord for a city outside "the doors."

Fr. Seaman left All Saints to return to the East after eight months. So when Fr. Carthy returned to Indianapolis in June 1956 to talk to the vestry, it "was the occasion of anxiety and prayer" as to whether or not he would accept the vestry's "unanimous" call to All Saints.

He did accept. One of the conditions was the purchase of a house (at 540 Central Court) for use as a rectory. In July, Bishop Kirchhoffer wrote to the Standing Committee of the diocese to get the necessary approval for the parish's purchase and loan. The bishop says, "John Craine ... has been in on this whole house deal for All Saints', who are buying it in order to secure a new Rector. Frank Carthy has accepted with this in view." A 13 year loan for $8,500 was obtained in August.

Also in August, Jerry Belknap was in correspondence with the bishop about division of the moving expenses between parish and diocese. Belknap, a lawyer in the firm that would eventually be named Barnes and Thornburg, had come to All Saints in 1946 and lived in the Canterbury Apartments across 16th Street from the Church. He had been a member of the vestry during Fr. Cirlot's years. Later he would serve the diocese as treasurer and the community as a member of the Indianapolis school board during the city's struggles with school integration.

All the details were finally settled, and Fr. Carthy moved with his family from Cranford, New Jersey, to Indianapolis in the middle of September. An article in a local paper gave an extensive biography in its announcement of his arrival:

An active worker in the social relations field Father Carthy during his 11 years at Cranford served as board member and chaplain for the Youth Consultation Service of the denomination and as a member of the Committee of Philosophy and Function of the National Episcopal Service for Youth. Father Carthy also has been a member of the New Jersey Diocesan Board of Christian Social Relations and represented the Episcopal Diocese of that state at the National Conference on the Churches and Social Welfare. He was vice-president of the Cranford clergy council, and member of the Union County (N.J.) Association for Mental Health and chaplain of the Cranford Fire Department. The new All Saints rector, his wife, and three daughters will reside at the rectory, 540 North Central Court.

Paul Moore (who would become Dean of Christ Church, then Bishop in first Washington, D.C.. and later New York), in his autobiography titled **Presences**, described his friend Frank Carthy as "another imported Easterner, who was more radical in his views than we. He was a rotund, humorous black-haired Irishman who grew up in the labor movement. He, too, had read Dorothy Day and the worker-priests."

The new rector's first Sunday at All Saints was September 16, 1956. The leaflet for the 9 a.m. Solemn Mass is preserved, along with other bulletins of the era, in the parish archives. It listed pages in the Prayer Book only for the Collect, Epistle, Gospel, and Creed, perhaps an indication that the remainder of the service was from the Anglican Missal. (An altar copy of the Anglican Missal is still in the possession of the parish.) Minor propers (Introit, Alleluia Verse, and Communio) were used, and the service music was the Missa de Angelis (plainsong). The leaflet said,

> Today we welcome to our parish family Father Frank V.H. Carthy and his family. The rector for whom we have so long sought has finally come to us in answer to all of our prayers. We are full of grateful joy and happiness to Almighty God for His true blessing on all of us. We offer to him our hearts and our hands, trusting that our Lord will give us the Grace to join with Father Carthy in this great venture for All Saints', Jesus Christ and His whole Church. May God bless Father Carthy, his wife and daughters as they begin their life with us at All Saints' parish.

Included in the announcements was a notice of a meeting of The Guild of St. Mary with a pitch-in supper. There was a reminder that the meeting was an Ember Day and that menus should be planned accordingly (without meat). A parish picnic was also planned for the following Sunday at Waycross, the diocesan camp in Brown County (with no prohibitions in the menu).

On October 21, 1956, Fr. James Mote, one of the sons of the parish, returned to Indianapolis to visit his family. He said the 7:30 Mass on that day and preached at the Solemn Mass at 9:15. (Fr. Mote would become bishop in one of the Anglican churches splitting from the Episcopal Church after the 1977 ordination of a woman at All Saints.)

In the announcements for the day we find an example of the Carthy style of communication:

> A real crisis is facing the Altar Guild and the Rector feels that an admonition is necessary. The situation with respect to our linens is deplorable; many willing but forgetful folks have taken purificators and amices home to be laundered and have not returned them. The result is that the Rector had to say Mass without an amice last week! This may seem a trivial matter to some, but we can assure you that it reflects a serious state of affairs and at the very least a lackadaisical attitude toward altar guild work in a Catholic parish. Can we not have a little cooperation in this matter, please? If you have any linens at home, will you get in touch with Miss Mary Lockwood immediately?

The leaflet for the All Saints Day celebration of Fr. Carthy's first year contained the following statement in its announcement of the plans for his Institution:

> Small in numbers, struggling with financial deficits, harassed by the problems of a changing neighborhood, weakened by the loss of parishioners to more prosperous parishes and locations, we still have enough "hope of our calling" to dare to install a new Rector and to plan positively for the future—come what may, cost what it will. May the example of the Saints in every age strengthen us in our temptation to despair; may their prayers before the throne of the Most High God avail mightily for our needs as a parish family.

A Choral Evensong on Sunday, November 4, 1956, saw the Institution of Fr. Carthy as rector. Richard Mote says the church was "packed". The Cathedral Choir of men and boys sang the service, under the direction of Robert W. Hobbs. The guest organist was Berniece Fee Mozingo (who would later become organist of All Saints). The bishop presided. The Master of Ceremonies was Canon Earl Conner. The officiant at Evensong was Canon Frederic P. Williams. The preacher was Dean John Pares Craine. The Bishop's Chaplain was The Rev. William L.

Casady. This list of names represents much of the leadership of the diocese and persons who would be important to the parish in the years ahead. A month later, John Craine would be elected Bishop Co-adjutor. Earl Conner and Frederic P. Williams would soon be serving on the new bishop's staff. William Casady was another product of Canterbury College. He would soon be working in the summer youth programs which became a feature of All Saints' life in the Carthy years.

This cast of characters met regularly at 7 a.m. on Tuesday mornings. Paul Moore recalled these gatherings fondly:

> Bishop Craine encouraged me to have a weekly Eucharist together with the other cathedral canons and the inner-city clergy. He celebrated the Eucharist, and then we had breakfast and talked at length. This was the cathedral chapter, and it became the group we relied on for support and stimulus. Frank Carthy regaled us on occasion with hearty labor-union songs. Henry Hill was there, a quiet black priest, rector of the only Negro parish in the diocese, St. Philip's … . Malcolm Boyd, who had been a partner of Mary Pickford's in Hollywood and who later became known as the "espresso priest," came as rector of a nearby inner-city church. A few years later, he was driven out of the Diocese of Michigan because on television, in an effort to emphasize the humanity of Jesus, he'd said that Jesus had … a penis … Luckily, he did not say that in Indianapolis … . This was the inner circle. Here we exchanged ideas, kidded one another, laughed, and comforted one another when things went wrong. Out of these weekly conversations grew the style and spirit of our ministry there.

An announcement in the service leaflet for the Institution invited the congregation to visit the offices of the Diocesan Department of Christian Social Relations in the All Saints' parish house during the reception after the service.

On the following Sunday, the congregation would find another admonition from the rector:

> The Institution was a grand affair which all who attended will remember for a long time to come. Now, however, what remains for us, the family of this parish, is to return with renewed vigor and determination to the tasks which are before us. The solemnity of All Saints' festival, the grandeur of the music and liturgy echoes in our ears; the hard daily jobs of building up our parish and insuring its continuance remain.

We also learn from the leaflet that Gloria Kemper was in charge of the United Thank Offering ingathering for the year. Phil Sourwine was in charge of contacting and training acolytes and would welcome more (boys) at the weekly rehearsals. The Altar Guild was to meet at the home of Mary Lockwood because there was "much sewing to be done on altar linens." There were two further notes from the rector in his no-nonsense style:

> Saturday's Requiem ought to find some present who made no effort on All Souls' Day. To pray, at Mass, for our loved departed is a great Catholic privilege; why do so many neglect it!

> The Sanctuary Light is now white and many have asked "why"? Because it is the proper liturgical color for the Blessed Sacrament. Red was used in some parishes in order that the Presence might be more readily known, but the usage was always frowned on by liturgists and in using the white light we are reverting to correct practice.

The leaflets for services during Carthy's first Holy Week and Easter in 1957 gave him an opportunity to teach "correct practice." The Palm Sunday leaflet tells us that the liturgy for Blessing and Procession of Palms is from the "Green Book." (Is this the Anglican Missal?). We also find the following announcements in the week's leaflets:

> Those interested in Holy Confirmation are expected to attend the Mass and Class each week.

> The Choir and Acolytes have rehearsed long and hard for the ceremonies of Solemn Mass. We hope you will attend the 9:15. If you must attend the 7:30 on Palm Sunday, notify us and we will save you a spray of palm.

> Everyone should strive to make a good confession before his Easter communion.

> Don't forget All Saints' Polio Clinic tonight, April 12 at 7:30. Those who have not been shot before "Stations" will be taken care of afterwards (*sic!*) and we hope to have some light refreshment for all attending this Clinic.

> Please fill out the Easter Communion slips and deposit them with your Offering Easter Day. We are anxious to have an accurate communicant list, and since Easter Communion is REQUIRED if you wish to remain a "communicant in good standing" you will, thus, insure (*sic*) being registered correctly on the Parish Roll.

The Queen of Seasons is drawing nigh and for us members of the corporate body of Christ this glorious feast is the occasion for great rejoicing. One lesser aspect of that rejoicing is the inner compulsion to make a special gift to Mother Church to mark the occasion. In our parish, where sacrificial giving is an inherent part of church membership, the making of a special Easter offering has been a matter of course without reference to the parish's need, for the offering is primarily a matter of the member's need to give rather than of the parish's need to receive. But let there be no misunderstanding, the need of All Saints for a good Easter offering is critical. Our financial situation is not disheartening by any means, but our regular offerings still do not meet our minimum needs. A good Easter offering is therefore vital. The rule of thumb for an Easter offering at All Saints is that it should be at least 5 times the regular weekly pledge.

Maundy Thursday.
Two chief ideas are put before us: that of the betrayal of our Lord by Judas, and that of the Institution of the Blessed Sacrament. Both are combined in the words of the Prayer of Consecration "who in the night that He was betrayed, took bread." Gloria in Excelsis is sung, bells are rung and then remain silent 'til Easter. At the end of Mass, a Procession is formed and Hymns 199 and 200 are sung as the Sacrament is bourne to the Altar of Repose. The Stripping of the High Altar follows as the Choir chants Psalm 22. The Watch begins to continue until noon of the next day.

Good Friday
Today's Liturgy begins with the Lessons, the Passion, and the Solemn Prayers. Next follows the Veneration of the Cross in which all the faithful will wish to join if they are able, making a single genuflexion before kissing the feet. Hymn 63 is sung. Then a procession is formed during the singing of Hymn 66, the congregation kneeling and the Deacon goes to the Altar of Repose and brings the Blessed Sacrament to the High Altar. Following the "Our Father", the Priest consumes the Sacrament and everyone flees the Altar. The remaining time until 3 p.m. is occupied by the Devotion of Stations of the Cross and Meditation. So we leave the bleak and bare Church.

Holy Saturday
Today's worship consists of the commemoration of the Christian Passover. It begins with the Blessing of the New Fire and Paschal Candle, the beautiful "Exsultet" is sung, and then follows the Lessons or Prophecies. Following the Blessing of the Baptismal water we renew our baptismal vows preceded by the first part of the Litany of the Saints, all kneeling and join in the response "Pray for us" and, later, "we beseech thee hear us." During the renewing of the vows we respond "we do renounce" standing. After renewing our Baptismal Vows, the Priest sprinkles the congregation as a

reminder of our Baptism. All is in readiness now for the beginning of the Glorious Easter Mass.

There is but a short time remaining for those who wish to contribute to the purse for Dean Craine's car as a gift to the Coadjutor-Elect from the laity.

We have cause for Easter rejoicing: Mr. and Mrs. Rudolph Schulte and family have transferred to All Saints' from Trinity; also Mr. and Mrs. James F. Blande and son, James P., have transferred from St. Paul's.

Did you sign for the Watch? Unless we get some names for late night and early morning hours we're going to have to "lock up" and I want to avoid that if possible. "Could ye not watch with me one brief hour?" Our Lord asked His Disciples during His Agony in the Garden of Gethsemane; those who love Him will surely wish to spend some time in loving Meditation and Adoration before His Eucharistic Presence.

Father Carthy obviously had no difficulty in getting to the point or stating what he thought! And he very quickly began to implement "Plan No. 3" as the guiding vision for the parish. According to the Mote history,

The year 1957 was to witness much activity at All Saints'. In February the first board meeting of the Christian Social Relations Department, organized by Fr. Carthy, was held. Mrs. John Harvey, a communicant of the parish, was engaged as a social service worker to help carry out this program, long needed in the diocese. The first task of "C.S.R." (as it was thereafter to be called) involved the organization of a city-mission type social agency, which would serve all priests and their parishes in the Central Deanery.

Mrs. Bonnie Harvey was not only the social worker assisting Fr. Carthy; she would also be, at various times, secretary, clerk, vestry member, and friend to an entire generation of neighborhood children.

Another activity in the sphere of social work was the formation of the Urban Mission Council, on March 25, 1958. Its purpose was to coordinate the evangelistic and neighborhood outreach program of the three downtown parishes. Among its contribution has been the "Camp-at-Home" program, running for a six week period beginning with the summer of 1958. It has been expanded each successive year, and now [1964] is a year-around activity of the Department of C.S.R, utilizing seminarians and college students, plus many needed volunteers ... . In May, 1958 came the incorporation of a new agency, Episcopal Community Services, with the Bishop Co-Adjutor president, Fr. Carthy executive director, and Mrs. Harvey social worker. One of its first tasks was the creation of a food and clothing bank, to help the needy, regardless of creed or color.

The maze of inter-related agencies located at 16th and Central that would mark the Carthy years was now in place—CSR, ECS, Urban Mission Council, and parish. It was not always clear which organization was doing what project or which pocket was paying for it. The recipients of service in the neighborhood, of course, did not care about such details.

Bishop Kirchhoffer made his visitation to the parish on October 6, 1957. The open offering of $14 on that date was given, as is customary, to the Bishop's Discretionary Fund. In his letter of thanks, the bishop says, "It was wonderful day and I am so proud of all of you people there and your fine rector."

In the summer of 1958, the Urban Industrial Churchwork Division of the National Council of the Church granted "several thousand" dollars for an assistant for Fr. Carthy. The assistant was The Rev. Robert T. Jenks, who started work on October 1, 1958. He was assistant director of CSR. In 1959 he became director of ECS. Fr. Jenks resigned in the summer of 1961 to become rector of St. Peter's, Chelsea, in New York City. A reception for Fr. Jenks and his wife Marie was held on July 27, 1961, with an invitation issued jointly by Jerry Belknap (Senior Warden), Mrs. Robert (Gloria) Kemper (President of the All Saints Churchwomen), and Claude M. Spillman, Jr. (President of ECS). Jenks was later replaced by The Rev. Peter C. Moore, who had been vicar of St. Timothy's on the south side of Indianapolis. Fr. Moore's title was Executive Director of ECS and Priest-Associate of All Saints.

With the addition of national church dollars to diocesan (CSR) and parish funds, the financing of the program at 16th and Central became even more complex. The budgets were also growing. The Camp-at-Home program cost $1,000 in 1958; in 1963, $18,000. CSR's first budget was $250 (in 1956); in 1963, it was $14,000. ECS grew from a budget of $900 in 1957 to $27,000 in 1963.

On September 13, 1958, John R. Russell, Clerk of the Vestry, wrote to the Bishop and Council of the Diocese about the repair of the roof of the church. Given the complicated finances, the question arose about which pocket should pay. The vestry voted

> to accept 1/3 of the cost of roof repairs to the old Cathedral structure as our parish's share. It was our understanding that this is to be paid by our treasurer in three equal installments over a period of three years beginning in 1959. The Diocese, we understand, would pay the total amount on completion of repairs … We wish it were within our power to pay more toward this major repair, but our financial situation remains precarious and our heat bill, for example, will rise 80% this year due to an increase recently granted to the steam Utility Company.

All Saints was the "end of the line" for the steam heating system of downtown Indianapolis, which terminated at 16<sup>th</sup> Street, and problems with the steam heat marked the history of the All Saints building until nearly the end of the 20<sup>th</sup> century. The original steam radiators in the nave were placed in niches which have since been enclosed. A boiler system had heated the building at first. The unused boiler was still in place in 1962, when there was a bid of $2,650 to remove it. In 1965, the Diocesan Property Committee wrote to Fr. Carthy warning that escaping steam from the city line was threatening the valves of the system.

The bid for the repairs in 1958 was $1,900. Donald B. Davidson, chair of the Diocesan Property Committee, wrote to the bishop saying "this acceptance of responsibility by All Saints in sharing a rather large maintenance item is commendable." Evidently everyone understood that the property was owned by the diocese and that the parish was unable to maintain the property without help.

Life in the inner city meant other problems, too. There was, for example a burglary of $110 in cash on December 29, 1960, which was covered by insurance.

The Rev. Alden W. Powers joined the staff as a third clergyman in July of 1962 (making weekly Solemn High Masses possible with the roles of priest, deacon, and sub-deacon all filled by clergy). He was to be Curate of All Saints and director of the neighborhood youth program.

Fr. Powers, however, was not a stranger to All Saints. He had started as youth worker for CSR in January 1958 and had then become a probation officer for the Marion County Juvenile Court. It took some financial juggling to pay Fr. Powers. A letter from Fr. Carthy to the bishop dated March 13, 1962, says,

> In proposing $1,000 be paid by the Diocese in 1963, the parish should be asked to pay that amount to Al Powers and some provision should also be made for a part time parish secretary. Al will want to go to work in August so there is the added problem of All Saints' paying him from August to December 31, 1962 until the "switch-over" is made on my $1,000. We can probably work this out satisfactorily if the vestry will "buy it."

A note in the Bishop Craine's handwriting indicates that the vestry approved the arrangement on March 14.

The Talbot Fund was an endowment established by Eli Lilly "to assure that Christ Church can remain on Monument Circle" and with the hope "that until such time as the Protestant Episcopal Diocese of Indianapolis may be able to construct and support a Cathedral, Christ Church ... may be designated as the Pro-Cathedral." Paul Moore recalled how Eli Lilly had approached him wondering how he might give more money to the church.

> Imagine the excitement this caused at the next cathedral chapter breakfast. Through the general good feeling, Carthy mumbled something about capitalism; Boyd thought this could fund a television documentary; the bishop showed a mix of satisfaction, puzzlement, and deliberation on his long-jawed face. How much should I ask for at my next lunch with Mr. Eli? "I'm not talking about chicken feed," he mumbled. "Prepare something for a million dollars."

> So it was that the Talbot Fund ... was established to finance work done by the church in the city of Indianapolis. The money could not be used for Christ Church parish except in a dire emergency. We were on our way in a substantive way to the city.

The budget proposed to the Talbot Fund for Fr. Powers was a salary of $4,200 (the $1,000 from All Saints plus $3200 from the Talbot Fund), plus pension, car and utility allowance, and medical insurance. Fr. Carthy's application says:

I have pastoral charge of a congregation which in the last few years has been able to adjust to the violent changes in this neighborhood in an increasingly progressive and Christian way. Despite the fact that there are still a few members of the old families who keep a sentimental attachment to the old parish and its ways, give it some financial support, and try to keep the old pattern, the old traditions in place, there is still the wonderful exhilaration which has been felt throughout the parish in recent years in the "vocation" which the parish has sponsored with my coming in 1956. This led to the formal foundation not only of the Department of Christian Social Relations, but of the inauguration of the Episcopal Community Services, Inc. Both these entities are now firmly established in the life of our city and Diocese. While I no longer have any relationship other than that of an officer of the Board of Directors of Episcopal Community services, I am still part-time Executive of the Department of Christian Social Relations, and am finding the work in this area increasingly demanding on my time and talent … . The Rev. Alden W. Powers, presently part-time Curate of All Saints Church has been studying for the past year at the Indiana School of Social Service. This young man has been known to the writer for some years as a person with deep interest in the inner city and its problems. He has served in the Urban Mission Council Summer Program, has worked as a probation officer at both the Juvenile Court and as a Caseworker at the Children's Bureau of Indianapolis … . I can think of no person more fitted to assist me in the rapidly growing neighborhood program among the children and families in the area immediately surrounding All Saints' Church.

Despite (or perhaps because of) all the exciting developments at 16th and Central, the parish experienced some rough moments during these years. In his Lenten letter to the congregation on Ash Wednesday, 1959, (now in the diocesan archives), Fr. Carthy says,

From time to time, I hear complaints (usually at third hand) about myself or some staff member and the way in which our office is administered and our time spent. The truth is, of course, that I am a fallible human being as is every other person who works at 1559 Central, and, undoubtedly, mistakes are made by us as often as by anyone else. In an attempt to deal firmly and fairly with the resulting tensions, I have recently established a Parish Council made up of representatives of each group in the parish, who will help me plan the parish calendar. May I ask, therefore, that complaints, criticisms, and suggestions be channeled through the Vestry and this Council whenever possible? Unlike most parishes, All Saints' has a dual or triple job on its shoulders every day of the week and the physical and emotional demands on the staff are enormous.

During that Lent of 1959, each Friday was observed by Stations and Adoration followed by a discussion around the theme "The Church and Family Life." Clergy of All Saints and the Cathedral were the leaders.

Through the efforts of Canon Earl Conner, the large crucifix which had been at St. George's Parish (now closed) was given to All Saints in 1959. This crucifix is now the focal point of the strikingly plain brick apse constructed in 1964. Jack Eltzroth, Clerk of the Vestry, expressed the thanks of the parish to Bishop Craine for the gift of the crucix:.

> Both our visitors and parishioners have remarked how its presence has enhanced the beauty of the interior of our parish church. It is our hope that you, in your visitations around the city, might express our appreciation and delight to the many individuals who attended Saint George's.

The crucifix, however, was not so beloved by Malcolm Boyd, the last rector of St. George's, who wrote in his autobiography **Gay Priest: An Inner Journey**:

> When I arrived at St. George's, a life-size figure of Jesus nailed to a wooden cross was hanging over the altar. Indeed, the stark emblem of Jesus' suffering reflected the hunger, crime, broken homes, racial hatred, and human deprivation that marked life in the neighborhood surrounding the church. Yet I felt that St. George's remained locked within the experience of Jesus' crucifixion, overlooking the joy and fulfillment of his resurrection. The rhythm and symbols of the church year, moving from Advent to Christmas and from Lent to Easter, unite the fragments in Jesus' life. But at St. George's, on Easter, we had no symbol of the triumphant Christ to mark the end of Good Friday's pain and death. When I sought the backing of parishioners to keep the figure of the suffering Christ over the altar only in the penitential seasons of Advent and Lent, and to replace it in other parts of the year with an empty cross or a triumphant risen Christ, I encountered only anger and resistance.

The issue of Fr. Carthy's salary and how it would be split between diocese and parish was raised again in 1960. Mrs. Marjorie Dorsey, chair of the Department of Christian Social Relations, wrote to the Senior Warden, Robert Nowicki, that the diocese was increasing its share by $500 for 1961. The vestry was asked to match this increase all, or in part. Since the responsibility of Fr. Carthy's stipend is a joint one between your Parish and the Diocese, the members of our Department feel that your Vestry would want to share equally, if possible in improving his very modest stipend. We feel that both we and you are most fortunate in having and sharing the services of this capable, devoted, and faithful priest and it is to our mutual advantage to do all we can toward insuring (*sic*) his continuance with us for many years to come.

Fr. Carthy may have been "high church", but he could be practical about his churchmanship, perhaps more practical than some of his congregation. He felt constrained to write the following letter to the parish on March 28, 1963:

> The Bishop has dispensed from the normal Lenten and Friday Rule for the [Central Deanery] Rally Dinner. Some of you have expressed yourselves as being opposed to his decision, but you may be interested to learn that he made it only after careful consultation with the Board of Health of the City who take a very dim view of fish as a main entrée at any amateur Church dinner to be served by volunteer Church women. Every woman worker has to be examined before working on the dinner and the "Spoilage" factor of fish made authorities dubious. This is the <u>real</u> reason for the dispensation. In any case, if your conscience forbids even after Episcopal dispensation, please follow S. Paul's advice in Romans 14—"Let no one over his meat, mock at him who does not eat it or the second, while he abstains pass judgment on him who eats it." Our Bishop would be the last person in the world to ask you to violate your conscience. And the Bishop should receive our support by attendance at the Rally whether we eat or abstain. I know our people will not give cause for offence.

The consultant's report in preparation for the call of Fr. Carthy had outlined a joint project of parish and diocese to serve the neighborhood. With that plan now implemented, the parish and diocese turned attention to the lack of adequate parish house facilities to house the program. This problem began to be addressed in 1960, but it was not to be solved quickly.

Bishop Craine asked Fr. Carthy and Claude M. Spilman, Jr. (president of ECS) to suggest names for a committee with representation from All Saints, ECS, and the Diocese to "study our building needs at 16th and Central." This committee had been suggested at a meeting of the Diocesan Council in June 1960.

A sketch of a proposed addition to All Saints by Donald B. Davidson dated January 1960. suggests the removal of the "temporary" wooden sanctuary still in use at that time. This would have required the moving of the altar into the present crossing. The organ and choir would be moved to the loft (as did, in fact, happen). Then a new, two story building would be built where the apse and the "new" (1990) Parish House are now located. Had this building been constructed, the appearance from the street would have been quite similar to that of the complex after the 1990-1991 construction. On the first floor of this proposed building there were spaces allocated for reception and reading room (with entrance from 16th Street), four offices, a choir room, dining and meeting room, kitchen, and sacristy.

At the Diocesan Convention of 1961, a Strategy Committee was appointed in preparation for a capital funds campaign. The Committee reported in December 1962, giving priority to expansion of the facilities at 16th and Central. The Campaign itself was named The Episcopal Advance Fund and took place during the spring of 1963. Richard Mote remembered:

> The banquet signaling the beginning of this campaign, was held at the Marott Hotel, on March 12, 1963. All Saints' delegates (indeed, everyone) present were pleasantly stunned when the bishop, in his concluding remarks, announced that $250,000 had been given anonymously, to be used for the construction of a new welfare center at 16th and Central.

(In Indianapolis in those days, Eli Lilly was often referred to as Mr. Anonymous.)

Evans Woolen III was hired as the architect of the project at 16th and Central. Woolen was an Episcopalian and also the architect of Clowes Hall and (later) of the Federal Building and Central Library addition. His design called for the removal of the old "temporary" wooden sanctuary, now fifty years old, and the construction of a new semi-circular brick apse and sacristy. The interior of the church was sandblasted to restore the brick and limestone to nearly original appearance. A building long before owned by the diocese was repurchased, renovated and renamed St. Francis House. The former Parish House on the corner was torn down in November 1963. Now All Saints could be clearly seen from both 16th

Street and Central Avenue (as had been envisioned in the proposal to the Church Building Fund in 1939). The renovated St. Francis House contained offices (for both parish and the other agencies) plus church school classrooms. Between St. Francis House and the church itself was the property upon which Knickerbacker Hall had once stood and which was now re-purchased (after "much negotiation and not a little anxiety" according to Richard Mote). Upon that property was built the new building called first Diocesan Hall, then Episcopal Urban Center, and now Dayspring Center.

Repurchase of the property had been under consideration as early as November 13, 1961. On that date W. Dudley Pratt of Uptown Realty wrote to Edward H. Grebe, diocesan treasurer, about the property at 1535-1537 Central and known as the Mid-Central Building. The building was described as "three story and attic solid brick office building with slate roof, comprising 14 separate units, 2 baths on each floor, city steam heat, on a lot 65 feet wide by 208 feet deep, with a 4 car cement block garage in rear plus parking for 17 cars." In 1958, this building (which would, after repurchase and renovation, be known as St. Francis House) had sold for $47,000. In 1961, the second floor and basement were empty; several tenants (business firms) on the first floor paid $277 in rent per month.

In addition to this 65 foot-wide lot, the lot immediately north (between 1535-1537 and the church) had to be repurchased for the new Diocesan Hall. This lot was 110 foot wide and was the site of a Standard Grocery. The diocesan property prior to the re-purchase had been reduced to lots 1 and 2 of the Wocher Addition, plus 25 feet of lot 3, which made a total of 139 feet 6 inches fronting on Central Avenue. When the repurchase was complete for the 1963-1964 project, the church would own the rest of lot 3, plus lots 4, 5, and 6. The original diocesan purchase in the 19th century had been of lots 1 through 4. The purchases of 1893 and 1894 had added lots 5 and 6; therefore, all the church's stake on Central Avenue had been reclaimed.

Beginning in June 1963, the Pilcher tracker organ was dismantled, the console rebuilt, 1684 new pipes were imported from Denmark, and the rebuilt organ placed in the west choir gallery. Aldo J. Bertorelli, who was both a parishioner (often a vestry member) and an organ builder, was responsible for the organ project. He was assisted by Rufo Lutes. While the organ was being reconstructed and moved, a reed organ was borrowed to provide musical accompaniment to sung masses.

According to Richard Mote,

> The warm, rainless fall of 1963 aided the swift pace of construction. The dirt and dust, the many inconveniences were borne cheerfully by all the faithful. The patronal festival on All Saints Day was of necessity more subdued than usual. But this was compensated for when, on Thanksgiving Day at the Mass, worshippers raised their eyes and for the first time beheld the beautiful free-standing altar, surrounded by the curving sweep of the new sanctuary. With the end of 1963 and the beginning of 1964 it was obvious that much remained to be done. The parish-diocesan hall was being hurried to completion, the first church school classes were ready to enter St. Francis Hall, and all parishioners eagerly awaited the completion of the organ.

The completion of the building project in 1964 coincided with the Centennial of Grace and All Saints. The first chance to mark the centennial came with an Evensong and Dedicatory Recital of the new organ on Sunday, May 10. The program lists Fr. Carthy, Fr. Moore (Associate), Fr. Powers (Curate), Robert Hobbs (Director of Music), Charles Everheart (Choirmaster and Organist), Choristers from Christ Church, and the All Saints Schola Cantorum. The dedicatory recital was given by David Koehring. He played *Prelude and Fugue in C Minor* by J.S. Bach, *Prelude Fugue and Variation* by Cesar Franck, *Prelude on "The King's Majesty"* by Leo Sowerby. A reception in the new Diocesan Hall followed the recital. David Koehring had been organist and choirmaster at All Saints while he was a student at Jordan School of Music (Butler University). After graduation from Jordan in 1962, Koehring had gone to Washington, D.C., where he was assistant organist at the National Cathedral and became assistant organist at the National Cathedral in Washington, D.C., and studied with Leo Sowerby and Paul Callaway. Later he would return to Indianapolis as organist and choirmaster of Christ Church (by that time the cathedral of the diocese).

The history of the organ was also given in the program for the recital:

> In 1889, a Pilcher tracker organ was installed in Grace Pro-Cathedral, which had recently moved to this site from St. Joseph and Pennsylvania Streets, where it had stood since 1864. Over the years the organ served well and was moved into the new All Saints Cathedral in 1910. Despite many changes in the neighborhood and parish, the organ continued to be played each Sunday, until the new building and renovation program required its removal to the West Gallery in 1963-1964. All Saints is fortunate indeed to have had the skilled and imaginative leadership of Aldo Bertorelli and Robert Nowicki in the rebuilding, and enlarging of the organ. These men donated their time and labor. The best of the old organ's pipes were retained and 22 additional stops were added. The organ case, designed by Mr. Bertorelli, was built by Rufo Lutes, another parishioner. The organ is dedicated to the greater glory of God in thanksgiving for the devotion of many hearts to the witness of All Saints parish over the years. The builders have also here memorialized departed members of their families: Frank Bertorelli, Dean Craft, and Ethel Nowicki.

Fr. Carthy wrote to the parish on October 27 about the celebrations (with, as usual, an admonition):

> Dear People of All Saints:
> None of us is 100 years old as an individual. As a congregation, however, we are 100 years old in November, 1964, and we are celebrating All Saints Day, Sunday, November 1 as a Homecoming for everybody who calls this his parish Church home.
>
> There will be a Processional and Solemn High Mass at 9:15 followed by a formal breakfast (eggs, juice, rolls—in short, the "works"). A special guest speaker, Mr Henry DeBoest of the Cathedral, will bring us a message of encouragement. There will be breakfast and special arrangements for the youngsters also. And, best of all, there are no tickets to buy, no reservations are necessary (thanks to an anonymous donor who is underwriting the whole affair). What could be better than to worship together (All Saints' Day is a required Holy Day of Obligation), meet old and new friends over a piping hot breakfast and have our sights lifted up by an inspiring speaker as we begin this joyful month of our centennial?
>
> Priests are people, too, remember, and we have all been somewhat discouraged by the poor attendance lately, especially at 9:15.

The Solemn High Mass for the Centennial Celebration was also the service of consecration for All Saints. (The church had not been consecrated—only dedicated—in 1911 because there was still debt on the building.) The service began with Bishop Craine's knock on the closed doors with his crozier. The new limestone High Altar was consecrated "to the glory of God and in honor of All Saints with water and oil"; likewise the chapel altar was consecrated "in honor of St Michael and All Angels." Then the altars were vested. At the Solemn Eucharist the minor propers were sung by the Schola Cantorum. The Book of Common Prayer, not the Missal, was used for the Mass. There was also a Blessing of the renovated St. Francis House and the new Diocesan Hall. The celebrant was Bishop Craine; Fr. Carthy was deacon of the Mass; Fr. Powers, subdeacon; and Fr. Moore, chaplain to the bishop. The preacher was Bishop Walter Klein of Northern Indiana; his chaplain was The Rev. William C.R. Sheridan (who would later become Bishop of Northern Indiana). The program leaflet was printed as a memorial to Paul Mozingo (1901-1963). Berniece Fee Mozingo was organist and director of music. Bishop Craine's copy of the rite (titled "The Opening of the Church, The Blessing of Ornaments and The Holy Eucharist") is in the diocesan archives, complete with his hand-written notes for when and how to do the censings.

In his 1964 Annual Meeting report as historiographer, Richard Mote summed up the centennial. "The church was filled to capacity with the bishop and clergy and laymen of both dioceses marching in procession." A catered dinner followed at which "touching remarks" were made by bishops, clergy, and devoted laymen."

Fr. Carthy had invited all the clergy of the diocese to the event:

> All of us who worship and work here hope that our brethren will want to come and participate (vested) in this joyful Centennial Celebration. Without your prayers and cooperation the development of the Urban Center and its program of Altar Centered Social Concern would have been greatly hindered. Because this historic place serves in its ministry the whole State of Indiana, especially in the field of social welfare and action, it is fitting that our Clericus has invited all the clergy of the Northern Diocese to participate as our guests—thus making this day our annual "Fellowship Day" with the Northern Clericus. Much as I dislike to invite you to a party

and then ask you to buy a ticket, I have no alternative but to do so. I hope you'll come anyway. Bring cassock and surplice and join the procession.

The price of the luncheon ticket to which he refers was $2.75.

The centennial celebration continued the next week with a conference on the theme "Morals and Man in Crisis." Dr. Margaretta K. Bowers, a psychotherapist and chair of the Pastoral Counseling Committee of the Episcopal Church, spoke on Monday night at the Marott Hotel. On Tuesday, the speakers were Dr. Russell R. Monroe (director of the Psychiatric Institute of the University of Maryland) and The Rev. Arthur Vogel (professor of theology at Nashotah House). These lectures were sponsored by ECS, CSR, and were offered to participants from the 13 dioceses of Province V of the Episcopal Church. The newspaper article listing the events described the "urban center complex" as consisting of "a meeting hall, gymnasium and administrative offices" designed by Evans Woolen III.

Once again there was a symbolic closing of a circle. Old Grace Church had once been turned into a gymnasium. Now All Saints had its own gymnasium!

In closing his centennial history, Richard Mote declares that the "vision" of All Saints is due to the leadership of Fr. Carthy. Mote also offers his reflections on All Saints in the year 1964.

> Gone are the conditions which forced [All Saints] to share its crowded facilities with the three social-welfare agencies. Although straightened financial circumstances have necessitated the "sharing" of Fr. Carthy between the entities present, this has not impeded progress nor destroyed the parish morale. These past years have seen the church school prosper. These years have witnessed the average attendance at late masses rise from 74 in 1956 to 144 in 1962. Where there was one clergyman in 1956, there are now three. If there has been an "Achilles Heel", in the parish life, it has been in the realm of finances, where successive dedicated vestries have struggled to keep the ship afloat, by balancing income (always keeping in mind that many parishioners were pledging sacrificially) with continually rising expenses.

The parish centennial year of 1964 was in many ways the high water mark of Fr. Carthy's rectorate and of "Altar Centered Social Concern". We have one snapshot of the work about this time in the application Fr. Carthy wrote to the Talbot Fund in 1963 (now in diocesan archives).

> The neighborhood work at All Saints Church has evolved since its inception in 1958 to the point where larger facilities and increased personnel are required to keep pace with the expansion. The first of these is being satisfied by the development of the physical plant at 16th and Central. The latter has been aided by the establishment of the position of group work supervisor in the parish by the Urban Mission Council … . At the present time, the neighborhood program includes a weekly Canteen of several hours duration superintended by the group worker and managed in large part by the teen-agers involved. Additional time is devoted to special interest groups maintained by volunteer leaders on Mondays and Wednesdays. This work for 6-12 year old children needs to be expanded, however, to meet a pressing need for the children of the neighborhood. The Group worker supervises a Mothers' Club and Teenage Cabinet. On Saturdays, a full scale program which integrates neighborhood and parish activities is carried out by the Group Worker and the present Curate. The Group Worker, Mrs. Bonnie M. Harvey, is engaged in house calls in the neighborhood.

A fuller portrait of the parish can be found in a spiral-bound book issued in 1965 with data from the year ending December 31, 1964. The book is called **The Way of the Saints.** In his preface Fr. Carthy introduced the book and its purpose:

> **The Way of the Saints** is a book written by and about the gathered community of Christians around the Altar of All Saints' Parish Church in the city and diocese of Indianapolis, Indiana. Because it is an inner-city parish, interracial and cross-cultural, with a sense of vocation and mission to "the last and the least" of Christ's brethren, this book breathes an atmosphere which provides a clue to our parish's character and motto: "Bear ye one another's burdens and so fulfill the Law of Christ." (Gal 6:2) I hope my brethren in Christ will "read, mark, learn and inwardly digest" the contents hereof. It is a manual for their life and work, which they have written, and will continue to write, all the days of our life.

A Directory lists, in addition to Fr. Carthy, the following staff: Associate, The Rev. Peter C. Moore; Curate, The Rev. Alden W. Powers; Group Work Supervisor, Mrs. Bonnie Harvey; Group Worker, Mrs. Mary E. Collins; EUC Sexton (the complex was called Episcopal Urban Center),

Mr. Albert Splatt; Assistant Sexton, Mr. Jacab Korbuly; Director of Music, Mrs. Berneice Fee Mozingo.

The first section is labeled "The Way of the Saints is a Sacramental Way." A paraphrase of the Chicago-Lambeth Quadrilateral is titled "The Four Essential Principles of the Anglican Communion" and reads as follows:

1.  The Bible as the Revelation of God.
2.  The Catholic and Apostolic Creed of Nicea as the basic statement of the Christian Faith
3.  The Sacraments as special vehicles of God's grace.
4.  The historic and apostolic ministry of Bishops, Priests and Deacons as the stewards of God's Holy Mysteries and the leaders of his people.

Seven sections detail each of the seven sacraments, telling what it means, what it does, when it is done, and what is required.

The following quote gives a taste of the teaching:

> The ideal is to begin each day with Holy Communion. Everyone who wishes to follow the example of the apostles will make every effort to do this ... . The minimum obligation for all members of the parish is "to worship God every Sunday in his church. One need not actually receive communion each time, but he should at least be "at the table" when the family sits down to this sacred meal, i.e. every Sunday and Holy Day of Obligation ... The apostolic custom of our parish is to receive no food before Holy Communion ... Any valid medical reason excuses from fasting, but you must seek the rector's approval. When the sacraments are brought [to the sick], it is more edifying spiritually not to talk with the priest unless there is an urgent reason. Do not ask him to stay for coffee, etc. You can always call him up later and ask him over for tea.

Requirements for baptism included a conference with the rector, two godparents of the same sex and one of the opposite sex (for children), and instruction on the meaning of the sacrament given by the rector immediately before the baptism. For Confirmation, faithful attendance at a special class (one for young people and another for adults) was required. "Those who were not baptized according to the form prescribed in the Bible and the Book of Common Prayer must be baptized at least conditionally by the rector."

In answer to the question "What is required for Holy Orders,", the answer includes "a Bishop whose consecration can be traced through an unbroken line of other bishops back to the apostles themselves" and "the correct rites and ceremonies required by Catholic tradition." Under the heading of Holy Penance we learn that "Confessions are heard, for those who avail themselves of this great spiritual gift, at 5:00 p.m. on Saturday afternoon and by appointment at any time." A note under Holy Unction and Visitation of the Sick tells us that the clergy "work from 65 to 80 hours on the job each week, but they will eagerly come to your aid at any hour of the day or night if you call or have some other member of the family call. They will rush to fight with you and for you against the enemy which threatens."

Directions concerning the Burial of the Dead include this note: "The funeral service is not meant to console the bereaved family. Our faith and our habits of prayer, study and the reception of the Holy Sacraments should sustain us now. We come to the funeral to do our duty toward the soul of the departed comrade and to see that his body is buried with dignity and solemnity as befits a vessel of the Holy Spirit. In the case of departed children under 7 years of age no Requiem Mass is said since no actual sins have been committed. Instead, a "mass of the Angels" is usually offered in thanksgiving for the child's assured entry into heaven." On the one hand, Fr. Carthy says that "It is inappropriate for persons who have not been members of the Episcopal Church to be buried from the Church itself." On the other, "It is expected that a faithful member of this church will wish to be buried from the church. The priest should be called before any arrangements are made with a funeral director."

Explicit directions are given about fasting. Eucharistic fast for morning Mass was to begin at the preceding midnight. For an evening Mass, the fast was to begin after the mid-day meal. On Ash Wednesday and Good Friday, "only one full meal should be eaten ... and meat is not permitted." On Prayer Book days of abstinence, meat was not permitted; but "the precise quantity of food is governed by the individual."

The next major section of the yearbook is called "The Way of the Saints is an Informed Way." Thirty-seven different groups are listed, each with a saint's name. Some of these groups are in the area of adult education; others are church school classes or service activity or youth group. The adult education offered included Bible Study, Theology, prayer, Moral Theology, History, Liturgics, inquirer's classes (fall), and confirmation classes (spring). Church school groups ranged from Nursery to Senior High. Service included the Parish Mission Council, Urban Mission Council Guild, Altar Guild, Mother's Club, two choirs, acolytes, and Episcopal Church Women. Youth groups focused on dance, homemaking, arts and crafts, manual crafts. There was a pre-teen club, a teen club, and Episcopal Young Churchmen. In addition to the three priests, 31 lay people are listed as group leaders. The Church School classes used the Episcopal Church Fellowship Series of materials.

The Parish Mission Council (St. Barnabas Group) is fully described. Its purpose was "to be the catalytic agent of All Saints' Missionary activities." It was composed of 12 persons representing leadership groups of the parish. The council was to "stimulate and elicit their support in the policies determined by the council."

St. Vincent's group was the acolyte corps of the parish. Classes of membership were listed as probationer, candidate, acolyte, and master of ceremonies. Each class had a *laborare* (work) duty and an *orare* (prayer) duty. Records of attendance were kept. At the close of each year a St. Vincent's award was granted for outstanding achievement and a Felix L. Cirlot award was granted for "Christian attitude." Older teen-aged members were eligible for a basketball team. Younger boys participated in Saturday recreation. "Eligibility for camping trips, cookouts, etc. will be based on attendance." After a period of several years, boys could obtain an All Saints blazer.

St. Cecilia's brought together 20 (and no more than 20) girls from the parish and neighborhood weekly to "learn to sing liturgical music and hymns for Sunday services and other occasions. At supper the choristers take turns in hostessing tables." Like the acolytes, the group was organized into classes (chorister, novice, singer in training). If a girl (and the choir seems to have been designed exclusively for girls) was absent for three weeks, she was placed at the end of the waiting list. Awards and promotions were made at the end of the school season.

The Altar Guild (St. Veronica's) met only twice a year for pre-Christmas and Lenten cleaning. Both men and women could belong. Making of new articles was one of the aims of the group.

St. Monica's was the group for mothers of children in the parish youth program. Mrs. Pauline Clements was the president. The group encouraged social action and civic responsibility, raised funds for the youth program, and assisted at parish meals.

The Urban Mission Council was the umbrella organization for youth work at All Saints, Christ Church, St. Philips, and St. Matthew's. A guild to support the work composed of All Saints members was called St. Anne's. They provided lunches for the summer youth program and assisted with holiday projects. Women from other parishes could join St. Anne's.

St. Leo's or the Episcopal Young Churchmen met two Sundays per month during the school year following Evening Prayer. Six officers were elected (including Sergeant at arms).

A Group Worker led the St. Martha's Homemaker's Group in "learning the Christian view of home life." Both boys and girls could join St. Anthony's group to "exercise skills in manual crafts." Volunteers supervised St. Joan's group for artistic crafts, which aimed to "develop a greater understanding and appreciation for God's creation in a group setting." St. Joan's was for girls only. St. Catherine's was formed so that children of the neighborhood could learn ballet and folk dancing, with three ranks of membership (principal, ballerina, and prima ballerina). St. Peter's was a pre-teen club (ages 8-12) limited to 15 boys and 15 girls from the neighborhood; since membership was limited, absence led to probation and dismissal. For the teens, St. Hubert's was available to 24 boys and 12 girls; "club members attempt through democratic methods and the aid of trained advisers to achieve new insights into the quality of life obtainable to them to take steps toward their manifestation." All members of the basketball team (sponsored by Urban Mission Council) had to be certified members of St. Hubert's Club.

The annual report of programs was titled "The Way of the Saints is an Active Way." Church attendance figures for recent years were given: 1960 - 7,160;1961 - 8,923; 1962 - 9,176; 1963 - 9,634; 1964, 14,277.

Bonnie Harvey's Group Work Supervisor's reports tells us that some meetings and activities were curtailed because of building construction and remodeling early in the year. Mrs. Harvey then listed program statistics for the year: registered for the winter program, 195 boys and girls; for the summer "camp at home", 275; for the Vacation Church School, 40.

The St. Hubert's Club for teenagers was a "new work" during the summer of 1964 (coinciding with the new gymnasium in the Diocesan Hall). The All Saints basketball team was undefeated. In addition to basketball, the group had guest lecturers (in social health, civil rights and race relations), formed a dance group, prepared Christmas baskets, and visited "vocational training spots in the city." The members raised money through dances and candy sales.

St. Catherine's was starting its fifth year of dance activities. Two exhibitions of ballet were given by the girls, with one also including folk dance. Fifty-six were registered, and average attendance was 25.

Mrs. Harvey noted that not all the groups were able to meet throughout the year because there was a lack of group supervisors.

Members of St. Monica's, the mother's group, had been active in voter registration, tuberculosis prevention and social activities.

Mrs. Harvey concluded her report this way:

> Our efforts are constantly to carry out the principles of the Urban Mission Council of which we are a part—service witness and evangelism for our Lord. As we report to the parish, we hope that you understand that while objective measurements of our work are necessary and justified, that much

is immeasurable in our time and in worldly terms. We attempt to serve without reward to aid others in finding God immanent in His world. Their search is often a struggle needing direction; our efforts, sometimes traditional, frequently experimental and new, are nevertheless an attempt to help others to discover God's revelation of Himself through His Church.

St. Matthew's Guild was established in 1964 to raise funds for the youth programs. During 1964 they held a pancake supper (which brought in $64), a bridge party ($76.50), and a carnival ($60.37). These funds were used to buy acolyte blazers and junior choir robes. But the dance group still needed sashes, leotards, and shoes; the basketball team needed uniforms; more blazers and sweat-shirts were needed; the clubhouse needed carpentry work; and the pool tables needed repair.

The women of St. Margaret's Guild reported many activities for 1964: a party for the aged at Julietta Home; meals served to a conference of the Urban Training Program; helping with noonday lunches in Lent, offering guided tours of the new and renovated facilities; serving refreshments to a group of Roman Catholic visitors and for the Dedication and 100th Anniversary Celebration; serving election day meals as a fund-raiser; and "packing baskets for needy families" of items donated to ECS. The United Thank Offering was $47.23.

The Altar Guild's extra activities included participation in the dedication of the new organ, in the tours of the facilities, and in showing vestments and vessels to a group of Roman Catholic for whom St. Margaret's provided refreshments.

The acolyte's report mentions some "extra-curricular" activities: a pancake supper, a trip to Nashotah House seminary (which cost $20), an Investiture ceremony, a father-son cookout and ballgame.

The Parish Mission Council first met in October 1963, under the guidance of Fr. Powers. Members were instructed to read literature about the church, and representatives were sent to conferences on "Religion and Race" and "Our Diocese Faces an Industrial Culture." The Council sponsored a neighborhood open house in June 1963 and planned a Mission called "Encounter 65" for the year 1965.

The Urban Mission Council was organized to coordinate the inner-city work. An executive board was composed of the clergy of All Saints, St. Philips, and Christ Church, plus two laymen from each of these parishes. All Saints' representatives were Tim Hall and Bill Hering. Future plans included the hiring of a full time executive director. All Saints' assessment for membership in the Council was $150. The total budget of over $30,000 was largely supported by the Talbot Fund. The Urban Mission Council contributed to the maintenance of the facilities at 16th and Central and allocated $13,000 to the completion of Diocesan Hall as a part of the Episcopal Advance Fund. Urban Mission Council sponsored both the summer neighborhood programs and year-round programs.

Within the remodeled facilities of St. Francis House, one room was made available for a parish library. Gloria Kemper, in her Library report, said that it contained a restored portrait of Bishop Francis "so that many could feel at home in the new surroundings and new friends and parishioners could be aware of some of our heritage." The library contained free copies of **Christ and Divorce** by the former rector, Fr. Cirlot.

Berniece Fee Mozingo reported on the music program. She regretted that "it has been necessary to curtail the regular services of the schola." The St. Cecilia choir sang the mass "with some success, but this can only be on occasion." Mrs. Mozingo noted, however, that some good was coming of the loss because "the congregation is taking more responsibility in the singing of the ordinaries and the hymns." However, "a means must be found to create quicker responses doing away with some of the lag and retardation of the liturgy." She says that rehearsal time for St. Cecilia's choir is spent learning the way through the Hymnal and that this is "no small task." There was a waiting list of girls wanting one of the 20 places (because there were 20 red vestments).

Educational Warden Truman Moyer reported for the Sunday Church School. He says that Fr. Powers had prepared a teacher's workbook and that the curriculum was better organized than ever before. A new system of team teaching was tried; but pupil attendance was poor, particularly in classes for ages nine and up: "There is an apathy on the part of the older children which seems to reflect an apathy and lack of interest on the part of the parents." Moyer also notes, "The school operates on a sub-minimal budget and the teachers, who labor under extremely difficult circumstances, receive little, if any, encouragement or co-operation from parents."

The Vestry Report listed the major accomplishments of 1964 as "completion of the church, Diocesan Hall and St. Francis House. The demands on the parish and vestry have been great."

The Finance Committee reported that 57 pledges had been obtained for approximately $365 per week or $6.40 per pledge per week. This was thought to be the highest average pledge in the diocese.

The Property Report indicates parish pride in the new and remodeled facilities:

> Having been cleaned and completed, the church stands proudly for all to see. The old Parish House is gone. In its place, the beginning of a lawn shows to the passersby. The stone arches of the church entrance are clean and the doors invite all to come in. Within the church are new oaken acolyte benches and lovely green carpeting beyond an attractive new altar rail, companions to the truly beautiful stone high altar, which with stark massive simplicity, stands beneath the great crucifix in the sanctuary. The mighty organ with its grand and impressive array of pipes trumpets the glory of God in our wonderful All Saints Church.

Not all was perfect, however. Window repair was not completed except for the balcony. The roof and skylight leaked (as they still did some 30 years later). The kneelers and pews needed to be tightened and repaired. And the rectory needed attention.

The Episcopal Advance Fund, which was the capital campaign of the diocese, took place in May of 1963 and paid for the building project at 16th and Central. All Saints Parish had 70 pledges for $22,275. By the end of 1964, only $9,945.50 had been received in payment of pledges, with half of the pledges in arrears.

Fr. Peter Moore began his report as Executive Director of Episcopal Community Services by addressing the question of the relationship of the agency to the parish. The question was to arise time and again. Here is Fr. Moore's response to it:

The mystery of who I am and what I do in the Diocese of Indianapolis continues to plague at least me if not all the Board of Directors of Episcopal Community Services. So often I am introduced with the remark that Fr. Moore is down at All Saints'. Now that, of course, is an accurate geographical description. It also describes my canonical, parochial connection. But, alas, I do not think it describes the nature of the work which we try to do at Episcopal Community Services. So if you find that I am not as much in evidence Sunday by Sunday I hope you will attribute this to my attempts to relate the work of Episcopal Community Services to all the parishes and missions of the diocese.

Our new Quarters in St. Francis House have had a marked effect on our ability to serve those who turn to us for help. There has been a definite increase in the number of persons who come to the agency seeking help from it. In the year 1964 we saw 100+ persons in long-term helping relationships. We saw about 650 persons in short term relationships. Both these figures mark a definite advance over the year 1963. We continue to see, as the Psalmist says, "high and low, rich and poor, one with another."

We continue to offer the services we have always offered: the social casework services of Mr. James Thurston; pastoral counseling; the diagnostic and treatment services under the direction of Dr. Phillips; a referral source for help from other agencies for the clergy and laity of our community; emergency relief services. It is terribly important to me that you understand that we do something other than give out food and clothing. That is a service which we render—an important service—but it is by no means the only thing we do.

I would also want to comment on the way in which Episcopal Community Services is supported. Contrary to what everybody seems to think, we do not get any money from the diocese. The work of Episcopal Community Services is supported in the same way as a parish, by contributions for its work. In 1964 almost 400 persons contributed to the work of Episcopal Community Services. This is a shockingly small figure against the 17,000 baptized persons in the Diocese of Indianapolis. I should also report to you that 21 persons from All Saints' gave $462.17 amount of money for our work. In addition, the vestry made a corporate gift of $100, and the Churchwomen of All Saints' $15.00.

Finally, I could only conclude this report with the statement that without the altar of God unto which I go in the Church of All Saints' it would not be possible for me to carry on as Director of this agency. The Communion of Saints in the horizontal plane as well as in the vertical dimension both support and go before us in our work.

The Urban Mission Council Guild reported on how it had fed the children in the summer "Camp at Home" program. Government surplus food and milk were procured. Volunteers prepared, transported, and served the sandwiches. In addition the Guild sponsored a Christmas party for program participants.

The Young People's report notes that 1964 was the first year for the organization. Mr. and Mrs. Tim Hall were sponsors, and five officers were elected. At the last meeting of 1964 (on December 31) there were "16 regulars and a few visitors." A goal for 1965 was "to have a few more teenagers." Meetings were held two Sundays a month. Mr. Anthony Thurston talked to the group about his Civil Rights trips to Mississippi. Truman Moyer and the rector's wife gave the group a music recital. The one party during the year was a Christmas party.

A portion of the yearbook was devoted to the evangelism effort called "Encounter 65: The Twentieth Century Apostolic Mission of All Saints' Church." This section began with a theological and historical background for mission and concluded:

> During the first week of March AS Church will have a Mission. This Mission, however, will be a completely new approach to evangelism as we know it. For several months we have been including in our prayers, our mission, and for several months preparations for this mission have been offered to God in the Daily Mass. We as a Parish are going to tell all of Indianapolis about Our Lord and the Catholic Faith. This will be a time of bringing many people to the faith and it will be a time when all parishioners will be working to bring these people into the faith. You as a parishioner will want to do your part as a Catholic Christian to present your faith to others.

Fourteen committee chairs had been appointed.

A diagram of the three floors of the remodeled St. Francis Hall was included. There were nine class or multi-purpose rooms plus offices for the parish, ECS and its programs, Urban Mission Council's group workers, Christian Social Relations (Fr. Carthy, director and Anthony Thurston, executive secretary).

Upon receiving his copy of **The Way of the Saints**, Bishop Craine wrote to Fr. Carthy that it was

> the most magnificent booklet I have ever seen concerning the purposes and work of a parish. It is both imaginative and attractive, and I can assure you that I read every word of it. I know that Father Powers must have been responsible also for much of the work, and must also receive credit. I was so impressed with the involvement of the laity in both the planning and work of the parish, and they told the story well in each case. I expect that you may have the highest level of pledge giving in the Diocese, and will be interested to learn whether this is the case.

(Fr. Carthy often said that All Saints had both the highest per capita giving as a parish and the lowest per capita income as individuals in the diocese.)

Some monthly financial reports for the Episcopal Urban Center for this period are still in existence in the diocesan archives. Albert Splatt was the janitor and was paid $200 per month. $175 was the monthly payment on "Claymon Mortgage Interest." Operating expenses were allocated between All Saints, ECS, CSR, and Urban Mission Council.

Service leaflets complete our picture of All Saints at the high water mark of Fr. Carthy's years. For example, Easter 965 began with the Liturgy for the day from the "Green Book" at 10:30 p.m. This apparently was the Blessing of the New Fire and Vigil leading up to the First Mass of Easter at Midnight. On Easter morning there was a Low Mass at 7:30, Morning Prayer at 9:30, and Sung Mass at 10 a.m. This late Mass used the Minor Propers from the "Green Book." Instructions in the leaflet noted that

> Priest and People say together: Receive, O holy Father, Almighty and ever lasting God, this bread of our lives, now to be made spotless by the Son's atoning power, and which we offer unto thee, our living and true God; and may this offering be lifted up to thing eternal kingdom within the Resurrection and Ascension of the same thy son, Jesus Christ our Lord

When the chalice is offered, we say:
We offer unto thee, O Lord, this wine of our lives humbly beseeching thy mercy; that thou make this offering to have its portion in the eternal humanity of thine Incarnate Song at thy right hand in glory.

Further announcements were as follows:

We welcome Bishop Skelton of Matabeleland, Central Africa.
Fr Carthy will attend the Executive Council of province of Midwest.
Fr. Young is at Pendleton and Julietta on Easter Day.
Fr Powers assists at St. Timothy's.
We gratefully acknowledge a pair of candlesticks for St. Michaels Chapel, the gift of Jon Roper in memory of his parents. The new tabernacle veil is the gift of Earl Mertz in memory of his mother.

In this era, divorced and remarried persons were not admitted to communion without dispensation from the bishop, as the **Way of the Saints** made quite clear. However, the diocesan archives contain many letters requesting restoration of communicant status from All Saints. The letters reflect both Fr. Carthy's and the bishop's pastoral style. For example, Bishop Craine wrote to one All Saints couple,

The Church is a redeeming fellowship, and it is also her task to receive and support those who are earnestly seeking to do God's will. It is never the intent of the Church to pass judgment on past actions after people have paid their own price and made their peace with God and His Church.

Favorable judgments on re-marriage, however, were not automatic. Fr. Carthy informed the bishop that a communicant "was repelled from partaking of the Lord's Table by personal advertisement"; this person had been married by a civil magistrate without notifying the clergy and "further married during a prohibited season unaccompanied by extenuating circumstances a divorced person without seeking episcopal judgment which caused scandal and embarrassment to the Vicar and people of the church." The person had been informed "that the parish clergy of All Saints' Church sought primarily her welfare and would aid and counsel in her return to full legitimate status in the church." The bishop replied, "I would fully concur in this parochial action as you have outlined it."

The diocesan archives also contain a touching letter from Bishop Craine to Joyce (Mrs. Richard) Mote.

> I would not want this occasion to pass without expressing to you my deepest appreciation for the beautiful work you did in changing the clasp for my Cope. Your prompt willingness to take on a difficult job, and your graciousness in doing it so readily are wonderful acts of kindness to your bishop. I was also pleased to realize that this was the carrying on of a family tradition since your mother had done similar services for Bishop Francis.

Planning for the Parochial Mission called "Encounter 65, which had been referred to in the **Way of the Saints,** appears to have been largely the responsibility of Fr. Powers. He asked Bishop Craine to attend the opening ceremonies on March 6 and the closing on Sunday March 14. The Bishop replied that he would be present: "I should imagine you would want me to appear in cope and mitre." Fr. Powers' invitation says that Indianpolis Mayor Barton would also be present on March 6, that the evangelist for the Mission was Anthony Zeoli, and that Gertrude Behanna would be the featured speaker on March 14. (Behanna was a well-known Episcopal speaker on evangelism in the 1960s.)
Fr. Powers closed his invitational letter with the hope that "God will bless this Mission and that many people will find a means here to express their worship to Almighty God."

Fr. Powers' successor as curate was The Rev. Henry L. Atkins, Jr., who started work in September 1965. More financial juggling was required before he could be hired. Fr. Powers had lived in Kemper House, a historic building on Delaware Street given to the diocese by Mr. Lilly, at a rent of only $50 per month. (Kemper House later became the headquarters of Indiana Historic Preservation.) By the time of Fr. Atkins' arrival, the diocese had other plans for Kemper House. Because no other housing could be found at only $50 a month, All Saints requested and received $40 a month in diocesan assistance so that Fr. Atkins could have a housing allowance of $90. A note addressed to Bishop Craine from an unknown source but dated August 11, 1965, reported that

> Dean Lawson [of Christ Church Cathedral] and Paul Moore knew a young clergyman named Henry Atkins from Richmond, Virginia. Canon Carthy has just talked to him on the telephone and he is interested and Canon

Carthy said he asked him come here next week and was paying his expenses out of his Discretionary Fund ... Mr. Atkins is a young man just ordained recently to the priesthood, married, with a baby on the way.

The Rev. John E. Steeg, Jr., the General Missioner of the diocese, also worked out of the 16th and Central complex (primarily among the black community). In 1966 he wrote to Fr. Carthy an appreciation of the way Henry Atkins had handled an emergency. "I wanted you to know I have never had more complete or better follow through on church business. Thought you would be glad to know how well he handled the problem."

In 1965, Bishop Craine described All Saints to a prospective parishioner newly arrived in Indianapolis as "a good Anglo-Catholic" and "inner city parish", which was "a most fascinating congregation with most competent clergy leadership."

The exact date when All Saints became racially integrated is unknown. The original mission of All Saints Cathedral had been to be "open to all races." Louis Howland remembered a sermon by a "Negro priest" and commented that "it is a frightful sin to hate their neighbors and fellow-citizens because they belong to a certain church, come from a certain bit of territory or have dark skins." We have also seen that there were black members by the time a dinner was held at the Riviera Club during the Cirlot years. The usual pattern in Indianapolis, however, was for black Episcopalians to worship at St. Philip's. Then, during the rectorate of Fr. Carthy, the parish became more and more intentional about integration, attempting to live out the notice posted over the front door: "Everyone is Welcome."

Black parishioners and the year in which they first appeared on a roster (the first available roster being 1960) are Birtie Smith, 1960; Roberta Slatter, 1961; Clifford Henderson (brother of Roberta Slatter), 1963. Black members of the congregation very rapidly began to take leadership roles. William Finister was on the vestry in 1967; Ida Edelen, in 1968; William Coleman, in 1969. Annie Mae Greene came to Indianapolis in 1962. Shortly thereafter she became a faithful worshipper and active in many groups. Other names were those of the three generations of the Mallory, Clements, and Johnson family. The Bingham family also included at least three generations of parishioners.

The appearance of the name of Ida Edelen on the vestry list is doubly significant. She was also the first woman to be elected to the All Saints Vestry after the Canons of the church were changed to permit women to serve.

These years were marked by the deepening involvement of the country in the Vietnam War and by growing protests against that war. In the summer of 1967, Fr. Atkins agreed to let a national group working for peace use his office and his address. The program was called "Vietnam Summer." A note from the bishop to his secretary informs her that "he has talked this over with Fr. Carthy and he has agreed with Fr. Atkins in these decisions."

Vietnam was not an abstract issue. It was hitting home. On August 24, 1966. Canon Carthy called the bishop "to report to you that Shirley Johnson Duke's son whom you baptized down at the Cathedral was in Vietnam. He slipped going over a footbridge with rapids underneath and fell into the rapids and the body has not been found yet."

Throughout the 1960s, the parish also became more and more associated with the Black Power Movement. On March 12, 1968, Fr. Atkins wrote to the bishop asking that he concur in allowing the Radical Action Project to use the gym in the Episcopal Urban Center. He warned the bishop that

> Hand-bills will be circulated which will say roughly the following: "Hey, Black Brothers and Sisters. It's time that we start being proud of what we are—and that's being Black. The RAP organization would like to unite all Black folks into one black power structure."

The bishop approved the use of the building.

All Saints' clergy also did not duck another controversial issue—namely, homosexuality. An Indianapolis newspaper clipping of March 4, 1967, quotes Fr. Powers as saying, "The church must go to homosexuals with her hat in hand and ask forgiveness ... Rather than ministering to them, the church has excluded them. She has failed to reach out to those who need her." Fr. Carthy was also quoted: "Like any large city, Indianapolis has a large homosexual community." Carthy also mentioned that one club "frequented by homosexuals" was located only a few blocks from All Saints. Fr. Atkins attributed the lack of ministry to this community in Indianapolis to lack of funds and "fear of the personal risks." The article defined homosexuality and gave two competing theories for its origin—"psychological and emotional sickness rooted in the person's past" or "a matter of genes." "In either case," said Fr. Atkins, "laws against homosexuality are unjust … Whether homosexuality is a sickness or a natural thing, it doesn't make sense to pass laws that jail two consenting adults." (Indiana' sodomy law did just that.) Fr. Carthy pointed out,

> Homosexuality is considered a sin by the church, but there is no reason why a sinful act should be considered unlawful. And this sin is one of sex, and in many cases a sexual sin is far less serious than other sins, such as uncharitableness. The clergyman has no right to turn his back on any sinner, and it is his job to help not to condemn. If a homosexual comes to me for confession, the same rules apply as for any other penitent. He cannot be refused. And if he consents, a series of counseling sessions will be set up in an attempt to help him.

Carthy added that he had never met a clergyman or psychiatrist who could claim to have truly "cured" a homosexual.

The sexton during these years was Rufo Lutes—who was the father-in-law of Richard Mote and had been at various times Warden and Vestryman. He had also assisted Aldo Bertorelli in the rebuilding of the organ case. He resigned as sexton in 1968.

Finances were always difficult. Fr. Carthy applied again to the Talbot Fund for a grant of $6,200 in the year 1969 to be applied towards Fr. Atkins' support. (The amount requested for 1968 had been $5,000.) The rector's application letter noted

> a steady increase in the participation of the parish toward the assistant priest's costs … The reason for the increased request from the Talbot Fund is, of course, the Diocesan Convention's mandate placing the minimum

clergy salary at $6,700 beginning January 1, 1969. It would be impossible for our budget to absorb the impact of this increase.

According to the application, the proposed parish budget for 1969 was $30,951. At that time, the parish was paying only $2,300 of the rector's salary. ECS was paying him $7,904, although he was contracted only for 20% of his time to ECS. (Fr. Carthy had become director of ECS in November 1965.) The All Saints share of Episcopal Urban Center expense was $3,600. The parish owned the rectory at 540 Central Court (where Fr. Atkins now lived). Fr. Carthy had now moved to 3944 North Delaware, a residence owned by ECS.

When Fr. Carthy became director of ECS, it became necessary to spell out once again the shifting relationships among entities of the program at 16th and Central. The vestry wrote the following letter to Carthy on February 2, 1966:

In connection with your assignment as Executive Director of Episcopal Community Services of Indianapolis, and the compensation arrangements being worked out jointly by Episcopal Community Services, the Department of Christian Social Relations and us, we propose the following:

1 You will continue as Rector of All Saints' Church, Indianapolis, giving a reduced portion of your time to the matters required by such position. We understand that you will be available to conduct services no more than two Sundays a month and that your availability for other parochial duties will be correspondingly lessened.

2 As its part of the over-all compensation arrangements to be paid you, All Saints' will pay you a stipend of $1,872 a year, payable in monthly installments of $156 due on or about the first day of each month for the previous month's service. All Saints' will, of course, pay the related pension premiums, now estimated at $64 annually.

3. In addition, All Saints' will pay you a travel allowance of $180 a year, payable in installments of $15 a month concurrently with the monthly stipend payments, and will bear the cost of your major medical premiums, now estimated at $64 annually.

4. You and your family may take up residence in the premises at 3944 North Delaware Street, Indianapolis, held for the use of the Executive Director of Episcopal Community Services. It is our understanding that

the Department of Christian Social Relations and Episcopal Community Services will pay your moving expenses. Upon the completion of your move to 3944 North Delaware Street, we will make the All Saints' parsonage at 540 North Central Court, Indianapolis, available to the curate, Father Atkins, and his family, and we will pay his moving expenses.

5. Other matters, such as the settlement for certain of your personal property which is to be left at the parish parsonage, will be handled on the basis approved at the special meeting of the vestry held on January 30, 1966, which we understand is acceptable to you.

6. The foregoing arrangement shall be deemed effective as of February 1, 1966.

It is our understanding that this arrangement involving your reduced duties and compensation as Rector of All Saints' Church and your assumption of additional duties with respect to Episcopal Community Services is being made on a one year basis and will be subject to review by each of the parties thereto at the end of this year. Unless and until other mutually satisfactory terms are agreed upon, however, the foregoing shall continue in effect notwithstanding the expiration of the one year term.

Dr. John R. Russell, a faithful member of All Saints and frequent vestryman, was one of the trustees of the Talbot Fund in these years. The Talbot Fund trustees also received annual, separate requests to fund ECS. For 1960, $900 had been requested to support a discretionary fund for the caseworker; $4,050 was asked for three part time workers (in the three neighborhoods that surrounded All Saints, Saint Philip's, and Cathedral House); $3,000, toward Fr. Jenks' salary as Associate Director; and $3,000 for caseworker and secretarial expenses. For 1961, the request was $7,000 to support, in part, salaries of the Executive Director, the full-time caseworker, and the office secretary. In addition $5,230 was requested for the Urban Mission Council program in the neighborhoods, which was to be administered by ECS. Even so, ECS started the year 1962 with a deficit of $3,878.50; however, a gift of $6,000 had been received for a caseworker; and an endowment of $25,000 had been established. Board members of ECS in 1963 included All Saints parishioners Mrs. Meredith Nicholson, Jr. (Roberta) and Jerry Belknap. The budget for that year was $25,700. (Fr. Peter Moore was then Director of ECS.) The request to the Talbot Fund for 1964 was actually a decrease (from $10,950 in 1962 to $9,500 in 1964), and the request for that year was granted. The Talbot Fund was drawn upon by other entities besides those at 16th and Central, but the focus was upon ministry in Indianapolis. Grants in 1966 and 1967 were to ECS, Urban Mission Council, All Saints, Christ Church, and Bishop Craine's Discretionary Fund. ECS, in addition to its grant, conducted fund-raising in the diocese. For example, $7,774 was raised in 1966. Canon Carthy was largely responsible. He tried to preach in other parishes once or twice a month about the work of ECS.

A talk he gave at a diocesan convention, as remembered by Gordon Chastain, illustrates Fr. Carthy's fund-raising style. Alluding to its former cathedral status, Carthy compared All Saints to "your old and disreputable mother." She "smells a little funny and wears too much perfume [incense]. She associates with the wrong people. She wears 'gaudy clothes' [vestments]. But she is your mother; you still love her; and you don't want to see her starve."

The Annual Meeting held on January 21, 1968, reflects both the health of the parish and some warning signs of danger ahead. The nominees for the vestry were Max Brydenthal (President of the AFL-CIO chapter and former city councilman), Richard Clark (attorney and former vestryman), Ida Edelen (social worker with IU Housing), and Philip VanKersen (senior Project Manager for Pittman-Moore). A motion was carried changing the voting age from 21 to 18. Fr. Carthy reported that the Urban Mission Council formerly made up of All Saints, Cathedral and St Philip's had been phased out at the end of December. An Urban Task Force had been set up to replace it, but it would be impossible to conduct a summer program this year without the $6,000 formerly provided by The Talbot Fund—unless All Saints could somehow do the program alone. In 1966 average Sunday attendance had been 117; in 1967 it was 118. The 241 communicants reported marked an all-time high in 1968. Editors of *The Voice,* the parish newsletter, were Phil VanKersen and Fr. Atkins. All Saints' and the Urban Center were "fairly teeming with activity." There was a pre-school program five days a week; clinics (pre-natal and well baby) three days a week; after-school tutoring program two days a week. The Property Report noted that the All Saints share of utilities and other expenses for parish use of Diocesan Hall and St. Francis House were "covered in our flat payment of $295 per month to the diocese." Altar Guild acquisitions in 1967 included a thurible on stand (gift of Tim and Linda Hall), a ciborium (gift of Robert Nowicki Memorial Fund), and a Jerusalem Bible (gift of Fr. James Walker). The Christian Education Committee was composed of Bonnie Harvey, Philip VanKersen, William Finister, and Fr. Atkins. L.H. Bayley had organized a graduation exercise in the spring of 1967 for the church school students.

The 1968 ECS application to the Talbot Fund answered the question "What do we do for this money?"

> Casework and Counseling Servicesare headed by Mr. James Thurston, MASW, Director of Casework. He is assisted by a consultant, Mrs. Norman A. Beatty, MSW, and by two young diocesan priests, The Rev. C. Michael Annis and The Rev. John Roof, who serve without remuneration ... Sources of referrals are too varied to enumerate; but many come from the Bishop, the clergy and the parishes. Still more come, on referral from public and private agencies. In counseling, alone, the agency has carried 118 cases during the first ten months of the year.

> The Food and Clothing Bank is open two days a week to people who are referred from a variety of agencies. It is completely staffed by volunteers from our various Indianapolis parishes ... .

> The Tutorial Program aids children after school from School #10 ... Volunteers from eight Indianapolis parishes work with ... nearly 50 children in the program.

ECS also sponsored the following "auxiliary programs": The All Saints Pre-School Center (Headstart), a Maternal and Child Health clinic (at the Urban Center), the Urban Evangelism and Recreation Program (formerly run by the Urban Mission Council and now administered by ECS), basketball programs (involving 175-200 young people), cooking and personal health classes (for girls), dance classes, and musical programs. This list represents some simplification of the organizational structure. The old CSR and Urban Mission Council had been dissolved and now Canon Carthy, Joan Moyer (his "faithful secretary"), Elizabeth Jay (administrative assistant), and Bonnie Harvey were all to be paid through ECS. The total request to the Talbot Fund for 1968 was $15,000. It was granted.

The request for 1969 was again $15,000. Fr. Carthy appended a letter to the request quoting the minutes of the December 1968 ECS Board meeting:

> The Budget Committee for 1969 drew up a proposed budget only at the request of the Bishop that they do so. This committee recommended a 4% "cost of living" raise for all employees over the objections of the Executive Director. This proposed budget is (roughly) $45,000 for the year 1969. The Committee felt that they were only fooling themselves and decided to present to the Board a six-month budget and proposed a self-study of the agency before the end of the six-month period. The Bishop was present at the Executive Committee meeting and understood the problem—he is planning an Episcopal Charities Fund Drive in April 1969 with professional supervision and anticipates an income of $50,000, $30,000 of which will be earmarked for ECS; he hopes to know the results of the Drive in May ... If the money is not available for continuing the present on-going programs—the programs will be re-evaluated at that time.

This time the full amount was not granted by the Talbot Fund. The Trustees approved only $10,000 of the $15,000 request. It would not be enough. A letter dated June 27, to the Trustees stated that, even with the funds from United Episcopal Charities, the agency's funds would be depleted by August. Clearly, there was trouble ahead.

1969 also marked the year in which Bonnie Harvey retired. The effective date was March 31. Another loss occurred on July 1, when Fr. Atkins left. Once again Fr. Carthy's duties had to be "re-aligned." And the parish had to go begging once again to the Talbot Fund, increasing its request to a total of $6,920.30 for the year. And to top off the losses of 1969, James Thurston resigned as Casework Director for ECS. As a result of all the changes, Fr. Carthy reduced the ECS portion of his time and salary to 20%. Some ECS services (Institutional Ministries and casework/counseling services) either ceased to exist or were transferred to the bishop and cabinet.

Senior Warden Ed McPherson wrote again to the Talbot Fund on September 30, 1969, with a detailed account of the complicated inter-relationships of entities, of another "restructuring." and of another financial crisis. The request was for $6,500, the difference between the selling price of 540 Central Court and the appraisal of 3944 N.

Delaware. (The departure of Fr. Atkins had made possible the sale of Central Court.)

> The Trustees ... will be aware of the complete re-structure and budget reduction of ECS in July of this year. In the process our Rector who had been serving as Executive Director of ECS, 80% of his time and salary, is now only 20% of time and salary committed to ECS. The All Saints rectory is currently being sold and the proceeds of the sale will be about $12000 ... . This sum will be given to ECS—which desperately needs them—and the parish would like to "pay off" the balance right away so that it would own its own property at once. Our finances will not permit our seeking a diocesan loan for the difference between the two properties and we've already been informed that the diocese has no money for "grants" to us ... It's all rather complicated, but All Saints' and ECS have a real problem. Each wants to continue the work and witness of the other; neither can afford the money which is needed to erase the discrepancy in housing value. Already there is tension between the two official bodies and Canon Carthy, trying to serve both, is embarrassed that he is caught up in a situation (along with his family) about which he can do nothing.

It was at this time that Fr. Carthy began to think seriously about leaving All Saints. He must have felt like he was back at the starting line. Once there had been three priests to do the work. Now he was alone, just as he had been at the beginning, with the dual responsibility of ECS and the parish. He was without the support of Bonnie Harvey. Both ECS and All Saints were in financial crisis. The grants from The Talbot Fund, which had kept the program going, were declining. And he was personally embarrassed by the tension between the agencies over the house at 3944 Delaware.

His letter of resignation to the parish was dated November 30, 1969.

> Dear People of All Saints:
>
> Today the Church Universal begins a new liturgical year and I must now tell you that All Saints' faces an Advent of unusual significance in our common life around the Altar of God.
>
> Yesterday, at a special Vestry Meeting, I announced my resignation as Rector of All Saints' effective the latter part of January, 1970. I have accepted a Call for the Parish of Christ Church in the City of New Brunswick, N.J. and will become the Rector there on or about February 1, 1970.

I know that this announcement will cause sadness to many of you. I want you all to know how much I appreciate the devotion and loyalty of so many through the past 13 years. In the closing weeks of my rectorate, I look forward to recounting the many blessings, joys and sorrows we have experienced together.

The bulletin for that same 1st Sunday of Advent, November 30, 1969, gives an indication that there were other changes to come to All Saints, too—namely, liturgical ones. The Sung Mass at 9:30 used the new Trial Liturgy. And the leaflet contained a note about "Passing the Peace" from the altar through the congregation: "this ancient greeting symbolizes brotherhood."

Change was coming; however, All Saints, thanks to Fr. Carthy, was in the neighborhood to stay. He had "slugged it out."

CANON FRANK V. H. CARTHY, RECTOR

Fr. Carthy in 1964

Fr. Peter Moore, Director of ECS

FATHER ALDEN W. POWERS, CURATE

Graduate of Bentley College, University of Massachusetts, Nashotah House. Advanced studies at Harvard University, Amherst College, Boston University, General Theological Seminary and Indiana University School of Social Work.

Served in U.S. Marine Corps during Korean conflict. Married to Nancy Lee, a Registered Nurse, father of three children.

Also experienced in the fields of research accounting, judicial probation, professional social relations and urban reclamation.

Fr. Powers in 1964

"Bear ye one another's burdens and so fulfil the law of Christ"
Galatians 6 2

Mass 1964 (after the building of the new apse)

# CHAPTER NINE

## We're Gonna Go. We Got To
## All Saints Parish: 1970-1976

The first task of the year 1970 was to say goodbye to Fr. Carthy and his family. Bishop Craine received a letter from Joan Moyer on January 17 outlining the plans for the party to be held the following Sunday.

> Dr. Don Moore and Claude Spilman have cooked up a skit. I have given them what "dirt" I dared give—and they have a lot of material on their own. Dr. Moore is going to portray Father in the year 1980. The Vestments, which were specially ordered at Krieg's, have arrived and are beautiful (cloth of gold with red lining!!) There is enough to give Anne a silver tea service (which according to our sources she has wanted for a long time) and the balance in cash. Priests and people from all over the diocese have accepted the invitation to be with us ... . The big event, as far as I am concerned, that evening [at a smaller party after the parish reception] will be that Father has promised to sing—one more time—"On the Road to Senior High"—which, as you know, he is most famous for.

Not long after the farewell celebration, Joan Moyer, as the faithful "volunteer secretary" of the parish, informed the Bishop that the Carthys' move to New Jersey had not gone smoothly. The van had not yet left Indianapolis. "Father can't stand much more taxing of his nerves at this point. But the family did arrive safely in New Brunswick after a drive through bad weather." This trouble was in addition to the fact that Fr. Carthy had just had a "sudden trip to the hospital" which served to "slow him down and scare him into a sensible diet." (Fr. Carthy was very heavy.)

Without a rector, busy life continued at 16th and Central. As Moyer reported to the bishop, Bonnie Harvey was "sparking" the food and

190

clothing bank volunteers and re-organizing emergency assistance. "Our phone receptionist can hear the stories that come in off the streets—and hear [Bonnie] gently draw these people out and do the wonderful education job that only she can do." All the other agencies were going "full tilt", too. All this activity was a "wonderful tribute to Fr. C. A lot of places lock up when a priest leaves."

The contributions of Bishop Francis to the congregation were symbolized in the pulpit dedicated to his memory. Fr. Cirlot's contribution, the continuation and strengthening of Anglo-Catholicism, was reflected in the statue of Our Lady given in his memory. The permanent marker of Fr. Carthy's influence was to take the form of the dramatic stained glass windows in the Michael chapel. The windows were designed by Margaret Kennedy, an artist from Richmond, Indiana, who also executed similar windows for the National Cathedral. The large upper three windows portray St. Michael and the archangels winning the battle in heaven. Their piercing jewel-like eyes look down upon the cowering and defeated Satan. In the lower three windows the battle is won in a city. A woman, looking much like the single mothers of the 16th and Central neighborhood, sings *Magnificat*. A man is crucified in the midst of a city at the intersection of streets named Bigotry and Greed. And a group, much like a church committee, is on fire with the Spirit; over them the "blue marble" of the earth seen from space is orbited by satellites. Fr. Carthy's vision had been of a ministry to the poor—like that single mother. His passion was for justice in the city, for the defeat of Bigotry and Greed. During his rectorate, the perspective upon the earth had changed forever.

Change at All Saints came quickly after Carthy's departure. The newly appointed Screening and Nominating Committee wrote to the parish on December 18, 1969 that they did not want All Saints "to be without a rector any longer than is necessary." The Committee (Jerry Belknap, Don Bose, Ida Edelen, Bonnie Harvey, Dr. John Russell, and Ed McPherson) certainly kept their promise of acting speedily. On February 6, the Committee made their recommendation to the vestry that The Rev. Harris C. Mooney (nicknamed Mike) be elected the next rector.

The Committee had prepared a list of "Qualities That We Are Looking For In A Priest":

1. Someone who plans to stay awhile
2. Someone who is a family man
3. Someone who knows who he is—a seasoned man
4. Someone who not only has a feel for the problems of the inner-city but who is also capable of understanding suburban families
5. Someone who has the ability to speak the Word—attract people especially neighborhood people
6. Someone who can keep the parish integrated—not too much one way or the other
7. Someone with executive ability
8. Someone who is … 35 to 45 years of age
9. Degree of churchmanship very important to some on the committee— unimportant to others

By February 15, a call had been issued. On that date, Ed McPherson, Senior Warden, and Philip VanKersen, Treasurer, wrote to Father Mooney that the vestry had approved a salary of $7,700, a travel allowance of $1,500, one half of Social Security contribution, and heat and maintenance at the rectory on Delaware Street. Mooney's acceptance letter was written on February 18. He noted that he would be "entering the hospital here tomorrow for a yearly physical and psychological examination to insure (*sic*) my fitness and vitality to serve you."

Unfortunately, circumstances would soon deprive him of "fitness and vitality." Fr. Mooney would not, in fact, be able to "stay awhile."

The new rector was from the Diocese of Eau Claire, Wisconsin. He had been serving Christ Church in LaCrosse. In keeping with his new parish's growing involvement with peace and justice issues, he had been active in both the Peace and the Civil Rights Movements.

Father Mooney, his wife (Mary Lou) and their family left LaCrosse on March 31. The rectory was painted and new carpet installed for their arrival.

The call to Fr. Mooney had been to be rector only. Episcopal Community Services would again be separated organizationally, although it was still to be located at 16th and Central. The next Executive Director (beginning in June of 1970) would be The Rev. R. Stewart Wood, who was from the Diocese of Indianapolis. The Wood family became active participants in the life of All Saints.

The annual meeting of the parish took place on April 26, very shortly after Mooney's arrival. At that time, the staff consisted of a sexton (George F Herdock) and two volunteer secretaries (Harvey and Moyer). In addition to the vestry, organizations were listed as a Young People's Fellowship with 20 members meeting six times a year and St. Cecilia's Choir with 30 members and an average attendance of 25. At the meeting, a Youth Representative to the vestry was established—an action which was to have unexpected consequences. Accompanied by applause, Judge DeBruler complimented Father Mooney on the first issue of the Newsletter. Fr. Mooney suggested goals for the year as follows: establishment of a liturgical commission, vestry training, and a vital youth program. Immediate needs included staffing for a Vacation Church School and a summer tutorial program. Evangelism was another high priority.

Fr. Mooney's emphasis upon establishing a liturgical commission was undoubtedly a response to the opportunity to use Trial Liturgies now authorized by the national church.

The next milestone in parish life was the Bishop's Visitation on May 31, 1970. In thanking Philip VanKersen for the check for $32 representing the offering for his Discretionary Fund, the bishop said, "How grateful I am for your fine new rector and the wonderful devotion of so many there like yourself." One of the young people confirmed on May 31 had been Kathy Moyer, who also was a student at St. Richard's School, attached to Trinity Parish. Her mother (Joan) wrote to the bishop, "Where but at St. Richard's can an All Saints' child learn Morning Prayer." Obviously the Mass was still the center of worship at All Saints.

Fr. Mooney was soon busy with the needs of the parish. Correspondence in the archives from July 1970, for example, documents his advocacy for a parishioner who was in difficulty with the Internal Revenue Service.

Then, suddenly, the new rector was taken from parish life for a period of months. On August 20, L.H. Bayley, the Senior Warden, wrote the parish that

> Father Mike was seriously involved in a car accident Wednesday evening as he was leaving Church. We further wish to report that as of this writing he has been placed from the "Critical List" to the "Satisfactory List" at General Hospital. We are announcing a special Eucharist of Thanksgiving for Father Mike's deliverance and prayers for his full recovery to be held Saturday, August 22nd at 9 a.m.

The rector was still in the hospital on September 19. Fr. Wood, Canon Earl Conner, and Fr. Anthony Thurston stepped in to assist the parish during the crisis.

During this time, the parish was being visited by a member of the Diocesan Standing Committee as a step toward diocesan assistance in finding solutions to the perennial financial problems. Bishop Craine prepared a memo in preparation for the visit. Although some of the dates and details are wrong, but he gives a good overview of the parish.

> This church was started in 1912 by Bishop Francis to be his Cathedral. It still carries this recognition on its cornerstone, and the Diocese has title to the building. As Indianapolis expanded northward, in 1920 a group of these people founded the Church of the Advent at 33rd and Meridian, now Trinity Church, and many of the wealthy members left All Saints. It should be noted that there have been two or three mission churches in the area between the Circle and 16th Street, which merged into this congregation in 1912. It has been a marginal operation probably all its years. With the coming of Fr. Carthy in 1956, the Diocese was able to give considerable support on the basis of his work in addition to the rectorship … In the EAF, money for the Diocesan Hall and the purchase of St. Francis House was raised. This latter building had been built by Bishop Francis to be a girls school, but the Diocese had sold all but the church building and the rectory which huddled next to it in 1940. It was this land we had to purchase back at a rather exorbitant figure. We have made a strong commitment to work in that community, and the development of that congregation under Father Carthy, continuing under Father Mooney is dramatic. While it has

increased in communicant strength greatly, a considerable part of the new membership consists of people from an exceedingly low income group, and they really have to stretch to meet their budget. In the past few years, this was accomplished by Talbot Fund grants and Diocesan assistance directly or indirectly. Father Carthy drew half his pay as Director of ECS. Father Mooney has only one source of income, as rector of All Saints.

As life at All Saints continued, important events were happening in the lives of its people. Ed "Mac" McPherson retired from his work at Fort Harrison on October 30, 1970 and was honored with a surprise party. McPherson had been Senior Warden, chair of the Search Committee, Deputy to General Conventions in 1969 and 1970, property chair for the Urban Center, and chair of the Every Member Canvass. According to a note in the bishop's correspondence file, he had "kept the acolytes together" during the rector's hospitalization, and he was "famous for keeping the singing going" at Mass.

By November, Fr. Mooney was again involved in parish life. On November 28, he prepared for the vestry his ideas for the next year's budget:

> Because a request was not made for additional aid in 1970, we have used roughly $6,000 in our savings ... You will note that we need $11,000 a year more than we take in simply to operate. I have added $650 toward a summer neighborhood program not now provided."

A copy of the materials was sent to the bishop, who replied, "I trust that the Talbot Fund will come through for you. I think we all realize the strategic importance of assisting All Saints, serving so many people in straightened financial situations."

At the annual meeting of 1971, Fr. Mooney presented an address on the State of the Parish. He began with a paraphrase: "He that seeks his own Soul shall lose it; a Church that lives to itself will die by itself." He listed four characteristics of All Saints that "mean will we never enjoy the stability and growth of some of our neighboring parishes." All Saints is "Catholic Mass-centered parish"; it is "truly integrated both economically and by color"; it is "committed to serve a neighborhood populated by the poor and the oppressed"; it is "dependent on those who wish their experiences and those of their children to reflect the entire city and not just the world around their house." The rector shared his thoughts about liturgy also:

> Ceremonial will change as music does within the limitations of our ability and staff to do them, but we remain firmly Catholic ... If you believe our liturgy, music, or ceremonial will impress or convert the lonely, the oppressed, and the alienated you are wrong—those become things rich with meaning ONLY if they discover here ... that we different kinds of people love each other.

He had strong words about the youth program, too.

"The days of our wonderful summer programs are over. The money is gone; new ways must be found. The Youth are older and militant." In order to reach them, two directions "present themselves immediately." The first was "increased coordination with Forward, Inc., whose president is a member of our congregation." The second was to structure the youth group "about things of interest to them and in their language"—for example, drugs, abortion, alcohol, and sex. He urged translating the Eucharist and the Gospel into street language.

Reporting on finances, Fr. Mooney said that, despite "the best ever" canvass, the parish could not operate without the sharing of expenses with the other agencies using the facilities and the grants from the Talbot Fund.

Two commissions were operating—Liturgical (chaired by George Hight) and Transportation (chaired by "Scotty" Selch). The choir, under the direction of Berniece Fee Mozingo, was still composed only of girls and was also a project of ECS. Money for new vestments for the acolytes had been raised in 1970 by Sarah ("Susie") Mallory and her daughter, Pauline ("Polly") Clements.

Also at the 1971 Annual Meeting, the Young People's Fellowship reported 20 members and had met 12 times in 1970. Pledges from 18 families, 37 individuals, and two Church School students had been recorded. Ten pledges were under $2 per week, and 10 were over $10.

The rector was adding a mass on major holy days which fell on week days

> to meet the needs of those who have adopted fasting before communion
> as a part of their rule of life. I encourage fasting before communion, but
> it cannot be required by me because the Prayer Book doesn't, and because
> many simply couldn't make it to an evening Mass much earlier than 7 or
> 7:30 and I want good congregations of families on the major holy days.

Fr. Mooney also talked about his own humanity and about the
expectations of clergy.

> I am not surprised to discover that here, as in every parish, we have a gap
> of 18-23 year old persons who ought to be here with us and are not. I have
> met some of them and have heard the remarks I expected, for they are
> said about all priests—we are hypocrites, phonies, liars—these are the nicer
> words. That age group throughout the Church has been raised to believe
> the myth that a priest is God-like; holy, too holy really to live. Then they
> discover various priests have tempers, drink too much sometimes, commit
> sexual sins, are gossipy, bitter—the reality of our humanness hits their
> illusions and they are hurt. I hope that over the years I get to know and
> work with your children and those in our neighborhood … . They will grow
> to understand and love me as a man like themselves with mixed elements of
> sin and good. I make no claims except to be a Christian, which is to admit
> to being a sinner.

Fr. Mooney closed his remarks to the Annual Meeting by referring to the
need to change: "I work from day to day." Then he quoted an African
American woman's statement at the funeral of The Rev. Jack Steeg (the
priest who had been Urban Missioner of the diocese, working out of
16th and Central): "Father Mike, we're gonna go. We got to. We'll do
new things, old things. But we're going to make it."

Another Special Parish Meeting was held on May 9, 1971. Its purpose
was to discuss a suggested age for admitting children to communion.
Liturgical change was in the air—and not just at All Saints. One of
the repercussions was re-examination of the centrality of baptism in
Christian Initiation. Father Mooney gave a part of this background,
stressing that confirmation was "not a gate through which one must
pass to be able to receive communion." According to the minutes of
the meeting, someone asked, "Why do we need a suggested age if the
parents can decide?" The answer was, "Perhaps you are right." Another

question: "Why do they have to go to class?" Answer: "Perhaps not. The rector has a kit of material for parents to use at home." Fr. Stew Wood mentioned that the General Convention of the Church had stated that receiving Communion is receiving the love of Christ and "we cannot restrict Christ's love."

It became apparent that the rector was not fully recovered from his accident. He experienced pain while being on his feet for long periods of time—as, for instance, during the administration of communion. On March 7, he wrote to the bishop requesting permission to train lay chalice administrators. Two men and one woman were ready to start instruction. The canons of the Church now permitted "lay persons' to be licensed by the bishop for this purpose. The bishop responded affirmatively, mentioning Ron MacIntosh as a potential candidate for this function. (MacIntosh was the young man who had asked Fr. Atkins for use of the facilities for the Black Power meeting. He had been associated with the ministry of Fr. Steeg and was the leader of Forward, Inc.) The bishop also suggested that Fr. Mooney tell any upset parishioners that "this is done regularly now in the Roman Catholic Church."

In that same letter, Fr. Mooney talked about his enjoyment of a ministry at the Masonic and the Methodist Homes in Franklin. "We visit for a long period of time, as well as celebrate the Eucharist." He reported that Mrs. Cora Thompson (83 and the longest attending member of All Saints) was in the hospital. Also, "our youth group (really ecumenical—the president is A.M.E.—and cross parish—one Saint Paulite and one Saint Albanite) runs around 15 or 17." They were using a liturgy developed by Forward, Inc. The sermon was a rap and discussion of "Ron and Ernest's paraphrase" of the Gospel of John.

In March 1971, the rector received a request from the Free University to use All Saints' facility space. Since anyone could offer any course he or she wished, Free University was possibly controversial. Fr. Mooney asked the bishop for counsel. He replied, "I have nothing at stake in this, and it is for you to decide, with such other support as you feel necessary."

Another opportunity for ecumenical cooperation arose in March 1971, when a Unitarian-Universalist group asked to use the facilities from noon to 1:30 on Sundays. The vestry raised several issues—time of use, wear and tear on the organ, insurance issues, and application of the $125 monthly rent to the All Saints share of Episcopal Urban Center expenses. Finally in November, L.H. Bayley, acting as Senior Warden, informed the bishop that agreement had been reached. The group would begin their usage at 1 p.m. on Sundays and would obtain insurance protection.

Fr. Mooney experienced even more health problems, this time related to a gunshot wound he received while visiting a local restaurant and bar. He was able to attend a Baptism (where the Bishop was the officiant) at All Saints on August 7, 1971, but did not feel well enough to attend the party afterward. He wrote the bishop the next day, "It appears that I won't be able to handle Sundays until mid-September. The short time yesterday really wore me out." He was keeping his finger on the pulse of the parish, however, because the purpose of his letter of August 8 was to alert the bishop to a problem developing between All Saints and the Episcopal Urban Center. The problem was cleanliness and maintenance. Some of the vestry "feel not enough responsibility is exercised by the Forward street leaders." The toilets in the gym were frequently "filthy." Therefore, "some kind of understanding will have to be reached to reduce the increased antagonism which is growing among our laity." The bishop answered that despite the problems, "it is still more important to have people being served."

On September 19, 1971, Father Mooney was back at All Saints for Sunday service; however, he was still not well. The Rev. Dom Leo Patterson, OSB, was the preacher for the day. Dom Leo was used by the bishop as a chaplain and confessor to the clergy (and many laity) of the diocese. The liturgy for the day was one of the Trial Services. A special announcement was inserted in the bulletin:

> Receiving Communion at 9:30 Mass: Beginning today, to allow the Rector the chance to conserve strength and you to participate more fully in the Mass, we will receive Communion at the Altar Rail with each communicant moving and the administrator remaining still. This is already done at Nashotah House and in some of our parishes in this country. The Rector

will administer the Hosts near the pulpit, the communicant receives (kneeling or standing, as you wish), then moves to a position near the Lady Statue and receives the Wine from the Chalice held by a priest or a person licensed to administer. He then returns to his seat. You will find this form of receiving helps with a good crowd and it certainly eases the strain on the Celebrant. Our older forms of receiving are not dictated by the Book of Common Prayer, but just grew up as whatever was useful was tried and adopted. Those receiving a blessing only should go to the Celebrant, kneel, hands down, and return directly to their pew.

At Thanksgiving of both 1970 and 1971, the Indianapolis *Star* had carried a column complaining that All Saints and other churches in the neighborhood were locked. Fr. Mooney felt compelled to respond:

The day following last Thanksgiving, I read your column which concerned this church among others in our neighborhood. I decided not to write and tell you that we <u>were</u> worshipping at Mass here on Thanksgiving Day, 1970, but to see a repetition of the column with another nagging complaint, requires an answer.

At 10 a.m. and for something more than an hour, 60 people, rich, poor, black and white offered a Mass of thanksgiving and then shared their love for one another for some forty minutes more after Mass. As a church building, we are locked when Mass is not being celebrated, to protect persons from danger in a lonely, cut-off building and to prevent irresponsible destruction of Prayer Books, crosses, etc.—all bought by a poor congregation which can rarely afford to replace anything.

However, your problem is you and your friend don't know what a church is. It begins in worship and fellowship, but if it is Christian, it goes beyond that. This small congregation (250 members) is a part of the Episcopal Urban Center and shares its support—both in person and financially—with a variety of other agencies. By All Saints gifts, with those of other agencies, people are fed, clothed and counseled with their need being the only consideration. In addition, a Pre-School occupies one entire floor in our office building, and we provide offices for a branch of the State Employment Service whose personnel break their necks to find employment for the last hired, first fired of our city. Forward, Inc. joins Episcopal Community Services in offering guidance and help, to the young black; to the old who feel so hopeless they want to die now; to the affluent white middle class run away; and those who are trying to break out of the trap into which race, religion, drug or alcohol has placed them. All Saints parish church ministers pastorally to a wide variety of persons, in neighborhood and out of neighborhood, in addition to its share in the structure of the Episcopal Urban Center.

I have some questions for you and your friend, so easily critical. Where were you when the young blacks from Forward, Inc., were sorting their share of the food collected by Young World Development, with 100 turkeys, to feed 100 families, black and white? Where were you when 23 families were fed and another 15 clothed by Episcopal Community Services on Wednesday? Where were you when as parish priest I took food to families when agencies had run out or closed on Wednesday, or talked to a young couple in the neighborhood about baptism, or spent several hours with an alcoholic fighting the shakes and himself, or for that matter where were you and your friend when an overdose had to be ministered to on the churchyard a couple weeks ago? The tavern you went to is always open—but does it reach out?

Yes, our church building is frequently locked, but the church isn't. The church is we baptized people, strengthened by our weekly acts of worship, going out to minister, to feed, to heal, to love, to convert. We don't lock that in.

Just where were you? We always need help.

Reading through Fr. Mooney's anger, we find a real description of life at 16th and Central. Altar Centered Social Concern did not depart with Fr. Carthy. It just took some new forms.

As 1971 came to an end, the rector shared with the vestry his personal goals for 1972:

1. A two week summer neighborhood program, utilizing our parish young people
2. Effective use of continuing education money in the budget ($200)
   a. An intensive course on the use and abuse of drugs
   b. Phase I and Phase II of Leadership Training ("Sensitivity Training").
3. More intensive training of our young people for confirmation
4. Strengthening our Commission system
5. Begin a youth program for our parochial youngsters, grades 5 through 7
6. Consistent effort to have each Sunday's sermon a life giving word
7. Learn to shut up, stop being so eternally "doing" things and sit and listen to God.

Further, he shared with the vestry his health concerns:

A handicap of mine is that I look so well. There is a very great deal of constant pain which relates to a surgical technique done on my ribs. It involved no serious organs—those are all fine—but does involve wires used to put me together again. If the pain continues this bad for another two or three months, it may require minor surgery to remove the wire.

Nevertheless, he was "eternally doing things." His visits to the homes in Franklin took two days a month. He was the diocesan representative to the Indiana Inter-Religious Commission on Human Equality, and its various sub-groups. He was a reader used by the Standing Liturgical Commission of the national church in the process of preparing the Trial Liturgies. And he reviewed books for various publications.

Also in Father Mooney's year-end thoughts in his report to the vestry was the continuing problem of cleanliness and security at the Urban Center. "So far in 1971 we have had stolen a vacuum cleaner, a riding lawn mower, and our floor buffing machine (twice). For now, please help us all to bear with the present mess."

There was risk in programs so deeply involved with neighborhood youth as those at 16th and Central. Complaints reached the rector and vestry about drinking on the part of All Saints parishioners at a Diocesan Youth Division event January 29-31, 1972. One consequence was the resignation of Ron MacIntosh.

Father Mooney celebrated the 15th Anniversary of his ordination to the Priesthood on February 24, 1972. The 7:00 p.m. Mass used the Trial Service I with Baptism.

The liturgical high points of the Christian year are the services of Holy Week and Easter. The schedule for the years 1971 and 1972 included a Maundy Thursday Mass. Good Friday was observed with Veneration of Cross and Mass of Pre-Sanctified plus opportunity for Confessions. There was no Mass on Holy Saturday, but at 7 p.m. there was the Lighting of the Paschal Candle and Renewal of Baptismal Vows. Easter Day was celebrated with Sung Mass and Procession.

On Maundy Thursday of 1971, Fr. Wood and Fr. Mooney were concelebrants. John Russell acted as sub-deacon. Marian Jones read the Epistle, and Phil Johnson was Master of Ceremonies. The Passion was read with congregational participation. And the rite for Holy Communion was from the 1929 **Book of Common Prayer**. The Peace was exchanged (not included in the Prayer Book rite).

The Good Friday services contained a Hymn, Veneration of Cross, and Dramatic Reading of the Passion. The *Sursum Corda* and Consecration were omitted before the Peace, and Communion of the People of God. The following announcement respected those in the congregation whose piety preferred that the Good Friday Mass be non-communicating: "At each service today each communicant should feel free to receive from the Reserved Sacrament or not as he feels it would be most useful to him. There is no obligation to receive."

At the Easter Eve service of 1971, the New Fire was struck at west end of the Church. Candles were lit three times in response to the Deacon's chant: "The light of Christ." Then the *Exultet* was sung. The Renewal of Baptismal vows was based on the 1929 **Book of Common Prayer** Vows. Ushers passed out candles to those "from the 4th grade up" so that light could be passed throughout the congregation. Then came the Dismissal and Blessing. The Deacon for this service was The Rev. Thomas Honderich, then curate at Trinity but later to become Priest Associate of All Saints. The 1929 Prayer Book had made no provision for such an Easter Eve service. Its appearance in the schedule for 1971 reflects the rector's interest in Liturgical Renewal and his efforts to combine the existing Prayer Book with renewal.

Yet another liturgical addition on occasion was dance. On Pentecost, 1972, the bulletin announced that "between the Blessing and the Final hymn Quinon Mimms [would offer] a 2 ½ minute ballet ... which he created himself to interpret the Holy Spirit."

Although the Trial Liturgies were used regularly during Fr. Mooney's tenure as rector, the bulletin for Ash Wednesday, 1971, again illustrates how the rector combined Catholic ceremonial and practice with the 1929 Prayer Book rite. Sung Mass was at 7:30 p.m. An introit was sung; thereafter, Holy Communion was celebrated using the Book of Common Prayer. An announcement said, "All desiring imposition come forward after the Blessing of ashes before the Liturgy begins. Late arrivals may receive the imposition by kneeling at the Altar Rail after the liturgy." The Lenten schedule was to include Stations and Benediction at 7:30 p.m on Fridays. Coffee and discussion programs would follow in St. Francis House. The rector also had suggestions for Making a Lenten Rule:

Everyone of us should make an effort to fashion a Rule for Lent.

1. Fasting and Abstinence: Cutting down on amounts of food and drink. Why not give up one meal a day—or eat only what a person on welfare has?

2. Prayer: If you don't already say daily personal and family prayers, Lent is a good time to begin.

3. Worship: Added opportunities for this are available in Lent. If you are not already keeping the basic precept of assisting at Eucharist, Lent is the time to start doing it.

4. Good Works and Charitable Acts: "Almsgiving", not only of food, clothing and money—but of yourself. Deny yourself some time to give to others.

In the bulletin for Pentecost, 1971, the rector announced the first session of a Lay Reader's Class. The topic was "The Theology of the Mass." In addition:

All Saints is happy to share three of her children next Sunday with Trinity for their 10:00 a.m service as Jeanice Hight, Katherine Ridley, and Kathy Moyer act their parts in the play "Noah". The play is enacted by members of the 6th grade graduating class of St. Richard's School, with Fr. Tom Honderich directing. It makes a little parish feel good to be able to share her talent with a larger one.

We congratulate our newly confirmed and baptized (including) the first priest's grandchild I'd ever instructed, Dawn Bose. The congregation was good with 68 communions—but, we missed a number of regulars. I trust your reasons were good, because it is important for a whole congregation to welcome its new brothers and sisters in Christ and share the Holy Meal together. Congratulations to Nancy and Kelly Shaw, Annetta Parnell, Pauline Dillon, Lisa Wood, Mary P. Mooney, Dawn Bose, Margaret Rabbitt, Barbara Bingham, Ercle Washington, Theresa Packwood and Forest Packwood, and to Rex Hume.

The Cry Room at the back of the Church is open and available during the
service to mothers with hungry or fussy babies or small children.

At the Annual Meeting held on January 23, 1972, Kristin Wood,
the wife of Fr. Wood, acted as Clerk. Her minutes record that "Mrs.
Murtz suggested that the men help in cleaning up the hall and
setting up tables Saturday night as this has been a problem. There is a
possibility of using a janitorial service for cleaning during the week."
Ron McIntosh presented the report of the Youth Division. On behalf
of the youth he presented a resolution to lower the voting age to 16
for confirmed members and that the youth group be autonomous at
All Saints. Mr. Mote asked that the resolution be separated into two
sections, but the youth representatives opposed this suggestion. After
much discussion the resolution passed. These two issues, maintenance
of the parish hall and youth, were the focus of much parish attention
and tension at the time.

The February, 1972 issue of the newsletter, *The Saints in Action*, also
reported on that annual meeting and added a "thank you" to Sadye
Harris who had been the first youth representative to the vestry during
the preceding year. Thanks were also given to the Unitarian Fellowship
for being "perfect tenants" and cleaning up the area around the gym
each Sunday. The newsletter also carried a little article by the rector
giving a foretaste of the future for All Saints. It was titled "Women in
the Priesthood?"

> The Anglican bishop of Hong Kong has ordained two deaconesses to
> the order of priests this past month. In World War II the parent Chinese
> Church also ordained two women to the priesthood. This month's issue
> of the *Episcopalian* has two able articles, Yes and No, on the subject of
> the ordination of women to the priesthood. In this reader's mind, the Yes
> article is the more substantial in its scholarship. There will have to be a
> good deal of serious study to face this issue without prejudice either way.
> As a church we have evaded the issue far too long in spite of the fact we
> have had intercommunion with a church which has ordained women to the
> priesthood for some time, the (Lutheran) Church of Sweden.

Another women's issue, that of female chalice bearers arose again.
Apparently, a woman had not yet been licensed; and some women
were asking, "Why not?" So it was decided to take an "advisory vote"

at an upcoming special Parish Meeting that took place on March 5, 1972. The vote in favor of women chalice bearers was 23; opposed, 19. Fr. Mooney wrote the bishop, "Damage has been done to my job as rector in the eyes of many who do not understand the complex background." He asked for the bishop's help. Consequently, the bishop wrote a "Pastoral Letter from the Bishop to the Faithful at All Saints' Parish":

> Father Mooney has reported to me the very close vote taken at the special Parish Meeting last Sunday on the subject of women being licensed to administer the chalice. As I am sure you know, the Rector is in charge of the worship of his own congregation by canon law, and the Bishop's task is to counsel with him and then support his decisions. With such an evenly divided vote, I would have to agree with the Rector that a change of this magnitude at this time would be more divisive to the congregation than simply to maintain the present position on this issue.
>
> You should know that there is no canonical restriction against women being licensed to administer the chalice, or girls serving as acolytes, and these practices are followed in many places, even in this Diocese. However, I do support the Rector's decision that this change at this moment would not be in the best interests of All Saints Parish. I do not need to remind the people of your congregation that our primary loyalty is to Jesus Christ, and that our presence at the Altar fulfills a deep need in us. Keep the Faith and do not hesitate to work for any change you believe will support God's work and the dignity of personhood more fully.

In a letter to an All Saints parishioner of the same date, the Bishop said, "There is no reason why a woman cannot serve in any capacity in the life of the Church." But he also said, "It is clear that the Church is not emotionally ready to accept this rather great change." For the next five years (and after), the issue of women's ministry would be a topic of national church debate. All Saints would, at a high price, decide in a most dramatic way that "there is no reason why a woman cannot serve in any capacity." But not all the congregation would be "ready to accept this rather great change."

At that same special meeting in March 1972, the issue of youth representation was also hotly debated. Phil Johnson moved that the governing body of the Youth Group of All Saints be allowed to elect the person they wished to represent them on the vestry, regardless of church affiliation. The motion was seconded by Ron McIntosh. L.H. Bayley moved to limit debate to two minutes by any person and that no person speak more than twice on one point. Twelve spoke to the issues on both sides. The result of the vote was 33 no; 12 yes. The motion to allow youth representation to vestry to come from outside All Saints Parish was voted down.

On February 23, 1972, the rector convened a meeting of various agencies serving the neighborhood defined as "Model Cities Areas 1 and 2." The purpose was to create a "congress" or umbrella group to speak for all the groups. Bonnie Harvey was also active in this effort. For the months of January and February, Fr. Mooney reported in the newsletter (in the parish archives) 42 masses at All Saints, 8 at the Franklin homes, 3 at the women's prisons. He had made 16 house calls, 17 hospital calls, led 5 confirmation classes, and conducted 1 sick communion, 4 confessions, and 39 interviews. He had gone to 15 meetings and driven 2252 miles on business. All this was in addition to attending a course on drug abuse. And this was a man with chronic health problems!

Of course, mundane affairs continue to demand attention even during times of change. In March 1972, Fr. Mooney wrote the bishop, in another of his very frequent letters, that the parish had purchased a "decent used VW bus" for $400 plus $200 needed to "get it in shape." The purpose was to "haul kids." In the June 1972, newsletter, Fr. Mooney calculated that 9 of the 14 persons baptized so far during the year lived in the neighborhood; and 5 of the 12 confirmed or received were "neighborhood". By this time there were two youth groups—one for older and one for younger youth. July 1972 activities included a trip to King's Island Amusement Park for the older group and a car wash for the younger. The rector also took the "Chanters" (girl's choir) to King's Island in September.

In preparation for the bishop's Annual Visitation in May, Fr. Mooney sent him some liturgical notes. The Sursum Corda was to be sung. The Lord's Prayer was said in the (contemporary) Trial Service II language.

The "cleanliness" and "security" issues continued to plague the parish and the rector. On August 7, 1972, Fr. Mooney put into a letter his response to the "complaints made to me personally or among members of the parish which relate to the badly deteriorating condition of the Episcopal Urban Center." The letter also touches on other complaints and comparisons to the way matters were conducted were under Fr. Carthy. Here is his response:

> It must be clearly understood that Father Carthy <u>did</u> have complete control over the entire Center—who used it and when. Now the Center is governed by a Board consisting of myself, Father Wood and Mr. McIntosh. The change in governing the Center was made by the Bishop. The aim was deliberately to separate agencies.

> The authority which Father Carthy had no longer exists in your present rector. The only portion of the Center over which I have complete authority is the Church building and my office. This is precisely the reason that while I was ill, the locks were changed on the kitchen and the keys restricted. It reminds us that if All Saints wants to use the kitchen, the gym, the conference room or any other part of the Center other than my office or the Church we must go through channels. That channel being Canon Conner, the Chairman of the above mentioned Board of the Urban Center. If a gym, kitchen or toilet is left dirty it becomes the duty of the organization who had signed up to use it to clean or if that is not done, a complaint is lodged with canon Conner who attempts to put pressure on the offender. Believe me, I have complained several times already this summer.

> Episcopal Community Services is a separate agency just as is All Saints and that has created some changes not always clearly understood.

> A) Mrs. Moyer could no longer do our secretarial work as she did for Father Carthy who was both rector and director—we relieved that problem by hiring Mrs. Egnall to work for me one day a week as All Saints secretary. (Note, however, that Joan Moyer continued as the bookkeeper for the Urban Center.)

> B) The choir was affected. It was not just an All Saints choir but also an ECS project which allowed Mrs. Harvey to handle it—but not with each agency cooperating but separate—her ECS work load has to come first. We can't ask Father Wood to release his staff to do All Saints work.

C) That raises another issue about the choir—partly dictated by money. We can only afford $1,200 a year for an organist—that means we are tied to the Cathedral to offer an attractive salary and it ties us to their practice date: Thursday.

D) Do we need a choir supper? I like it—some parents have said they do not. But if we have a supper WHO will cook it with all our working mothers? ...

A word about finances. Our budget is roughly $32,000—of that $13,500 comes from two sources. $8,500 is a grant to which we must approach the Talbot Fund each year—and with such approaches there can be no infallible guarantee we will get. That means, like your home budgets, ours is a wee shakey, too.

Fr. Mooney was obviously feeling considerable stress. The combination of constant worry about money and tensions between agencies had finally ended the rectorate of Fr. Carthy. Now the same problems appear to have intensified, and the rector felt that he had even less control over the situation than his predecessor had.

He wrote to the bishop on August 14 about the possibility of getting more money from the Talbot fund and added even more concerns:

We have lost two large contributors to St. Alban's. Progress is being made. Most of our baptisms are neighborhood. They recognize me even without collar; but if these are the people we get, they can't pay the freight. As to the future, I've not had the program I want because Forward just takes over everything in the summer.

To this letter he added a hand-written postscript: "I love it here and I want us here."

In addition to everything else, Fr. Mooney's health was still precarious. However, the bishop tried to be encouraging. "I am most grateful to know that the medicine is meeting your needs and that you are so well on your feet."

The problems did not go away. On September 18, a parishioner wrote to the bishop with more—and quite specific—complaints about the dirty condition of Diocesan Hall when parishioners came on Sunday morning to fix the choir breakfast and about members of Forward having access to keys and causing damage to the building. Another parishioner wrote a similar letter on September 27.

The deteriorating situation and the rector's health brought about a decision that he should be relieved of his responsibilities. The bishop wrote to the congregation on November 30, 1972 (almost exactly three years after Fr. Carthy's resignation),

> After extensive consultations over the past few weeks, it is my sad responsibility as Bishop and Chief Pastor of the Diocese to announce my decision to terminate Father Mooney's Rectorship of All Saints' Parish. I do this in view of his great physical limitations and his need for hospitalization.

The Bishop's Cabinet (Canon Conner, Canon Jack Potter, and Archdeacon Fred Williams) would see that regular services and pastoral and administrative matters were covered. They would also consult with the vestry.

Many seemed to be relieved that this step had been taken. L.H. Bayley wrote to the bishop,

> We, the Vestry and congregation of All Saints parish, wish to express our gratitude to you and to your cabinet officers who have so courteously served and guided us for the benefit of our parish and Father Mike. We wish to especially mention, Archdeacon Williams, Canon Conner, and Canon Potter in their personal assistance.

After he left Indianapolis, the final tragedy in the life of Fr. Mooney involved another gunshot wound, this time a fatal one which occurred during a hold-up at a store where Fr. Mooney was working.

In the meantime, Episcopal Community Services was not only continuing its work, but thinking about expanding in a new direction. Fr. Wood's cover letter for the ECS request to the Talbot Fund Trustees dated March 24, 1971, tells us that

> Our United Episcopal Charities request included the expectation that we would receive during the calendar year 1971, $10,000 from the Bishop Talbot Fund. While this is a substantial amount, your continued support of

our agency in the past in similar amounts has enabled us to offer substantial services both to the poor and to those of our own congregations requiring psychological and psychiatric assistance ... . You will notice under the budget an item called Development. It is the hope of our Board that some truly significant ministry to "alienated" young people can be begun and sustained by our agency. In this regard we are presently examining the possibility of providing a residential program for runaway young people ... . During the last year our agency has had to stretch to meet the increasing needs of the poor created by our economic recession. Approximately 60 families a week have been assisted temporarily with food, clothing, rental assistance and a variety of other ministries. At the same time, we have maintained the counseling services of the agency and where appropriate have referred people needing deeper psychiatric care to our volunteer professionals.

The proposal for a program to address the needs of runaway youth would eventually become Stopover, a separate agency which outlived its parent (ECS) and celebrated its 30th anniversary in 2001.

Fr. Wood's request to the Talbot Fund for $15,000 in 1972 explains that Stopover was inaugurated during the summer of 1971, "using volunteer homes and the experience of Karen Townsend, our staff worker who had had earlier been on the staff of The Belden Street Youth Help Center in Chicago." His letter also describes the need: "The police in Indianapolis are apprehending 200 runaways a month. By providing short-term housing and counseling for the runaway and his family, we believe that we are offering a significant service." Fr. Wood also calls the operating principle of the food and clothing programs: "no red tape."

In October 1972, a request was made to the Mayor's Youth Commission for $43,480 to rent, staff, and maintain a residential facility for Stopover.

Concurrently, the Standing Committee of the Diocese endorsed a plan of Bishop Craine to implement an experimental street ministry in Indianapolis, beginning July 1, 1972, and with an outside evaluation to be carried out after July, 1973. The Talbot Fund was, again, the source of funds. The person appointed to the job was The Rev. Fritz Wiecking, who was ordained at All Saints on October 4, 1972. Concerns were raised by the ECS board about his involvement in the "Inauguration of Conscience" held on January 20-21, 1973, in Washington, D.C., a protest against the War in Vietnam. Wiecking had worked on publicity for the event but had not been present at it. He said in a written statement to the board: "I was excited about this because I saw in it an opportunity to have a wider dialogue among people concerned about Values and Beliefs ... And so I quickly became the defacto chairman."

Another clergyman associated with ECS at the time was The Rev. Lloyd C. Williams. After his ordination in 1971, he served ECS as a part-time counselor. He was working two days a week at ECS, two days at St. Philip's, and two days at the Indiana University Purdue University Indianapolis (IUPUI) campus. As Fr. Wood said in a letter to Archdeacon Williams, "His cultural heritage as an American Black, offered us the possibility of extending our counseling services beyond our basically white, middle-class clientele."

The Bishop's cabinet, especially Canons Jack Potter and Earl Conner, maintained the service schedule after Fr. Mooney's departure. On Maundy Thursday 1973, for example, The Rev. Canon Jack C. Potter was the celebrant. The Easter Even service began at 11 p.m. with the Lighting of the New Fire and continued with Renewal of Baptismal Vows and First Mass of Easter (using the Prayer Book rite). At the Easter Day Sung Mass, Ian and Caroline Mitchell and their family provided the music. At Pentecost, Canon Potter was again the celebrant. No introit was sung and the service was taken from the **Book of Common Prayer**.

As part of a process of a search for a new rector, a document titled "Potential Rector Attributes" was developed. Bishop Craine dated his copy June 20, 1973 and preserved it in his All Saints correspondence file. Priority Number 1 was "A strong Anglo-Catholic who will continue the long tradition of Eucharist-centered worship." Eight other statements used such phrases as "mature individual", "charismatic personality", "effective tactician who can engineer transition of a neighborhood-related program from ECS to All Saints." An attached statement was called "General Background."

All Saints, a parish comprised of a total cross-section of the Indianapolis community—racially, culturally and economically—is located in the midst of the central city. The parish, unique for its genuine reflection of Christian love among its parishioners, is at the crossroads in terms of its relevance both to itself and to the community in which it is situated. At one point in its history, the rector of All Saints was also the director of Episcopal Community Services (ECS) which provided neighborhood outreach. Based on this dual role of the rector, the parish has enjoyed the reputation of serving the central city whereas, in fact, it has ministered almost exclusively to itself. This is not to deny, however, that individual parishioners have contributed consistently and effectively to the neighborhood as individuals and through ECS. Currently the role of the parish is being carefully reassessed in close coordination with the bishop. The approach on which we have achieved consensus envisions that All Saints, in addition to continued ministry to its parish, will assume responsibility for neighborhood-related programs. This approach will of necessity require, in addition to a rector, minimal staff including professional social work expertise, and a staff of active volunteers both from within the neighborhood and from other church groups throughout the city. The latter reality must be faced in view of the fact that a significant percentage of potential volunteers for service within the parish are fully employed outside the home.

The parish began to consider asking Fr. Wood to serve as rector, as well as director of ECS—returning to the arrangement of Fr. Carthy's last years. The ECS request to the Talbot Fund for 1974 funds ($20,000 to supplement the $30,000 expected from United Episcopal Charities) details the history of the proposal:

In July of this year (1973) the vestry of All Saints Episcopal Church ... approached Bishop Craine with the request that he consider talking with the Board of Episcopal Community Services about drawing theses two bodies into a more advantageous union. It was their hope that the present director of ECS could be called as Rector of the parish and with a priest-associate would administer a unified program of Christian worship, education and outreach using the total facilities of the Episcopal Urban Center. On September 6, 1973, the ECS Board accepted this idea in principal and authorized its Executive Committee to negotiate details of this staff merger with the Vestry of All Saints. Under the proposed plan, there would be one staff person hired not presently employed at the Center. This person would act as Staff Secretary and would be responsible to the Rector-Director for all general secretarial duties. A Financial Secretary would keep the five sets of books now kept by three people: ECS, All Saints, Stopover, Youth Outreach and the Episcopal Urban Center.

A July 17, 1973, resolution of the Vestry read as follows:

> The Vestry of All Saints accepts the Episcopal Urban Center concept which will combine the ministry of All Saints Parish and the ministry of Episcopal Community Services, Inc. with an Administrative head. The concept also includes the establishment of a Liaison Committee composed of equal number of All Saints and Episcopal Community Services representatives to develop and maintain the Episcopal Urban Center concept.

The copy of the resolution in the diocesan archives has the word "maintain" underlined in red. Evidently someone remembered the previous tensions over building maintenance and hoped the new plan would address them. The liaison persons appointed to the committee from All Saints were listed as L.H. Bayley (Senior Warden), George Hight (Junior Warden), Maurice Edelen (Treasurer), Dr. John Russell, and Joan Moyer (Alternate).

After "averaging two meetings a week for one year." the vestry was "excited to call a Parish Meeting" on September 18, 1973, to announce the decision to join the agency and the parish under one head and to select Canon Wood as the rector.

Re-joining ECS and the parish under the same leadership was not, however, to be a return to the "one man show" that had exhausted Fr. Carthy in his last year. There was to be an Associate, a priest who would share leadership in both the agency and the parish. That person was The Rev. John H. Eastwood, known more familiarly as Jack. Eastwood had been ordained in the diocese (coming from Good Shepherd, West Lafayette) and had served at St. Thomas, Franklin (now Whiteland). Fr. Eastwood's first Sunday at All Saints was the First Sunday of Advent, 1973.

The sharing of leadership was highlighted by a Celebration of New Ministry instituting The Rev Canon R. Steward Wood, Jr., as Rector and The Rev. John H. Eastwood, Jr., as Associate on Thursday, January 17, 1974. Bishop Craine presided. The preacher was the Rt. Rev. Samuel J. Wylie, D.D., Bishop of Northern Michigan. The invitation (in the diocesan archives) to the celebration spoke of the renewed mission:

The Diocese of Indianapolis and All Saints Church in particular are committed to touching the life of the inner city with the whole of the Christian Gospel, a concern for man's total needs. Joined in this single ministry are the members, staff, and volunteers of All Saints and Episcopal Community Services. They invite you to join in celebrating this on going ministry under the leadership of Canon Wood and Father Eastwood.

Implementing that vision of "touching the life of the inner city" through "concern for total needs," both Fr. Wood and Fr. Eastwood became active in neighborhood issues. In October 1974, for instance, they were writing letters advocating the apprehension of an assailant who had raped a neighbor. In addition to the clergy efforts, two parishioners, Mary Green and Karen Debruler, became involved in the effort to assist the victim.

The beginning of the Wood and Eastwood era coincided with growing tensions in the national church over Prayer Book revision, the ecumenical conversations called Consultation on Church Union (COCU), communion administered to those not confirmed in the Episcopal Church, and the proposals for the ordination of women. The 1974 General Convention of the Church, which took place in Louisville, Kentucky had included a preliminary vote on the ordination question. Momentum was building for both approval of women's ordination and approval of a new Prayer Book which would include material from the Trial Liturgies. Among those who were unhappy about these developments were some parishioners of All Saints. The issues, particularly that of ordination, were not an abstract concept in the parish because The Rev. Jacqueline A. Means, a deacon, was working at 16th and Central and was "waiting in line" for ordination to the Priesthood. As director of Institutional Ministries for the diocese, she was assigned to All Saints. (Her work at the Women's Prison, as well as other institutions, was in the tradition begun by Mrs. Francis half a century previously.) The vestry's vote to endorse Jackie Means took place on May 11, 1975. Bishop Craine responded about this issue to one of the parishioners (Richard Mote) as follows:

We are a Church under God and under law, and it is my responsibility to follow the decisions of General Convention, and once the Diocese has expressed itself, to be loyal in my representation of their point of view. You certainly must know that the General Conventions of 1967 and 1970

215

authorized the Ordination of Women to the Diaconate, and that has been
followed in many parts of the Church already. Our Diocese with almost
unanimity not only favored this, but also endorsed the principle that women
should be eligible for the Priesthood and Episcopate.

Another parishioner, Henry Hull, also wrote the bishop after the
Presiding Bishop predicted on television in February, 1976 that "we
will ordain women to the priesthood."
Mr. Hull's position statement said,

> The Apostolic Succession was established by Jesus Christ and though
> many women were His followers He chose twelve men to be His Apostles.
> Although in the days of Our Lord women were not treated as equal to men,
> the writer believes that He would have chosen some women had He not
> wished all His Apostles to be men.

Appended to his statement was Henry Hull's biography:

> 78 years of age, was baptized and confirmed probably 75 and 67 years
> ago, respectively. Since World War I (1919) he has been reasonably active
> in the church having served in several capacities—church school teacher,
> vestryman, junior warden and senior warden. Due to a coronary attack
> several years ago and upon advice of his physician, he has had to become
> more or less inactive and one of "the silent majority." However, he feels he
> should make his position known to whomever might care to know.

And then he added a hand-written note to the bishop:

> These reflections were written to let those in authority know my feelings,
> but believe me, not to stir up anything. As I told Fr. Wood and Fr. Eastwood
> I tell you—you may be assured of my continued limited support. You
> conduct services as you believe they should be—I only am expressing my
> "druthers."

The bishop wrote back,

> Certainly I respect your position. The Episcopal Church has always
> represented diverse positions as you know, and it can be a healthy tension
> if we don't let it get us down. You are an old and trusted friend, and I know
> you recognize this and, like me, you will continue with your presence and
> support.

Henry Hull would remain true to his word. When others left All Saints following the ordination of Jackie Means on January 1, 1977, he did not. He attended regularly until the end of his life. However, he did not receive communion when a woman was the celebrant.

After having functioned for more than 10 years as both a gym and parish hall, the building once known as Diocesan Hall and later simply as the Parish Hall was remodeled in 1975. The work began on February 24. The March edition of the newsletter (*Sounds of All Saints*) said that construction was expected to last three months, during which the parish would not have use of the "gymnasium" building. "When finished, Diocesan Hall will be a two-story building for parish and ECS use, while the area where St. Francis' House now stands [after it is torn down] will become a playground area." The gym was remodeled to turn it into a two-story building with kitchen, dining room, and storage (for example, for food and clothing banks) on the first floor. The second floor contained offices and program space. Primary funding for the project came from a Lilly Endowment grant of $130,000 "sufficient to handle the essentials of construction". However, opportunities were promised for ways in which parishioners could help with "extras."

The 1975 newsletters also announced several drama programs. All Saints parishioners (including Bonnie Harvey, who was in charge of costumes) were involved in a children's theater group called Talbot Area Performing Arts. Their presentation of *Rose White and Rose Red* (based on the Grimm Fairy Tale) had to be moved to Immanuel Presbyterian because of the construction. An adult production of the Jules Feiffer comedy *Crawling Arnold* beat the construction deadline and opened at All Saints before moving subsequent performances to other churches. The children's program also offered a Story Hour on Saturday afternoons.

The vision of All Saints parish as a focus of neighborhood outreach which had led to the "joining" of ECS and the parish found expression in a Community Outreach Commission. Once again, Bonnie Harvey was instrumental in implementation. In January 1975 she offered newsletter readers a list of 14 community groups or agencies with which All Saints had relationships. The Commission promised to offer information on each and encourage parishioner participation. The parish was also active in a Coalition to End Neighborhood Deterioration, which was an outgrowth of the Human Justice Commission (another group the parish had been involved with for a number of years). Other parish programs also had a social service focus. Lenten fasting was encouraged as a reminder that others were hungry, and contributions to hunger relief were connected to the fast. The young people's first project for 1975 was a spaghetti dinner on February 22 to benefit underprivileged children. In addition to Jackie Means' work at the Women's Prison, she and a group of parishioners met weekly with inmates of the Pendleton reformatory. Susie Mallory, Polly Clements, John Branham, and Rex Hume are mentioned in newsletters as participants in the Pendleton visits.

During these years, the parish implemented a "Commission System." The commissions were Stewardship (including maintenance of the building), Fellowship (planners of picnics, breakfasts, etc.), Christian Education, Worship, and Community Outreach. In January 1975, John Branham accepted responsibility for the acolytes. After consultation with the Worship Committee he was instructed to include both males and females in the acolyte teams. A needlepoint group, led by Joan Moyer, made kneelers for the sanctuary (which were still in use at the turn of the next century). Joan won awards at the 1975 State Fair for her church kneelers and stitchery. By December 1975, Judy Finister and Maurice Edelen had been endorsed by the vestry as chalice bearers. They joined John (Scotty) Selch, who previously had been endorsed. In other parish activity, an All Saints Prayer group met weekly on Tuesday evenings. The January 1976 newsletter announced that home liturgies would begin (again) on a weekly basis.

A major development during 1975 was the planning for a music program which would serve as a neighborhood outreach to the children of the neighborhood. An ad hoc Committee composed of Bonnie Harvey, Scotty Selch, Joan Moyer, Rex Hume, Gloria Kemper, Gretchen Mote, and Louise Jones was appointed to help meet the goals of the proposed program. In a letter dated May 5 to this committee (and found in the parish archives), Fr. Eastwood provided the following background:

Bob Goodlett has worked up a music proposal for All Saints' which would require significant support of the parish—both financial and personal. It involves, in the short range, going outside our parish for financial help to enable us to get started on what we hope will last for years to come. It means, as well, time and energy on the part of some of our parishioners in the project. The Vestry, in its April meeting said "yes" to the intent of the proposal. They would like to see it established at All Saints. They were not asked to agree in detail to it. It is now in my hands to see how we can "do it." So I am asking your help to strategize with me.

An attachment to the letter listed goals, objectives and outline of the program:

Goals
1. To strengthen the worship of the parish
2. To reach out to adults and children in the neighborhood
3. To provide and promote Christian nurture through music and worship

Objective: to produce excellence in music through a variety of musical offerings, emphasizing "doing well" what is done; by teaching music theory, vocal skills, reading music, religious education in worship; by having the "parish choir" as a way of life within the parish family—both children and adults, male and female, as a functioning unit representative of the parish family.

General Outline of the program
1) Involvement of children
   a) Max. number of 20 through High School age—12 sopranos, 8 altos
   b) Rehearsals—three days of the week
   c) Discipline and incentive built through money and merits $1 weekly to each child @ 25 cents per rehearsal and Sunday Attendance and improvement criteria for advancement to next level (e.g. novices, choristers, chanters, etc.)
2) Adults
   a) from the parish, not paid
   b) four section leaders, professional, paid to insure (*sic*) development and standards of music, until parish choir is "on its own"
   c) Rehearsals once weekly.

This proposal was one of the fruits of combining the work of ECS and the parish into one effort: it was directed at both parish worship and neighborhood outreach. And it built on the previous tradition of the girl's choir trained in plain chant. However, this new choir was purposefully designed to include boys and girls, children and adults. Bob Goodlett, the organist and music director of the parish, was also a member of the Indianapolis Symphony Orchestra (in the bass violin section). The budget (of $9,220 per year) he drew up included his salary, the cost of music and supplies, the paid section leaders, the children's salaries, and instrumentalists.

This proposal also had other roots. The previous music director, Charles Manning, had asked in 1973 for the appointment of a music committee. Meeting on April 8, 1973, the committee adopted a resolution to take to the vestry requesting a "mixed choir." Other music concerns discussed at that meeting would arise again later, and probably had arisen innumerable times before. Some did not like the "kind of music used at Mass." According to minutes of this meeting, Manning responded that parishioners came from varying backgrounds and, therefore, had varying expectations. Some said the music was "too slow." (Manning said that some things are written to be slow; other to be fast.) And there were "too many unfamiliar hymns."

Bob Goodlett succeeded Charles Manning in February 1975. By the time of the next annual meeting he could report that there was a parish choir of 15, with an average attendance of 10. His report continues,

> We have managed to do occasional anthems on more important feast days and have sung at several other special services combined with other singers not usually members of our choir ... . The Feast of the Pentecost was celebrated in a big way with Sung Morning Prayer—at the Eucharist Mary Van Mele of South Bend offered liturgical dance, and in the evening there was a service of Solemn Evensong and Benediction with a special choir assembled for the occasion. We have had several instrumentalists from time to time from the Indianapolis Symphony Orchestra perform at the Eucharist. The choir was fortunate in obtaining vestments through its own efforts and through a gift from St. Matthew's, Indianapolis. The choir raised its money by sponsoring a supper at the Hummingbird Café. The choir has recently become affiliated with the Royal School of Church Music, which provides help in program development and maintains a quest for quality in Church Music.

In the same report, Goodlett informed the parish that the proposal for the Children's Choir Program had been submitted to the Lilly Endowment, Inc. On April 14, 1976, the Lilly Endowment told Fr. Eastwood that a two-year grant of $13,700 had been approved "for development of a music education program for inner city youth."

Bob Goodlett immediately began recruitment of children. Tapping other sources of potential singers, he contacted nearby School #27. He also prepared a brochure titled "Vocal Talent Search: A Program of Music Education for Youth Aged 8 & Older."

> Our program will offer an arena in which talent can be identified and developed to an extent that is not presently available to many of the youth of the inner-city We see the arts as very important ingredient in the education of the total person, and the arts is one area that is often neglected in some of our public educational institutions. The participation in the program will primarily involve singing. The voice is an instrument accessible to everyone, and we hope to encourage the development of our native assets. The instruction will not only include the elements of singing, but the materials and structure of music and music history. Each week a professional artist will be brought in to demonstrate some aspect of music or the fine arts. The group will also be taking field trips and participating in other concerts and music festivals … . Auditions will be held June 28-30 at All Saints.

By June 14, 1976, Goodlett was able to inform the adult choir members of plans to implement the proposal. He also reminded them of the attendance and tardiness rule. Unexcused absence counted for one point, and tardiness for ½ point. An accumulation of three points meant suspension until after the next major feast. Adult members were also asked to provide the cost of their own vestments since the "hand-me-downs" from St. Matthew's were mostly children's sizes.

A by-product of the choir program was a project to improve the organ and the organ loft. Culver Godfrey, an architect, was Senior Warden at this time. He had drawn plans to extend the choir loft six feet into the nave to accommodate additional choir members. At the same time it was proposed to put plexiglas storm windows on the west windows of the building to protect the organ from temperature changes and moisture. In addition, some repairs were needed on the organ. (It was now 12 years old in its current configuration.) The total cost of the project was estimated to be $7,350. The parish asked the Standing Committee for permission to do the work (since the building was owned by the diocese), for permission to borrow approximately $3,200 and for a grant of $4,150. As support for the request, Culver Godfrey's letter to the Standing Committee mentioned "we have been experiencing an increase in attendance each Sunday of about 20% and our income for the first four month is ahead of both our budget and our actual expenses.

Despite that encouraging financial development the vestry was worried about a shortfall for the budget year 1976 and vestry asked the parish to reconsider its pledges. Culver Godfrey was able to announce in the March, 1976, newsletter that this appeal had increased income by $5,000. A deficit of $1,500 was still expected for the year and would have to be taken from savings. In the same newsletter Fr. Wood reported on "rotation" of the clergy's pastoral contact lists. The parish had been divided into thirds with each of the clergy (Wood, Eastwood, and Deacon Means) responsible for one of the groups. Three times a year the clergy would rotate; thus, in the course of a year all of the parish would have contact with each of the clergy.

Prayer Book revision was moving along in the national church. A Draft Proposed Book was made available in time for the 1976 General Convention. Use of it was actually begun at All Saints in March before Convention met. The newsletter article announcing use of Rite I pointed out that the words were almost the same as the 1929 Prayer Book and that the order was the one familiar at All Saints (but not in much of the rest of the church): *Gloria* "up front" at the beginning of the service, *Benedictus qui venit* after the *Sanctus*, and Offertory after the Intercessions rather than before.

Community issues remained in the spotlight. The January 1976 newsletter ran an article on "red lining" practices of financial institutions. The April issue announced that school board candidates from all three slates would present their views at the adult class on April 25, 1976.

The choir was invited to participate in services at St. John the Divine Cathedral in New York City on Pentecost 1976, joining other groups to comprise a choir of 700 voices. In order to raise money for the trip, the choir put on a chili supper on May 23. The June *Sounds of All Saints* gave a full report of the trip.

> Friday, June 4 at 4 pm marked the beginning of an unforgettable adventure as All Saints' Choir set out on its New York trip. Regina Allender, Barbara and Linda Bingham, Mary Greene, Rex Hume, Jackie Slatter, Ellen VanKersen, Valerie Vinson, and Choir Warden Scotty Selch all piled into the rented van and Father Wood offered a prayer for our safe return. [In New York] our quarters for the night were in one of the basketball courts in the basement of the Cathedral. The women on the trip were much more impressed with the fact this is the world's largest Gothic Cathedral than the men, since the women's restroom was located about a block from our quarters. After unrolling our sleeping bag and freshening-up we took what was for many of us our first subway ride down to Greenwich Village. We next headed for the Theatre de Lys, where we had tickets to see the Negro Ensemble Company's production of "Eden." On Sunday morning ... we attended Solemn High Mass at the Church of St. Mary the Virgin. Some of our younger members, exhausted by our rigorous schedule, fell asleep during the extensive sermon. While at "Smokey Mary's" we met Sara Davis and Karen Scott, two of our choir members who had traveled to New York a week earlier. After the service we rushed back to St. John the Divine, where we joined other choirs in rehearsal with David Pizzaro. The massed choir presented the Evensong Setting and 5 anthems in commemoration of the 75th Anniversary of St. John the Divine Choir School and the American Bicentennial Celebration of the Royal School of Church Music. [On the return trip] we had the first real problem when the right rear tire blew out. In order to put on the spare, we had to unload all of the luggage from the van and it caused a considerable delay while Scotty and Rex changed the tires. A second delay hit us 22 miles east of Columbus when our left rear tire blew. This presented a more serious problem as we had no spare at this time. While Scotty managed to get our crippled van into a Sohio station, they had no tires which would fit our van. Through the help of an Ohio State Policeman we managed to locate a tire at a truck stop three miles away. At our prayer of thanksgiving during the last meal of the trip we were all aware of the close ties of friendship and interdependence which had developed between us from our good and "not so good" times together.

In the midst of all these exciting and hopeful developments, Stewart Wood received a call to be rector of Christ Church, Glendale, Ohio. Fr. Wood was on the national Executive Council of the church. He had many connections throughout the national church and was often talked of as a "potential bishop." The Vestry scheduled a meeting with the bishop on August 31, 1976. At that meeting, the vestry moved to elect Jack Eastwood as the rector without a search process; and the bishop consented. The bishop wrote to Culver Godfrey on September 2,

> I was delighted that we were able to move so quickly on this, and that wonderful meeting with you and your vestry in your home Tuesday night was one of the happiest ones I ever had. Your tribute to Stew Wood's leadership and your instant selection of Jack Eastwood to replace him was a very moving joy to me.

The August 31 decision could not be made official, however, since Fr. Wood had not yet left. The formal vestry vote was taken on October 17, 1976 and was unanimous.

This decision meant that once again ECS and the parish could have different leadership. ECS would find its new director in the person of The Rev. Joseph W. Riggs.

The choir at rehearsal

The Rt. Rev. R. Stewart Wood

# CHAPTER TEN

## Get Thee Behind Me, Satan
## All Saints Parish: 1976-1985

The Celebration of a New Ministry and The Institution of The Rev. John H. Eastwood, Jr. as rector took place on December 6, 1976. The Rev Canon Earl L Conner preached at the Solemn Mass. The wardens were Culver Godfrey and William Morgan. The Venerable Canon Frederic P. Williams sang the Litany. The Rev. Jackie Means was deacon, and Judy Finister was sub-deacon. Lessons were read by George Hight and Carolyn Godfrey. Acolytes were David Clements, Kelly Wise, Michael Shutt, Kevin Finister, and Eric Bose. Presenters of symbols included Shirley Bradbury, William Coleman, Nancy Shaw, L.H. Bayley, Margaret Barnard, Lena Harris, and Mark Nicely. Those names include much of the leadership of the parish at the beginning of the Eastwood rectorate.

The new rector quickly had to address the parish finances. On December 15, he wrote to the Talbot Fund requesting $16,300 (in addition to $5,000 being requested from the diocese for property expenses). This represented an increase over the $15,000 which had come from the Talbot Fund the previous year. Fr. Eastwood said in his letter that the proposed budget

> represents an honest appraisal of our efforts to be responsible stewards of the property and program here at All Saints. We have kept in mind the recommendations of Charles Wilson in his study of the All Saints—ECS relationship while struggling with the increased burdens of property expense which were not apparent at the time of his study. Our life as a parish has begun to feel more vibrant. The new music program substantially funded by Lilly Endowment, the setting apart of All Saints—ECS and the

institution of a Rector devoting full time to parish activity, adult leadership now generated with our young people, and other factors have caused an increase of newcomers to the parish, requests for adult confirmation, and, in general, the parish taking an interest in itself and what its mission is in this neighborhood.

The "increased burdens of property expense" were expected to amount to over $19,000 in 1977. Also in the budget was a part-time salary for Jackie Means to be Priest Associate following her ordination planned for January 1. She was expected to devote one weekday plus Sunday to "liturgical activities, teaching, and outreach in the immediate neighborhood." Eastwood, Godfrey, and Clifford Henderson (Treasurer) told the Talbot Fund trustees, "We continue to affirm and support Jackie, the Ordination of women, and their ministry by offering to employ her at a reasonable salary for two days' time."

The Means ordination brought All Saints into the national spotlight. The General Convention's approval of women's ordination became effective on January 1, 1977. Bishop Craine's position was clear: he was strongly in favor, but was also strongly committed to acting "legally" within the canons of the church. Jackie had been the first woman ordained as a deacon (1974) in the diocese and was, therefore, "first in line" in a diocese determined to ordain a woman as quickly as possible. Since she would be the "first in the nation," she and the parish became the focus of media attention. The Louisville *Courier Journal*, for example, ran an article on New Year's Day 1997, under the headline "A first for church: Woman will become legal priest today." The article began,

> Amid the promise of ecclesiastical hoopla and the threat of a disruptive demonstration, the Episcopal Church today will break with a 2000 year old tradition by legally ordaining a woman to its priesthood.
> A special platform has been constructed in the All Saints sanctuary to accommodate the expected crush of photographers. And a group of traditionalist Episcopalians who oppose the ordination of women to the priesthood have made plans to picket the service.

Some of the protestors were All Saints members who left the parish immediately after the dramatic moment in the service when The Rt. Rev. Donald Davis, acting for Bishop Craine (who was ill), asked,

Dear friends in Christ, you know the importance of this ministry, and the weight of your responsibility in presenting Jacqueline Allene Means for ordination to the sacred priesthood. Therefore if any of you know any impediment or crime because of which we should not proceed, come forward now, and make it known.

One of the protesters read a statement declaring the ordination to be heretical. Bishop Davis continued the service, and the others in the congregation responded to his question enthusiastically: "Is it your will that Jacqueline be ordained a priest?" "It is."

At that point, the objectors walked out, some never to enter All Saints again. Jack Eastwood later remembered that the number who left All Saints at the time was 17. The ordination became the occasion of a split in the Episcopal Church. One of the sons of All Saints, The Rev. James Mote, removed his parish, St. Mary's in Denver, from the Episcopal Church on January 1. His statement to the press said, "It's no more possible to ordain women into the priesthood than for men to have babies."

Jackie herself recalled the tension of the day in a later interview:

"I had a bodyguard that day because we had expected some demonstrations," Rev. Means recalls somberly. "I didn't care what they did, they could march up and down, cry and shout, but I didn't want them to bother me or my kids.

Although it was a joyous occasion for me it was also a sad one. In the Episcopal Church there is a place for everybody and anything they want to do. The marchers had been members of the church and when I was deacon they had said fine. Now they were against me and it was a hurtful thing. One of the marcher's sons was supposed to be a server and had been tickled to death about the idea. But his mother wouldn't let him serve. Also I was very disappointed because Bishop Craine was sick. He had been such an inspiration and support to me that I found his illness more disturbing than the presence of the protestors.

I never will forget, I can see it yet, the moment when we came into the church. I guess it was so much stress—and at least that's what my psychiatrist told me later—that I thought I was somebody else, that I was standing outside myself watching what was going on.

I thought, look at that crazy woman, she has to be out of her mind. By that time I had been hounded to death by reporters, a UPI photographer had spent 10 days with me, and I was trying to get my family ready for the ordination, plus it was close to Christmas. I thought I was going to go crazy, worrying about if someone would get hurt or try to hurt the church."

There was an overflow crowd. Those who could not get into the nave were in the parish hall watching on closed circuit television. The Rev. Gordon Chastain remembered giving communion to the overflow crowd. Canon Jack Potter was the preacher. Presenters included Father Wood and Father Eastwood.

How did a parish which only five years before had been too divided to accept women as chalice bearers become the first parish in the American Church to ordain a woman as priest? Part of the answer was the strong support of the clergy. Father Eastwood. remembered that at a Vestry meeting considering endorsement of the ordination (a necessary step specified in the canons), Fr. Wood had stated that vestry refusal would force him to reconsider his presence as rector. Fr. Eastwood's support took the form of an offer to employ Jackie as Priest Associate of the parish, in addition to her duties as head of Institutional Ministries for the diocese.

One of the reasons the media focused its attention upon the Means ordination was the fact that her background did not match the image of "staid Episcopalian." *People* magazine (January 17, 1977), for example, wrote,

Means grew up a Roman Catholic in Peoria, Illinois. "The nun was my idol" she remembers. She needed one, for her parents were alcoholics living on welfare. At 16, Jackie married Delton, and in time they mutually chose the Episcopal Church. Delton, who drives an interstate truck, had a bad highway accident in 1963. Suddenly Jackie was forced to look at herself as an untrained, unschooled mother of three small children. "What would I have done if he had been killed?" she wondered, and shortly afterward began an educational blitz. She graduated from high school in 1968 at age 32 and later attended Indiana University.

A woman of volcanic energy, Means "sometimes puts people off with her power and lack of tact," a co-worker notes. The new priest hopes to establish a halfway house for women released from prison and in time to become more than a symbol of iconoclasm. "The church has become ingrown, parochial and comfortable," Means says. "We're too concerned about bricks and mortar." As she once asked, "Who cares if the parish house has drapes and silver if kids need food and clothing?"

The *Indianapolis Star Magazine* (August 10, 1978) observed, "Rev. Means is not a stereotype priest. She wears no collar in her daily rounds, her speech is colloquial, spotted with what an earlier age might consider profanity, though her usage can be termed more a plea than a damnation, and her manner can be folksy and blunt."

In a March 1978 newsletter article Father Eastwood reflected on the relationship between himself and Jackie.

> Months ago Jackie and I were talking about what we have given to each other. I said, "Jackie, you have given me spontaneity." She paused, then smiled brightly. "Jack, you have given me patience."

As the *People* article stressed, she was equally unconventional in her work at the Women's Prison.

> Father John Roof, chaplain at the prison, says admiringly of his 5'5" colleague, "Jackie's a dynamo in Big Mama pantyhose." The inmates agree. "She's my best friend," says a lifer. When one woman confided, "You know I'm gay," Means responded, "So what? You don't ask who I'm sleeping with. I won't ask who you're sleeping with."

Following the ordination, the vestry issued a statement which was printed in the January 1977 newsletter:

> The ordination of the Rev. Jackie Means to the priesthood in the Episcopal Church on January 1 was a highly significant event not only for our parish but many others both within and without the Church. We know that here at All Saints it has had a divisive effect. While many are affirmative of the actions of General Convention, regarding both the ordination issue and the proposed changes in the Prayer Book, still there are some who disagree, or at least question these actions. Two members of the Vestry have withdrawn from our services, and still others may not have withdrawn but do struggle with their consciences about these events. As the Vestry of the parish, we acknowledge and respect these differences among us, and the extent to which some of us want to demonstrate that disagreement. Yet, we are saddened by this division and pray earnestly for a reconciliation among us.

> There are many in the Church at large who disagree, yet find it possible to work and worship within the Church. We pray that by their examples we will find in all of us an increase in faith, hope, and charity.

> We re-affirm the actions of General Convention regarding both issues, and support the use of the proposed **Book of Common Prayer** as well as the ministry of Jackie Means as a priest in this parish. She will receive a salary appropriate to any priest serving a parish on a part-time basis.

Although the ordination, the publicity, and the pain of the congregational split seemed all-consuming, other things were at happening at All Saints in 1977. The choir program made possible by the Lilly Endowment Grant, for example, was blossoming. An article in *The Indianapolis Star* on April 17, 1977 pictured Antonio Love and Carmelita Byrnes, along with Robert Goodlett and J. Ryan Stephenson (vocal coach for the program). "Inner city youths are bringing forth lovely sound at All Saints Episcopal Church from vocal chords they didn't know they had," said the article, which also announced that the choir was giving a concert on April 24 at All Saints. The program was to be Bach's *Christ lag in Todesbanden*, Mozart's *Ave Verum Corpus*, and the spiritual *Ain't-a That Good News*. Another concert was planned for May 15.

In celebration of the 50th anniversary of the Royal School of Church Music, a Choir Festival was held in Indianapolis. The two host sites were North Methodist Church and All Saints. On Saturday, June 11, Evensong and Benediction took place at All Saints, sung by the Men and Boys Choir of Christ Church, Winnetka, Illinois. The Solemn High Mass on Sunday morning at All Saints was sung by the choirs of All Saints and the visitors from Winnetka. On Sunday afternoon there was a Festival Evensong at North Methodist. Music sung by the massed choirs included *O Praise the Lord* by Adrian Batten, *Magnificat and Nunc Dimittis* by Herbert Murrill, *Behold the Tabernacle of God* by William Harris, *Like as the Hart* by Herbert Howells, *Let All the Earth in Every Corner Sing* by Vaughn Williams, and *Festival Te Deum* by Vaughn Williams.

Each week the choristers were required to meet standards in the following areas: being present, on time, neatness, posture, attention, tone, diction, staying in place, small group work, and condition of music and vestments. The members also signed a pledge:

1. To be punctual at all rehearsals and services;
2. To take care of all items issued to me and see that they are kept in their places neatly and in good order, including my hymnal, music and folder, cassock and surplice;
3. To see that the Choir loft is left in good order after services, that no items are left behind, and that bulletins are filed away in waste basket;
4. To cooperate with my team captain and the choir warden in all matters and to notify both of them of any absence or lateness in advance;
5. To learn the music and spoken responses to the best of my ability, especially the simpler portions of the service;
6. To uphold my role of leadership of the congregation in the worship of God, and to set an example fitting to that office.

Although the choir program took a break during the summer, momentum was continued with a Workshop in the Arts for Youth Ages 8—16 held at All Saints from July 7-12, 1977. Guest artists included Dave Baker of the Jazz Faculty at the Indiana University School of Music, Denise Nicholas of the Indianapolis Museum of Art, Peggy Nicholson of Channel 4 TV, and Berniece Fraction, soprano. The week's events also included a field trip to see a dance performance. The programs lasted from 9 a.m. to 3 p.m. and included a free lunch.

A choir list exists from this period names the following members (both children and adults): Regina Allender, Barbara Jean Bingham, Sara Davis, Theodotia Hartman, Teresa McGarr, Jackie Slatter, Sandra Tyler, Ellen Vankersen, Valerie Vinson, Brenda Walls, Sharon Jones, Kathy Leamer, Janice Schilling, Karen Scott, Helen Small, Gino Agresti, Earl Furlow, Don Bose, Rex Hume, and Scotty Selch. Barbara Jean Bingham, one of young people in the choir, was still a member of the parish at the turn of the next century—as was her mother, her children, her grandchildren, and several other family members. Jackie Slatter, another one of the young members, would go on to complete her education at Indiana University School of Music.

The initial Lilly Endowment funding was exhausted by the fall of 1977, but the program continued with some modifications until at least 1980. At that time a document called "Summary, Conclusions and Recommendations" was prepared and submitted by the Music

Advisory Committee (Karen Scott, chair, Sara Davis, Earl Furlow, and Robert Goodlett).

> Recruiting was done initially by walking though the neighborhood and speaking with children who were playing outside. Later the choir members themselves proved to be the most effective recruiters. A total of 49 children participated in the program during the years 1975 to 1979. Originally the program extended from September through June and included four rehearsals per week. Two of these were with the adult choir members and one included a worship service and dinner. Due to budget limitations and a multiplicity of other problems the joint rehearsal was discontinued, and the calendar was shortened to October through May. Transportation was organized on a volunteer basis, but proved to be such a constant and time-consuming problem for clergy, staff and parishioners that it was dropped after the second year. At least 35 parishioners volunteered their time to assist with meals, transportation, and field trips. As many as 12 volunteers per week were required to maintain the original schedule with 20 choristers. Religious instruction was provided by both clergy and choirmaster. As a result, ten of the children were baptized and eight were confirmed or were receiving confirmation instruction by January, 1980. The choir enjoyed many outings ranging from lunch at Burger Chef to trips to New York City and Glendale, Ohio, to sing services. All of the choristers participated in the Diocesan summer music camp program. As a result of their participation in the Music Education Program, three especially talented choristers were accepted at intensive summer music camps. One spent eight weeks at the Interlochen National Music Camp in Michigan, and two attended a two-week RSCM camp in Lawrenceville, New Jersey.

The evaluation document reported that 59% of the choristers lived in the target area and that an additional 32% lived within the "inner-city." Twelve choristers were interviewed and "were unanimous in their feelings of being an accepted and respected part of the community at All Saints Church, and they all expressed a strong desire to see the program continue." Parents and guardians were also interviewed "and found to be pleased to have their children participating in a program that involved learning skills and going on field trips." The choirmaster "expressed both frustration and satisfaction with his involvement. The frustration grew out of discipline and transportation problems, a shortage of adult singers, a perceived lack of parental support, and budget worries." The clergy "felt their consciousness about the life situation of poor families in the neighborhood of the parish was raised. The support and maintenance of the program demanded a great deal of time and energy." A congregational survey was also undertaken. Eighty-five percent said that worship was enhanced by the program; 88% thought it benefited the children involved; 79% thought it was a good means of outreach; and 94% wanted it to continue. Some desired a wider variety of music—for example, folk, jazz and gospel. The general conclusion was that the program had been successful and enjoyed almost unanimous support. However, it was time consuming for staff and there were continuing budget problems. Expansion would "require an addition of a coordinator to oversee ... transportation, volunteers, pay, activities, and referrals for discipline."

In addition to the choir program, a Youth Outreach Program was housed at the Episcopal Urban Center complex. Harriette R. Snorden, a parishioner of St. Philip's, was the administrator. In her 1977 application to United Episcopal Charities (a source of funding after Talbot Fund grants to 16th and Central declined) she reported a total budget of $17,875 for services of counseling, legal referrals, summer camping, after-school program, recreation, and Black History provided to approximately 200 youth ages 4-14. The after-school component met Monday through Friday. Her report mentions an average attendance of 20 for activities including softball, skating, bowling, movies, and spelling tests. She also made family visits and did intake for ECS.

The social worker at ECS had been Margaret Barnard, M.S.W., who also served frequently as a member of the vestry and assisted with the parish youth program. Her responsibilities at ECS were advocacy, referral, casework and administration of the emergency program. That position was no longer funded after 1976. Also by 1976, Stopover was being operated by its own board of directors and was receiving separate federal and Lilly Endowment grants. The 1978 request to United Episcopal Charities from ECS was for $45,000 of a total budget amounting to $60,447. The request defined the agency program in the following terms:

> Emergency material assistance, food, clothing, prescriptions, rent, fuel—to persons whose urgent, temporary needs are not being met by regularly established agencies. This part of our program is considered almost indispensable by people and agencies in the community. Much of our effort is directed toward helping people to use other resources available for

long-time assistance, or to secure employment. Another facet of our program is serving as advocate for target groups in the population—the poor, aged, unemployed, etc. In these activities we may work alone, but more often we work in cooperation with other interested groups or agencies. We believe that one role we can play is that of innovating programs to meet unmet needs. Stopover, for runaways, was an example.

A proposal for a program to address the needs of women ex-offenders was related to Jackie Means' work at the Women's Prison. The idea would soon take shape as John P. Craine House, a residential facility on North Pennsylvania Street. The first director of Craine House would be Lena Harris of All Saints.

The ECS board was in the midst of reviewing its mission and objectives in the late 1970's. Mrs. Jane Johnson acted as Interim Director between the time of Fr. Wood's departure and the arrival of Fr. Joe Riggs as the next Director. Board members of ECS were appointed by the parishes of metropolitan Indianapolis, but there was a felt need by United Episcopal Charities to expand the role of the agency to an area beyond Indianapolis if diocesan support was to continue. The application for assistance in 1978 tried to address this issue:

> The emergency program has been under the immediate supervision of the social worker and since that position is no longer funded, the Executive Director, with the Volunteer Coordinator will have to assume this responsibility. The emergency programs, while essential, we believe, should not be the only, or even the major program of the agency. However, they can serve as models for other programs in the Diocese, as a training ground for volunteers, clergy, etc; as an opportunity for volunteers to participate in the social ministry of the Diocese.

Bishop Craine had conceived of United Episcopal Charities (UEC) in order to support outreach and service projects throughout the diocese by means other than the Talbot Fund. ECS had always made the largest demands upon UEC; and, when the Charities campaigns were not as successful as anticipated, the work at 16th and Central became the focus of concern and, sometimes, resentment. As a proposed remedy, the ECS board was to be elected at Diocesan Convention instead of being appointed by Indianapolis parishes. When The Rev. Joe Riggs became director of ECS, he was faced with the challenges of an agency with declining resources, no full time social worker, and a new project (Craine House) about to start.

As manager of the Episcopal Urban Center (EUC) building, Fr. Eastwood had the worry of maintenance. For example, in August of 1977 he wrote to the Standing Committee requesting a grant of $1,155 for repair of "numerous leaks" in the roof, now over 10 years old. His letter of request says that the next meeting of the EUC board in September would have to "give special attention to the discrepancy between budgeted income for '77 as against budgeted expenses for '77."

A year later, there were even greater worries for the EUC. A fire, caused by vandalism, broke out in the parish office portion of the building. Many parish records, including all the parish registers except one, were destroyed. The Rev. Tom Honderich was hired to help piece together the financial records and to help manage the reconstruction. The re-building turned out more complicated than was expected. As a matter of policy and in an effort to support the community in which the parish ministered, bids were received only from minority firms. After a contracting firm was selected, its owner became tangled in a messy divorce procedure and was unable to complete the contract. While the re-building was in progress, the nave itself was used as office space and parish hall. Pews were removed from the rear of the nave, and tables and dividers were set up. During Mass, the smell of brewing coffee sometimes overcame incense.

Fr. Honderich was available to help at this time because both he and Fr. Gordon Chastain had recently left the staff of St. Paul's. The reason for their departure was that they had helped to found an Indianapolis chapter of Integrity, an organization for "gay Episcopalians and their friends." One of the first activities of the group was the publication of a newsletter. Honderich was the editor and Chastain a frequent contributor. Through the newsletter, their involvement with Integrity became known to the rector and vestry of St. Paul's just as the rector, The Rev. Russell Staines, was planning to retire. Before he did so, Staines questioned Fr. Chastain about his sexuality and Chastain responded truthfully. Both Honderich and Chastain were asked to resign and did so at the end of May 1978. Immediately following their sudden departure, Fr. Eastwood invited them to participate actively in the life of All Saints. In several sermons in later years, Fr. Honderich talked about the impression made upon him on the first Sunday he accepted Eastwood's invitation. The altar party on that day included black faces and white, males and females, children and adults, persons in inter-racial marriages, an ex-convict, and at least one gay person. Above this group hung the image of the Crucified One holding out his arms to embrace all. Underneath and gathered around the altar was a community acting out that inclusive embrace.

Integrity scheduled regular Eucharists followed by social time or discussion. Several parishes were asked to host the group. Only All Saints agreed to do so. Thus, the weekly "Integrity Eucharists" were added to the All Saints schedule. Three Adult Education sessions on Human Sexuality were scheduled in May 1977. The newsletter announced the series by saying, "This is a topic that has been raised by members of the adult class as an area of concern. This will be an opportunity for us to examine our own individual attitudes, and to raise questions in a supportive atmosphere." The next month's newsletter reported on the sessions: "With strong attendance each time, the class focused on social attitudes and biblical insights, in both large and small groups. The area of homosexuality was treated for the most part throughout the discussions with a variety of opinions being expressed."

The decision to welcome Integrity and to accept a ministry to gay people as a part of the parish ministry came with a cost. The parish had just lost 17 members because of women's ordination; now three more families left because of Integrity and the presence of gay priests. Fr. Eastwood remembered that two were African-American and one white. He also remembered that in the vestry discussion, the issue was talked about as a fear of the parish losing its "social character." But the losses were matched by gains. Newcomers were attracted to the parish precisely because it had ordained a woman and welcomed gay people. In an article published in *Tidings,* the diocesan newspaper, at the time of his resignation in 1985, Fr. Eastwood recalled these gains and losses. He said,

The open public affirmation of gays in the life of the church, Eastwood said, "brought to the parish some new people who had not felt fully accepted. It took time to integrate them. Some members did some real stretching and growing."

The newsletter for June and July of 1978 featured an article by Fr. Eastwood on the various ways in which the parish was reaching out to gay people and lesbians. In addition to Integrity meetings, the Human Rights Coalition was housed in the Urban Center and had been formed to educate and advocate against discrimination because of sexual orientation. A group of Concerned Clergy sponsored a service of worship held at All Saints during Gay Pride Week in 1978. These services became an annual event, frequently held at the parish.

In the midst of all these changes, Bishop Craine died. He had been ill at the time of the Means ordination in January, 1977. After his call for the election of a Bishop Coadjutor, Edward Whitker Jones was elected (on March 26, 1977) and consecrated. Bishop Craine's death came before his announced date of retirement. Almost before he had unpacked, Bishop Jones was faced with the issue of gay priests in the persons of Fathers Honderich and Chastain.

Father Honderich had designed and woven the fabric for the colorful cope and mitre for Bishop Jones' consecration, which was held at Market Square arena. Needlepoint in bright primary colors was worked by a variety of volunteers and applied to the red fabric. Because of the weight of the vestments, Bishop Jones did not always use them; but he did wear them for his visits to All Saints (where there were stoles made to match). One of the favorite stories of the parish was about the bishop and these vestments. Here is the way Fr. Honderich related it in a sermon on May 6, 2001:

In the early 1980s, Bishop Jones made one of his first visitations to All Saints. It happened to be Good Shepherd Sunday. I remember it only too well. At the time, the parish had a bunch of kids between the ages of 9 and 13, and they used to sit in the first three pews. For the occasion, the Bishop wore his red cope and carried his shepherd's crook. That I remember particularly well because his theme for the day was "feed my sheep." The panel down the back of the cope had very stylized lettering which was difficult to read unless you happened to know it was there. It read "Feed My Sheep." In an attempt to elicit some participation from the kids, the bishop asked what the words were on the back of the cope. He got no response. So he gave them what was intended to be a clue to deciphering the letters—"the first word is a four letter word beginning with F", he said. We all sat mortified and apoplectic for fear that these inner city kids might actually know a four letter word beginning with F and might shout it out—and it would likely not be the one he was looking for.

Parish life in the late 1970's was busy. The Youth Group met on Sunday mornings under the leadership of Sara Davis and held annual retreats at Waycross. Church school and nursery were also available on Sunday morning. Perennial teachers included Gloria Kemper, Rex Hume, and Polly Clements. The Altar Guild was chaired by Ida Edelen. Another perennial was Cliff Henderson, treasurer. The second annual arts festival on September 17, 1977, was threatened by "dark clouds" of rain, according to the newsletter. However, crowds came to eat fish sandwiches and view the exhibits. Among the exhibitors were inmates of the Pendleton Reformatory. Barbara Bingham offered classes in karate and self-defense for women and children. The more than $1,800 raised was used to put new red carpeting in the sanctuary. In the summer of 1978, All Saints sponsored an Evensong followed by a program of Gospel Music presented by the choir of St. Rita's Catholic Church. The neighborhood was invited.

The presence of other clergy in the congregation allowed for an increase in programming. Fr. Chastain, for example, led the Adult Inquirer's Class for 10 weeks in early 1979. Fr. Honderich arranged for a weaving workshop for six Sunday afternoons in that same year. This was one component of "The Psalm 150" project, a program (like Bob Goodlet's choir program) based on the idea that the arts cross cultural and ethnic barriers to speak symbolically of the truths of human experience in God's world. Another "Psalm 150" component was a stained-glass workshop.

During the summer of 1979, The Rev. Eddie Blue assisted as Deacon at Sunday Mass. He had just graduated from Bexley Hall Seminary. The Rev. Fritz Wiecking, later Executive Director of Citizen's Action Coalition, preached on July 15, 1979, while Fr. Eastwood was on vacation.

In January 1979, a new secretary, Julia Collins, was hired for the Urban Center. She divided her time between the administration of the parish, the Urban Center, and the prison ministries.

A highlight of the music program was the performance of Vivaldi's *Gloria* before the Midnight Mass on Christmas Eve 1978. The February newsletter for 1979 announced that Jacque Slatter, soprano, had been accepted at Interlochen Music Camp for eight weeks during the coming summer. The vestry voted to pay her registration fee and a committee was formed to raise funds for other fees. The Shrove Tuesday pancake supper was one of these fund-raising projects. Folk Mass settings provided an occasional change in musical diet. On March 25, 1979, for example, the *St. John's Mass* (Chapel of St. John the Divine, University of Illinois) by Peter Carroll was used. The congregation had a chance to practice the setting during Mass and coffee hours of Lent. A Folk Mass setting was also used at the Easter Eve service in 1979 for the First Mass of Easter, following Vigil and Baptisms. About this time, the rector and choirmaster asked for volunteers for a "musical advisory group" to assist in reviewing options for anthems, hymns and mass settings. In Lent 1979, the service began with the Penitential Order. At the entrance of the ministers, the canticle *A Song of Penitence* (setting by Eric Routley) was used in place of an introit. To augment the children's music education program, a class in percussion was offered on Monday afternoons.

After 1980 the Talbot Fund ceased to be a source of support for the All Saints budget, and the diocese had to absorb the cost. When the diocesan budget began to reflect this new reality, there were questions (again) about why so much money was being given to 16th and Central. Fr. Eastwood's review of his ministry published in *Tidings* reflects this concern.

> Since all of that aid was funneled through diocesan Aid to Congregations, the amount appeared to increase dramatically, Eastwood said, due to inflation and the need to maintain the Episcopal Urban center (next to All Saints) where ECS had been located. "The increase is less dramatic when you consider the various sources the aid formerly came from."

Fr. Eastwood recalled that a diocesan official termed money given to 16th and Central as "money down a rathole."

ECS was also in transition. Craine House became a reality and soon consumed more of board's attention than did the continuing programs of emergency assistance, staffed by volunteers. There was no longer a full-time social worker on the staff (Margaret Barnard had left the agency on January 28, 1977), and other community agencies were providing counseling. In addition, Fr. Eastwood had begun a Doctor of Ministry program in Pastoral Counseling at Christian Theological Seminary and was providing supervised counseling services. The ECS board remembered the Stopover experience and how a "daughter agency" had grown up to operate independently. All of these factors eventually came together in a decision that the ECS board would disappear and be renamed as the John P. Craine House board. The new board would take the assets (the property on Pennsylvania Street used as Craine House) and would function as a Diocesan Institution. A major source of the funding for Craine House was payment by the state and the courts for the services provided to the women residents. The food and clothing bank would continue to be operated by volunteers at the Urban Centers. A new program called Parent Centered Education had replaced Youth Outreach. Other social service agencies were operating out of the Urban Center. It appeared, therefore, that ECS was no longer needed: the vision of Altar Centered Social Concern would continue without the expense of another agency. At nearly the same time that the decisions were being made to change the course of ECS, Fr. Riggs was diagnosed with cancer.

For much of its history, the ECS board had been composed of persons representing the Indianapolis parishes and had, therefore, been a means (not always effective, but always a possibility) for joint action in response to needs in the Indianapolis community. After ECS was disbanded, it was recognized that this function was still needed. The Indianapolis Episcopal Metropolitan Council was created to fill the vacuum. The "Metro Council" was composed of clergy and lay representatives of all the Episcopal parishes in the Indianapolis area. (Later it would be the "Metro Council" which would be the corporate body administering the feeding program and Dayspring Center in the Urban Center building.) Thus, a new chapter in the complicated institutional history of programs at 16th and Central began. Fr. Eastwood talked about these changes as a "New Mission" for the parish in an article in the February 1979 newsletter:

> We as a parish have a chance to minister more fully to the neighborhood; heretofore, ECS has done most of the local programming. Current ECS programs include a Youth Outreach program on the 2nd floor under the direction of Harriet Snorden and the ECS food pantry ... . There are classrooms which house Indianapolis Pre-School, a headstart program. All Saints' is presently operating its own neighborhood program in music education. Under the proposed actions, All Saints' would be given responsibility for the entire ministry on this corner, including decision-making about programmatic use of the Urban Center. I feel excited about this opportunity for the parish, and look forward to pulling the talent we have in the congregation to undertake this new mission!

A committee composed of parishioners Bill Scott, Carolyn Godfrey and Margaret Barnard was appointed to help assist in the transition of programs to parish oversight. By February 18, 1979, the vestry had already begun to make decisions about new programs at 16th and Central. At that meeting, space was offered to Offender Aid and Restoration (a national program focusing upon those released from local county jails) and a Gay Alcoholics Anonymous group. The vestry also approved use of the church by the Metropolitan Community Church on March 11 for that congregation's fifth anniversary celebration. (Metropolitan Community Church was founded by The Rev. Troy Perry in response to the needs of gay Christians rejected by other denominations.)

A special parish meeting was called for April 29, 1979, to inform the parish about the proposals, to allow for discussion, and to determine parish commitment before proceeding further. Father Eastwood, in his announcement of the meeting by way of the newsletter, said,

> The idea began in January, 1978, when Jackie Means, Archdeacon Fallis, Joe Riggs, Dick Wyatt [former rector of St. Paul's, Evansville] and I began to share frustrations about the ministry here at the Urban Center. For example, problems we have been encountering included competition between two youth programs, administrative tension around "lines of accountability" for both the program and property, and a lack of focus for the "whole" of the Urban Center. Out of further discussion, we began to raise larger questions,

and ideas (not really new ones) emerged. For example, it made sense that the community which gathers at 16th and Central have the opportunity to carry out the ministry there if it can and wants to. To ECS it seemed the time had come to relinquish responsibility for the neighborhood ministry, and to adopt a different set of goals for social ministry.

Fr. Riggs also wrote an article in preparation for the meeting:

> I am frequently asked, "If All Saints takes over neighborhood programming, what will happen to ECS?" Although this step would remove ECS from active involvement in some of its longest enduring and best known programs, we welcome the change as something appropriate for the parish and the agency. This seems to be a logical step in a process of change ECS has been undergoing for some time. The ECS board has tried to focus the work of the agency on area-wide programs (like Stopover, Craine House, our Youth Employment Program, and the volunteer Lawyer Program), and on helping parishes and other church groups respond to social issues and needs. Throughout the history of ECS we have operated programs at 16th and Central, and people have frequently seen our total identity in terms of these programs. Shifting responsibility for these programs to All Saints should help us achieve the identity we desire, as well as strengthening the parish and the neighborhood.

However, in the same newsletter was an announcement of yet another ECS program at 16th and Central—a garden project. Plots could be rented at either $5 or $10—including water, seeds, and access to tools.

Another parish meeting was held on June 17, 1979, to hear a progress report from the parish committee developing plans for neighborhood programs.

> The two main concerns were funding All Saints' specific investment of time and money …. The committee also discussed the current ECS programs. It expressed concern about the maintenance and effectiveness of the Food and Clothing Bank. The need for a youth program is urgent and the committee felt that the present choir program could serve as a model for youth programs which would reach into other interest areas. There is a strong concern that All Saints maintain a high visibility within the neighborhood. All Saints could be an active instrument of reconciliation between various factions within the community, and become a resource center for the community … It could also become a meeting area for various community groups …. It was also stressed that the Church should serve as an advocate against oppression. This is directly related to funding, for it is difficult to

be an advocate against the political and economic structures which oppress people if one is receiving funding from those sources.

The committee's final recommendations were presented at the next parish meeting on September 9, 1979. Parish program goals were listed as 1) Food Bank, 2) Youth Program, and 3) Housing Program. The Youth Program proposal was further broken into four components—cultural enrichment through teaching of skills to small groups in the arts; educational re-enforcement through tutoring, survival skills, and career education; positive social interaction; and recreation. The Housing Program's goal was to assist long-term renters towards home ownership.

There was still the question of managing the Urban Center. In September 1979, "by action of the Standing Committee and at the request of the Vestry of All Saints Church, Indianapolis, management of the property at 16th and Central was transferred from the Urban Center Board to the Rector, Wardens, and Vestry of All Saints' Church." Instead of a board, there would be an "Advisory Committee" of persons from other parishes whose purpose was threefold:

1. To nurture a spirit of cooperation between the Standing Committee and the All Saints Vestry in matters pertaining to the use of the property at 16th and Central.
2. To review the use of the property, with particular attention to three criteria: A) All Saints' needs for program space; B) Securing appropriate rental tenants; C) Use of the building to provide services to the community surrounding 16th and Central.
3. To confer with the Rector and Vestry of All Saints on any major plans for property improvement, in particular those which may involve a loan from the Revolving Loan Fund.

That need for a "spirit of cooperation" was already evident. In August, 1980, the Mission Strategy Commission responded to Fr. Eastwood's request for $5,000 to repair the parking lot:

The Commission feels that the diocese should be responsible for the condition of and the maintenance of the parking lot—but that $5,000 seems to be a high figure. Jack, to be perfectly candid, the Commission does not have this money available in our 1980 budget.

"The best" the Commission was "able to do" was to pass a motion stating its understanding of the need to maintain the property and requesting All Saints to secure two bids and take them to the Standing Committee.

One result of the organizational changes was that the rector of All Saints was once again a "one man show" responsible for the entire program at 16th and Central, particularly when The Rev. Jackie Means left to become rector of St. Mark's, Plainfield. Although there were other clergy to assist him on Sundays, the rector had the daily worries of not only the parish but, as manager of the Urban Center, all the agencies operating out of the building. In addition, Fr. Eastwood now became the focus of requests for emergency financial assistance. The *Tidings* article at the end of his rectorate said,

> Eastwood identified a question for the rector of All Saints yet to be solved: "how to provide leadership to both the parish and to social ministry issues."
>
> "Doing both spread me pretty thin," he said. "I would like to have taken more initiatives in pastoral areas."
>
> "I would like to have seen stronger social ministry programs, but the Diocese was not able or willing to support our requests for more staff."

In the midst of the changes in the still complicated organization chart of the work at 16th and Central, the parish was once again affected by events in the world beyond the parish. The General Convention of 1979 adopted a resolution on homosexuality stating that it was inappropriate to ordain persons who were "practicing homosexuals" or who were heterosexuals sexually active outside the bonds of marriage. The October parish newsletter reported that the vestry was "mindful of the pain" caused by this action and had adopted the following resolution:

> Resolved: That we, the Clergy and Vestry of All Saints communicate to Bishop Jones and our parish our deep concern over the loss and separation within the clergy and laity resulting from the attempts of both our Church

and society to understand and deal with issues of human sexuality. It is our intention to study and discuss further this matter, and see our role as one desiring to be a reconciler in the midst of confusing and painful differences and to communicate further with our Bishop and parish in this regard.

In the January 1980, newsletter Fr. Eastwood once again tried to answer the question "What are we doing down there at 16th and Central?" The question continued to be asked because the combined budgets of the parish and the Urban Center were nearing $100,000. The rector first listed his own involvement in neighborhood issues. He was active in the Citizen's Neighborhood Coalition which was trying to respond to the Preservation Plan for the Old Northside Neighborhood. He was also a member of the Metro Center (not the Metro Council but a separate program at 16th and Delaware) Commission operating that facility for the Church Federation of Indianapolis. Prison ministry activities continued to be focused at the Urban Center in the person of Jackie Means. A number of outside groups used the facilities. The rector noted that some were "risky" and controversial. The list included the following:

- Peace and Freedom Food Co-op (wholesale food cooperative);
- Welfare Rights Organization;
- Citizen's Action Coalition (dealing with issues related to public utilities);
- Indianapolis Neighborhood Development, Inc;
- Gay/Lesbian Union;
- United Senior Action Group;
- Integrity;
- Juvenile Justice Task Force and Indiana Consortium on Community Corrections;
- Karate and self-defense classes (taught by Barbara Bingham);
- Neighborhood forums to meet candidates for public office;
- Diocesan Urban Strategy Task Force.

All this was in addition to the "daily diet" of food and clothing bank and pre-school programs.

In Fr. Eastwood's list, the use of the word "neighborhood" is a sign that once again the area around All Saints was changing. When the diocese acquired the property at 16ᵗʰ and Central, the neighborhood was developing as a "suburb" of large and substantial homes. Later apartment buildings were built (for example, the Canterbury on the north side of 16ᵗʰ Street and the Cathedral Apartments on the church property). After World War II, the large old homes were converted to apartments and the residents became almost exclusively poor and black during the "white flight" to the new suburbs being built with VHA and other government funding. In the late 1970's the neighborhood began to "gentrify". Middle-class professionals were buying up the old houses and restoring them. Property values were rising. The largely African-American and poor residents began to feel squeezed out. The parish facilities were the scene of attempts to bring the new and old residents together—and also the scene of expressions of anger and resentment on both sides. The newsletter of June-July 1978 contained an article on the growing issue of Historic Preservation's effect on long-time residents of the area. In response to tensions created by the "gentrification" in the Historic District of the Old Northside, a coalition called the Citizen's Neighborhood Coalition had been formed as the lead agency to apply for city funds for the neighborhood. Fr. Eastwood was an active participant. His article says, "The Coalition is not against historic preservation as such, but it is against its effects."

The January 1980 newsletter also announced the resignation of Bob Goodlett as choirmaster. Paul Mueller and Marla Devendorff filled in as interim directors for the choir program. Another item in that newsletter announced that Beth Bose, a nurse and a parishioner, had gone on a mission trip to Guatemala for three weeks. The project in which she was participating was organized through the national church's Venture in Mission Program and was to bring health services and water to a small, undeveloped community. On February 10, 1980, the parish launched a campaign to raise money for Venture in Mission. The All Saints' goal was $27,300 over a three-year period. By July, $17,398 had been pledged by 37 units.

During Lent 1980, daily masses were offered Monday through Friday. Adult discussions on Sunday were on the theme of "Church and City".

A variety of music continued to be offered. On May 18, 1980 (the last Sunday of the "choir season"), Haydn's *Missa Brevis (Small Organ Mass)* was sung. Bob Goodlett returned to sing with the choir for the occasion. After the service he was presented with a silver pitcher and a scrapbook as tokens of thanks for his contributions to the music program. On May 25 (Pentecost) the Folk Mass setting by The Rev. Carey Landry was used. (Landry settings had also been used on Easter Eve.). The June newsletter noted that it was an "enthusiastic time 'in the Spirit.'" At this time folk or "contemporary" music was used on the last Sunday of the month.

As a part of the transfer of programming from ECS to the parish, All Saints planned a Summer Youth Program of education, recreation and cultural activities for the summer of 1980. Glenda Stewart of the Indianapolis Public Schools became the director and parishioners were asked to volunteer assistance. The Youth Choir enjoyed an overnight trip to Cedar Point amusement park on June 14 and 15. The trip was not all play, however; the choir sang at Christ Church in Huron, Ohio on Sunday, June 15.

At its July 1980 meeting, the vestry responded positively to the Citizen's Neighborhood Development Corporation's request for funds. The vestry granted $5,000 from savings as an interest-free loan to begin a "paint up and fix up" program for low-income area homeowners. Parishioners Culver Godfrey and Susie Mallory served on the board of the Corporation. The newsletter noted:

> The Vestry, well aware of urban problems and the need for the Church's strategic response, decided to risk some potential cash flow problems in its own budget in making this loan agreement. Because the city can no longer pay such expenses while waiting federal reimbursement, local groups such as Citizen's are expected to provide their own cash to start up re-development programs.

Within a year $4,200 of the loan had been repaid. There were 23 homes in the "paint up fix up" program. The money was used to reimburse homeowners for expenses or to purchase materials for homeowners who contributed labor. Contractors provided assistance for 15 of the homes.

All Saints Day in 1980 was celebrated with a visit from Fr. Ian Mitchell and his family to lead the congregation in his Folk Mass.

The Annual Parish Meeting for 1980 was held on September 14. At that time the following resolution was passed in response to violent threats and harassment against the YWCA for providing space to a group of homosexual persons: "We support the YWCA, and their Christian leadership, in the non-discriminatory action of providing space for homosexual persons to hold meetings."

Racism was also much on the parish's mind. Fr. Eastwood wrote a reflection for the newsletter upon his refusal to remain silent when overhearing racist remarks made in connection with a suit against a private club for its discriminatory policies.

On August 29, Birtie Smith was featured on a local TV station as Volunteer of the Week. Not only was she supervising the All Saints Food Bank, she was active in efforts to organize a metropolitan food bank to supply local pantries. The All Saints pantry fed 487 persons in 141 families during the month of July 1980, at a cost of $626.29. Fr. Eastwood reflected on "Food—A Christmas Value" for the December newsletter.

> Some of us have a great deal more than others but we do not operate the Food Bank because we feel guilty. If we did, we would need clients to make us "feel better." At times, we are able to help others so that they can help themselves. That is a special reward to our volunteers, but that does not always happen. That cannot be our main motivation for the tiring hours of service.
>
> As I return to that Bethlehem stable experience, I see again the themes of poverty: outcast, alone, insufficient resources for decent housing, all in the mystery of divine protection. God places a value on human life in such a lowly state as his Son Jesus. We sing about it at Christmas. It gives rise to the merry tunes, and pretty wrappings. It also gives rise to year-long efforts of Christians who believe in the value—the infinite value—of all human life no matter what circumstances.

Kathy Smith was appointed choir director, and took up her duties in November 1980. Kathy was on the music faculty of Butler University and had been part of the All Saints Choir during Bob Goodlett's tenure.

The next year began with financial problems for two of the parish's programs. In February 1981 both the Food Bank and the Music Program had to be temporarily shut down. Only a small grant from Episcopal Charities was now available for the purchase of food. It was simply insufficient to stock the pantry. Appeals for canned and packaged foods were made to Episcopal parishes and congregations of the Riley-Lockerbie Ministerial Association. The Music Program relied on special fundraising in the parish and a grant from the Talbot Fund which had not yet been received.

The response to the emergencies of the Food and Music Programs was good. The Food Bank was re-opened by April, and volunteers served clients on Tuesday, Thursday, and Saturday mornings. The Talbot Fund made its grant to the Music Program. By April Kathy Smith had ten neighborhood children enrolled. Sara Davis chaired a committee of the parish charged with raising an additional $6,000 for the program.

Parish life also continued in other areas. February was marked by an observance of Black History month. Parishioners Lena Harris and Nancy Shaw joined Fr. Eastwood in presenting a series of Sunday education programs. The Rev. Dr. Mwalimu Imara, Director of the Hospice at Methodist Hospital and associated with the parish, also led a session titled "Black People in White Churches: Vacant Symbols." The parish officers for 1981 were Nancy Shaw, Senior Warden, Bill Scott, Junior Warden, Cliff Henderson, Treasurer, and Sadye Harris, Clerk. Other vestry members were Wanda Reed, Louise Jones, Win Tackett, John Anderson, and Delbert White.

To celebrate the ministry of Jackie Means at All Saints and to send her to continue her ministry throughout the diocese, special events were planned for the weekend of April 25-26, 1981. A "roast" and banquet took place on Saturday night, and she was the preacher on Sunday morning, her last Sunday as associate to the rector.

In addition to the choir, Senior and Junior High Youth Groups remained active with Sadye Harris and Margaret Barnard as leaders. Outreach to children and youth meant that there were often un-accompanied young people in church. The vestry

> adopted an understanding about youth participation which parishioners are asked to adopt. Adults are asked to sit with non-parented youth in church, help them participate in the liturgy, giving guidance and direction. Distracting behavior during worship will be minimized through developing a relationship of caring. The "Cry Room" is off limits to young people during worship so that parents with babies may comfortably have access to change diapers or to nurse.

Some of the choir members were baptized on Pentecost, June 7, 1981.

On that same Pentecost, Fr. Eastwood became The Rev. Dr. Eastwood when Christian Theological Seminary granted him the Doctor of Ministry degree. In 1982, he reflected on his counseling ministry for the newsletter.

> When I came to All Saints in December 1973, as Associate Rector, a portion of my time was given to counseling clients who came to Episcopal Community Services. I quickly learned that the few short courses in seminary did not satisfactorily prepare me to deal with the unique problems I was facing. This occupational stress coupled with my interest and intuition about being an effective pastor motivated me on a six-year journey through training centers (CTS and Methodist Hospital) and course work at the seminary. In this process, what I appreciate most is the support of our parish vestries and others in allowing me the day a week to pursue this program. I see a small number of counselees (individuals, couples or families) each week—limited to five hours currently because of other responsibilities.

Initially the fees generated by the counselees were used to pay for Fr. Eastwood's course work. After his graduation, fees received beyond actual costs were turned over to the parish budget.

The summer program for 1981 was scheduled for eight weeks. Money taken from savings funded the hiring of a director, but parishioner involvement was also strongly emphasized. A newsletter article described a typical week of activities:

ied the request as too expensive and recommended using volunteers.
her Eastwood responded, "monthly food bags to families having
ay more with less is only bandaging a wound that continues to
d. Volunteers are important, but full-time professional training
direction is essential."

a result of the failure to receive funding, a special parish meeting was
ed on February 21, 1982:

> This gathering comes as a request from the Vestry that the parish be
> asked to respond to the fact that parish adopted programs in social service
> and youth ministry have not received outside funding. Dependency on
> outside-the-parish funding has been a frustrating experience for the Rector,
> Vestry and others who envision our congregation as having a strong social
> ministry with and for the neighborhood. Can we re-design our outreach
> focus? Shall we take a different approach?

rish concerns included the global as well as the local. The Lenten
ucation Program for 1982 focused on the arms race and nuclear
mament. Betty Riggs and others organized the Sunday series.
eakers included a proponent of the "just war" theory and a pacifist.
special liturgy on March 28 concluded the series "to celebrate in
sacramental context our trust in and unity with Christ, who is the
ince of Peace."

follow-up event occurred on Pentecost, May 30, when All Saints hosted
interfaith worship called a "Peace Pentecost" at 7:30 p.m. The service
nsisted of prayer and scripture readings with a sermon by The Rev.
osmas Raimondi of St. Thomas Aquinas Roman Catholic Church.

the March-April edition of the newsletter, *The Sounds of All Saints*,
olly Clements reflected on her service as Altar Guild Director.

> I love cleaning all the silver and washing the linen and ironing it; and the
> albs and the vestments that are used for the service, too. The Saturday before
> Palm Sunday, when the entire Altar Guild meets at the church to clean and
> drape the crosses in purple, is very rewarding. The contrast is so great when,
> on Easter morning the drapes are removed and the service is in full swing.
> Christ has risen and the Altar Guild has made everything neat and clean for
> Him. It makes me very happy. This is not a pitch for more people to get
> involved in the Altar Guild (although if anyone is interested please contact

On Monday and Thursday afternoons, the children are exposed to and
participate in various forms of dance. On Tuesday, they are learning about
literature through a trip to the Indianapolis Library. On Wednesday and
Friday, the story of people and nature will be introduced by exposure to the
State Museum. Parishioners like Gloria Kemper are giving their talents and
interest in teaching these areas. Sara Davis and Carolyn Salone meet weekly
with the staff for training and evaluation. Other parishioners are involved in
other aspects of the program. On Tuesday nights, Denise Senter and Sadye
Harris offer "teen rap" group sessions.

Another "parishioner involvement" project was the refinishing of the
wood floors in the nave. Under the direction of Win Tackett, a crew of
twenty worked during the week of June 7-14 and finished the project
in time for a wedding on Saturday afternoon.

In October 1981, All Saints co-hosted, along with Trinity Parish,
the Diocesan Convention. The Saturday morning Mass was held at
All Saints. The Fellowship Committee served a breakfast afterwards.
Sessions were held in a nearby hotel.

On the first Sunday of Advent, The Rev. Dr. Norman Pittenger
preached and addressed the adult class. Dr. Pittenger, well known as
an English "process theologian" and as a former member of the faculty
at General Theological Seminary, was a visiting professor at Christian
Theological Seminary. During his time in Indianapolis he also met with
the Integrity chapter at the home of Fr. Chastain and Fr. Honderich.
At this time, Dr. John Tofaute, parishioner and member of Integrity,
wrote monthly articles for the parish newsletter on various themes of
concern to gay and lesbian Christians.

Also in Advent, the Sunday Service schedule was changed to one
service. In explaining his decision about the schedule change in 1981,
Fr. Eastwood wrote for the newsletter:

> Our unity as a Christian congregation is what needs strengthening now.
> While this change does not affect a great many, it does show our intention
> as a parish to gather weekly for the basic unit of worship, fellowship,
> and education—the pattern followed in the time of the apostles and at
> other times in the life of the Church. We are a diverse people—that we
> demonstrate and appreciate. But what of our oneness in Christ? How do we
> show that? One gathering will strengthen us in our life together.

By January 1982, Treasurer Cliff Henderson reported that 54 pledges had been received for $37,486. The budget called for $40,000 in pledges plus an additional $7,000 from fundraising events. Later in the year one of the projects undertaken was a bus trip to Churchill Downs in Louisville. Susie Mallory and Polly Clements organized the event, which took place on May 22. Tickets cost $22 each. Eighty people made the trip, netting over $1,000 for the parish.

A new outreach program began in 1982, the development of low to moderate income housing on the lots south of the church to 15th Street. The proposal was a joint effort of Arsenal Technical (Tech) High School, the Mid-Central Deanery Clergy, and the Rector and Vestry of All Saints. A request was also made to Venture in Mission funds of the diocese for $12,000 to acquire and maintain the five full and two half-lots for the project. The idea was to train high school students in the building trades. These students were in Tech's Career Education Center Program. The church would acquire the property and transfer title when construction began on each new house. Claude Spillman agreed to act for the parish in acquiring the property. Some of the lots were owned by the city, but others were in private hands. Construction could not begin, however, until approval was granted by the city's Historic Preservation Commission. The Old North Side Neighborhood (whose northern border was 16th Street) had been declared a Historic District requiring such approval for all construction. The approval process became very involved when neighborhood objections were made to the "scale" and "mass" of the project, although considerable pains had been taken by the architects to design housing to fit the character of the neighborhood. Final approval was granted on May 10. Construction began in the fall. Mayor William Hudnut was present for a "brick laying ceremony" was held in September.

The objections and delays generated a series of meetings which, according to the parish newsletter report, "served to highlight the differences and conflicts within the neighborhood, and resulted in the design of more two-story houses rather than the one-story homes originally planned." Jack Eastwood later remembered that one of the meetings held with neighborhood representatives in the Parish House was opened with a prayer by Bishop Ted Jones: "Lord you know how hard it is to listen to

one another." One of the Old Northsiders whispered ...
people could be in your pews if you went along w...
Eastwood also remembered thinking, "Get thee behir...

*The Indianapolis News* featured the controversy in an ...
on November 2, 1982.

> "Now that we can actually see one, we think they're even l...
> than before," sighed Bob Phillips, president of the Old C...
> group. "But we tried everything we could think of to fight...
> nowhere."
>
> The students are building the "micro-neighborhood" ...
> supervision of professionals from the Builders Associatio...
> Indianapolis and Don Perry Associates. The volunteers ...
> not-for-profit Career Education Center Builders, Inc., a p...
> Indianapolis Chamber of Commerce and the Indianapolis Pu...
> Partners in Education program.
>
> This house—which eventually will have three bedrooms, two...
> room, country kitchen, parlor, entry stair hall, front and b...
> porches and a one-car garage with covered walkway—will h...
> need for low to moderate income housing in the neighborh...
> supporters say. The homes are expected to sell for $45,000 to $...
>
> The Old College Corners group fought the project becaus...
> considered the proposed dwellings "tract housing" and sul...
> structures not in line with the large, multi-story Victorian ho...
> neighborhood. They feared the micro neighborhood would d...
> properties.
>
> They filed a lawsuit against the Indianapolis Historic P...
> Commission for approving the project and temporarily halted co...
> In July, Superior Court Judge Michael Dugan upheld the co...
> decision.

As this new project was developing, the parish still str...
long-time needs. A request had been made to the Talbot C...
Christ Church once again to fund a full-time social worke...
Central. The food pantry had assisted 87 families with f...
during the Christmas season in1981. The request wa...
services to include client-follow through, advocacy, coordi...
other agencies, and counseling. Unfortunately, the Talbot...

me or Father Eastwood). What I'm saying is that I like coming over here on Saturday getting things ready for the Sunday Service ... So if you haven't found your rewarding job in the church, keep trying until you do, and then stick with it.

In the midst of controversy, fund-raising, education, outreach, and worship, there was also fun. An adult retreat at Waycross/Hickory Hill in Brown County took place in May 1982. The Parish Picnic was held at Eagle Creek Park on the afternoon of June 3.

Although some events like the trip to Churchill Downs were successful (as well as being fun), it was clear by the summer of 1982 that $7,000 was not going to be raised and that the Children's Music Program would have to be closed down. To the regret of both the rector and Kathy Smith, who had directed the program for the previous year, it was simply not possible in "the current economic situation" to continue it. Neighborhood youth programming would now have to be concentrated on after-school and summer programs, directed by interns from Christian Theological Seminary. Other changes in music were on the horizon, too. The organist, Mark Sweeney, was leaving to pursue graduate studies. Since January of 1982, Kathy Smith had been compensating for the lack of professional singers with resourcefulness and use of parish talent. Ernie Kiefer was hired as the new organist. Kathy assumed the responsibility of choir director. Another transition was the departure of Julia Collins as parish secretary to take another job after three and one half years at All Saints.

Also during the summer of 1982, Kelly Shaw and Tyrone Meriweather participated in the National Youth Event at Champaign, Illinois. Parishioner Sadye Harris, who was also one of the diocesan youth advisors, was the chairperson. The Youth Group also went to Hickory Hill in August and attended the Diocesan Youth Convention in October. Carolyn Godfrey was one of the leaders of the October event.

Keeping the pantry stocked with food was a continuing effort. Integrity members collected food during the city's Gay Pride Event. In October, 1982, Integrity had 24 members.

Parishioners were also asked to bring food as part of their offering on All Saints Day. The pantry was also a distribution center for federal surplus cheese and margarine. Pantry hours in 1982 were Tuesday, Thursday, and Saturday mornings.

The May 1983 newsletter announced staff changes in the music program. After the choir season was over Kathy Smith was planning to move from Indianapolis in order to work on a graduate degree. Also Ernie Kieffer was finding his medical studies at IU too demanding to be able to combine them with his duties as organist. He did, however, prepare a Handel organ concerto which he presented before the Ascension Day service. Also at the Ascension Day Mass, Earl Furlow and Jacqueline Slatter were vocal soloists. Guest instrumentalists also supported the choir.

This same newsletter reported some new tenants of the Urban Center building. They included Justice, a gay and lesbian rights group, and the National Organization of Women. And the parish secretary was now Deborah Dickinson-Ford.

The plans for the parish picnic in July 1983 included activities for all levels of athletic ability—Three Legged Race, Water Balloon Toss, Wheelbarrow Race, Balloon Race, Frisbie Tag, Frisbie Golf, Charades, Softball, Swimming, Pass the Orange—and, of course, eating. The location was Riverside Park. The activities were scheduled to last until 8 p.m.

The parish rejoiced when Lena Harris was recognized by the National Council of Negro Women as one of its "Outstanding Women in the State of Indiana" in 1983.

Fundraising continued to be needed to support the budget. The projects for 1983 were a Cooking School ($15 per person or $25 per couple and chaired by Chuck White), a trip to River Downs Race Course in Cincinnati (chaired by Susie Mallory), the annual Woodruff Place Flea Market, a Flower Sale in April, and an Arts and Crafts Fair on August 27. The Arts and Crafts Fair offered a cookbook for sale called "Loaves and Fishes." Parishioners Chuck White and Ray Warden had supervised this project. The introduction said, "The recipes in this book are a collection prepared by the parishioners of All Saints Episcopal Church, and range from original dishes, perfected through trial and error over long periods of time in home kitchens, some adaptations from other publications, and some deliberate plagiarism where a recipe didn't need improving." The "first edition" was sold out by 1987, when it was re-issued.

A grant from the Diocesan Revolving Loan Fund allowed replacement of the Urban Center roof. Bill Busse, Property Chair, spearheaded a group of volunteers who replaced kneelers in the church

Another outreach project with significant long-term effects was mobilized at this time—the Saturday lunch program. (Eventually the feeding ministry, under the leadership of Miss Nellie Gold, was incorporated into the operations of the Dayspring Center.) By the summer of 1983, more than 100 persons were being fed each Saturday. The Indianapolis Metropolitan Council operated the program. All Saints' first representatives to the Metro Council were Father Eastwood, Barbara Dove, Phil Coffey, Ray Warden, and Cliff Henderson. In 1984, the Diocese and the "Metro Council" renovated the Parish Hall kitchen to enable the feeding program to expand to six days a week. As a part of this renovation, Alice Usher painted the walls of the Parish Hall with murals representing bread and water.

Just as this new program was beginning, The Rev. Joseph W. Riggs, the last Executive Director of Episcopal Community Services, died on July 17, 1983.

A new choirmaster and organist was found in the person of Jim Keller, an architecture student at Ball State University as well as a master's student in organ.

One of the parish traditions during the Eastwood years was the presence of glazed donuts from Long's bakery at the Sunday Coffee Hour, and one of the jobs of the Fellowship Committee was to organize volunteers to pick up the donuts each Sunday. Failure of the assigned volunteer to follow through led to severe disappointment!

On December 3, 1983, the parish celebrated the tenth anniversary of Fr. Eastwood's ministry at All Saints. Fr. Chastain preached and many shared memories at a supper following the Mass. Fr. Eastwood had asked all the clergy present to vest in chasubles, and the result was, appropriately, a rainbow of colors in the nave and sanctuary.

The after-school program continued into 1984. In March, 15 children were reported as involved in tutoring, educational events, and recreation. There were also monthly parent meetings. The parish supported the program both through fundraising events (like the Shrove Tuesday Pancake Supper) and adult volunteer participation. The director, Elizabeth Nussmeier, used a system of rewards and punishments to maintain discipline. Children had to earn "smiley faces" in order to participate in events. In addition to this after-school program, Parent Centered Education was also operating out of the Urban Center. Directed by Shirley Brewer, PCE assessed student needs and then worked with parents to help meet those needs.

Christian Education during Lent of 1984 included a Tuesday evening Bible Study on the Gospel of John, Sunday morning sessions (also on John), a speaker from IUPUI on "The Changing Face of the Urban Community," a film on alcoholism, and a display of Indiana Black History titled "This Far by Faith." There was also an inter-generational session on the last Sunday of Lent in preparation for Holy Week (which undoubtedly included the making of palm crosses). Each Friday in Lent the Sacrament of Penance was available from 6 to 7 p.m., with additional times by appointment.

Spring brought a discussion in the vestry about renovation of the organ. Jim Vesper chaired a committee to gather information on feasibility and to present it to the parish at the Annual Meeting (September 29). The project was estimated to cost $30,000 to $35,000 and to take two years. After the presentation, the vestry decided to delay solicitation until the pledge campaign had met the needs for operating budget.

The kitchen renovation was nearing completion by April, 1984. A free lunch of hot soup and bread began to be served on Monday, April 2.

Fifty people per day was the average number fed in the first week of operation. The new kitchen was dedicated on April 7.

The November 1984 newsletter reported on children's education: "They have experienced a Near Eastern lunch, staged a skit about Noah (complete with a live kitten), and seen John Orton's slides of Abraham's journeys. They are beginning a unit on Moses and the Exodus, and they'll be learning an Israeli folk dance soon." (Gloria Kemper not only taught folk dances to parish children, but she also periodically conducted classes for adults.)

The vestry had undertaken an evaluation process called SWEEP. The initials stood for the areas of life examined: Service, Worship, Education, Evangelism, and Pastoral Care. Each of these areas, in turn, was related to one of the promises of the Baptismal Covenant. By the time of the November pledge campaign, the process was completed and reported to the parish as a part of the canvass. The budget proposed for 1985 called for pledges of $43,000, diocesan assistance of $60,000, and other income of $12,230. Expenses were budgeted at $122,145, leaving a deficit of about $7,000 to be addressed later by the vestry.

All Saints' life was never dull—and never just a matter of figures and statistics. In an interview in 2001, Jack Eastwood told stories which had stuck in his memory. When the Metropolitan Community Church (a church with predominately gay membership) requested to use All Saints' space, a vestryman said, "We're not ready for that. Maybe we're not Christian enough." In contrast, when Dr. Frank Lloyd heard about the proposal to build the houses south of the church, he said, "Now we're doing something really Christian." Part of the fun of parish life was the presence of the Eastwood children, Adam and Jessica. During one service for the Feast of Absalom Jones, in the presence of Bishop Jones, Adam's alarm watch went off very noisily. On one Ash Wednesday, the rector ran out of gas with Adam and Jessica in the car. When they finally got to church, Fathers Honderich and Chastain had started the service. The rector arrived in time for the sermon. Before a wedding, thieves broke into a car and stole all of the tuxedos. Instead of beginning the service with the usual, "Dearly beloved," the announcement came "Hold on while we get new tuxes." The wedding finally began an hour later. In 1975, Jack Eastwood was involved in a very severe auto accident. During his recuperation he grew a beard. When he returned to church, he began the sermon with, "My life has been a little hairy lately." In January 1978, one of the heaviest snowfalls of the city's history occurred. An emergency was declared, and many people were snowbound for several days. Jack posted a sign outside the church: "Service cancelled. Help your neighbor." Services were not cancelled, however, on a Christmas Eve so cold that the church could be heated only to a few degrees above freezing. Everyone, however, survived in hats and coats and long underwear.

The Eastwoods lived at 3944 N. Delaware, the house which had once been the residence of ECS directors and which had later become parish property. During his rectorate Jack proposed to the vestry that he buy the house and that the parish provide a housing allowance instead. At the Annual Meeting in September 1978, Treasurer George Hight announced that the sale of the rectory netted $25,090 but obligated the parish to provide a housing allowance. George said, "The parish is challenged to recognize that All Saints' is an aided parish." The rectory at this time was next door to the home of Jim Vesper and across the street from that of Fathers Chastain and Honderich. Alice Usher's address was in the same block on Delaware Street.

Although liturgy in the Anglo-Catholic tradition continued to be the norm, the rectorates of Stew Wood and Jack Eastwood were marked by a determination not to let the liturgy be "fussy." At the beginning of their shared ministry they made a retreat at St. Gregory's Abbey in Three Rivers, Michigan. At that time they worked out some simplifications—e.g., of the censings of the space—which became the norm in the parish through the turn of the 21st century. Fr. Eastwood also began preaching from the center aisle rather than the pulpit. Folk masses were celebrated from time to time. Fr. Eastwood provided guitar accompaniment—also from the center aisle. Another conscious liturgical decision was to make sure that the faces of acolytes and sub-deacons around the altar reflected the diversity of the parish so that the public face of the parish would not be seen as necessarily male or white or straight.

Fr. Eastwood had seen significant changes during his more than 10 years at All Saints—for example, the removal of ECS from the 16th and Central picture. Jackie Means had been ordained and moved on. Integrity and a visible gay and lesbian presence in the parish had been accepted. Yet in many important ways, the parish was recognizably the same as it had been at the time of his arrival. Even without ECS, neighborhood children's programs and concerns for such basic needs as food and clothing and housing were the focus of outreach. Some new things were on the horizon: The Metro Council's feeding program was now operating and the dream of a renovated organ was being talked about. But there were the same old worries about money and how one priest could juggle all the aspects of 16th and Central, the same sort of worries which had finally been too much for Fr. Carthy.

Fr. Eastwood's resignation came in December of 1984. He announced that it would be effective on January 20, 1985. He had accepted a call to become Rector of St. John the Evangelist in San Francisco, a parish with a similar tradition of liturgical style, social outreach, and of diversity in population.

The Rev. Jackie Means

# CHAPTER ELEVEN

## Oil and Water
## All Saints Parish: 1985-1989

All Saints had not lived through a "search" process for a new rector since 1970 when Fr. Carthy left. Fr. Wood had been well known to the parish when he was called, and Fr. Eastwood had been associate before becoming rector. In the intervening 15 years, the national church had developed a new kind of search process. In 1970 there had been no system for a search other than collecting names of possible candidates from the bishop and parishioners. Now, specially trained consultants assisted parishes in transition; and questionnaires solicited parish opinion. A committee was formed to write a "parish profile" and to interview potential candidates before making a recommendation to the vestry. And the national church maintained a computerized database of clergy interested in moving. The "process" was expected to take several months.

Jim Vesper was the Senior Warden at the time of Fr. Eastwood's departure. At its December 16, 1984, meeting, the vestry adopted a resolution asking Bishop Jones to appoint The Rev. Gordon Chastain as priest-in-charge during the vacancy. He was to conduct Sunday worship and provide pastoral care. He was also to meet with the vestry at its regular meetings, which would be chaired by the Senior Warden. Administration of the parish's facilities and finances was to be handled by Cliff Henderson, Treasurer. The bishop approved this plan. He also asked The Rev. Canon Mary Mail to be his liaison to the parish. The Rev. John Eberman of St. John's, Crawfordsville, was appointed consultant to the Search Committee. Nancy Shaw was made chair of the Search Committee, which early in its work decided to operate by consensus rather than official votes to ensure that all members were in agreement with actions.

Bishop Jones wrote to The Rev. Canon Harold T. Lewis of the national church office on April 11, 1985, "All Saints is an integrated congregation, and has specifically expressed an interest in receiving applications from Black clergy."

In the midst of the search, the parish continued to address current issues. In March, Jim Vesper wrote to the Bishop about a proposal from a group of young gay men (18-21) to use the parish buildings for meetings. The vestry with the help of Robert Burns, a parishioner and attorney, were proposing an agreement to be signed by the group setting forth rules (such as, no alcohol or drugs). The Bishop responded with approval and added, "Concerning ministries to homosexual persons, the Church has been generally supportive of such pastoral ministries."

Nancy Shaw reported to the bishop on May 16 that the committee had narrowed the list of candidates down to 23. By July 25, Bishop Jones wrote to Fr. Stew Wood (then at St. John's, Memphis, Tennessee) that the list had been narrowed to three persons.

The committee selected (and the vestry called) The Rev. Nan Peete. Nan (and she was often called that, rather than "Mother" Peete) was a curate at St. Mark's, Upland, California. Before ordination she had a career in business as a management consultant. She also listed on her resume: interest and experience in civil rights, community organization, political involvement, and women's issues.

The call of a black female generated a great deal of interest and comment in the city and in the wider church. All Saints, of course, had already taken a leading role in ministry of women priests. At the time of Nan's arrival, however, there were no other black priests in the diocese. St. Philips, the traditional black parish in Indianapolis, had been integrated and was served by a white rector. All Saints had been integrated long enough to have second and third generation African-American members. All Saints and St. Philips had shared leadership in the diocese in providing Martin Luther King and Absalom Jones services—usually with an invited Gospel choir. All Saints offered annual observances of Black History month. Much of its vestry and other leadership were African-American. It was not a shock to the parish that a black female had been selected, but it did surprise many outside the parish.

The announcement of the call came in a letter to the parish from the Senior Warden on October 8, 1985: "The long awaited announcement can now be made: We have a new rector. The Reverend Ms. Nan Arrington Peete has accepted the vestry's call and will join us on November 10th, when she will preach. The following Sunday, she will both preach and celebrate." Mr. Vesper continued with a thank you to the search committee:

> Laura Chastain, Maurice Edelen, Carolyn Godfrey, Reed Halliday, Lena Harris, George Hight, Gloria Kemper, Lynn Browning-Nance, Shawn Schreiner, Nancy Shaw, Win Tackett, and Charles White. Their work took many hours and displayed skill, patience, sensitivity to God's Spirit and each other, and a deep love for All Saints. They have pointed all of us in an exciting direction.

The parish had an "unofficial" first look at its new rector before her stated arrival date. On All Saints Day, Father Honderich and Father Chastain took their birettas out of mothballs. During the procession from the altar at the conclusion of the Liturgy, they stopped at the pew where the new rector sat *in cognito.* Fr. Honderich placed a spare biretta on her head as he brought her into the procession.

The official Celebration of New Ministry took place at 4 p.m. on Sunday, December 8, 1985. There was music for organ and brass before the service. During the new rector's sermon, there were interspersed responses from the Senior Warden and the Bishop. One of the hymns selected was the rector's favorite "Sweet, Holy Spirit." The words of the chorus seemed just right for the occasion:

> Sweet Holy Spirit, Sweet Heavenly Dove,
> Stay right here with us filling us with your love.
> And for these blessings we lift our hearts in praise
> Without a doubt we'll know that we have been revived
> When we shall leave this place.

The Peete rectorate would focus on significant issues confronting the Church. One of these was that of the place of women in the Church's ministry. Not only was it an issue of obvious personal importance to the rector herself, but it also became a vehicle for bringing her and the parish into an international spotlight.

A Committee for Women's Full Participation in the Church had been appointed in response to a resolution of General Convention "to study women's participation in congregational, diocesan, provincial, and national Church bodies and to review, evaluate, plan and propose policy on women's full participation in the life of this Church" Nan Peete was named to the Theology Work Group of the committee on June 25, 1986. She was asked to draft a theological statement which was to go to a small group for revision and then to the entire committee. (A large file of materials relating to Peete's work towards full inclusion of women is in the parish archives.)

Her paper was called "Women in the Episcopate." She pointed out that the course of the discussion to date had been "as if Women in the Episcopate is a male issue to be resolved by men. The fact that only men can currently consecrate a woman as Bishop and that the House of Bishops is all male does not give them sole authority to speak on the matter."

The Theological Statement was approved December 8, 1986. It began with a quote from Genesis 1:26a, 27-28 and then continued:

> From the beginning God charged both men and women with being stewards of the earth and all that is in it. Yet somehow through history we have created artificial barriers that denied equal opportunity to selected groups of people based on the color of their skin, their religious beliefs, their countries of birth, their age, and their sex. All of these barriers were justified at one time or another on selective religious and theological grounds ... Fortunately the theological arguments supporting these barriers were exposed as means to justify false positions. The Will of God is not be used to justify our beliefs. Our beliefs instead come from trying to understand the Will of God from the broad based perspective of scripture, tradition and reason.

As a result of her work on the issue, the rector of All Saints was invited to England to preach at a parish at a time when the Lambeth Conference of Anglican bishops was in session. The Conference was expected to make a statement on the ordained ministry of women. In a letter to The Rev. Barry Thorley, of St Matthew's, Brixton, London, and dated December 31, 1986, she said, "I am quite honored and flattered to be invited to England to celebrate and preach on Mothering Sunday, March 29, 1987. Before I give you an unequivocal yes, I have some major questions and concerns. I do not want to do anything that is going to be detrimental to the movement over there."

As a member of the Episcopal Women's Caucus, Nan convened an Ad Hoc Committee on Women in the Episcopate to increase the voice of women in the discussion. Yet another voice in the discussion was an Ad Hoc Committee for Black Women. Nan was also involved with this group.

Her participation in this work beyond Indianapolis was not without stress—within the parish and upon the rector herself. (It was the same kind of pull between national and local responsibilities experienced by Stew Wood when he was active in the national Executive Council.) In a report dated December 31, 1986, she commented, "I had been to two meetings just prior and wanted to get back to my parish. However, I realized that these women are part of the church gathered just as much as my congregation is."

The plans for the trip to England began to take shape. She wrote to her host, Fr. Thorly:

> My plans are now finalized. Our plane arrives at 9:40 p.m. September 15th at Heathrow. We depart on September 30th. I do have an appointment with The Reverend Canon Samuel Van Culin on September 17th at 10:00. I am planning on preaching at St. Matthew's, doing the Bible Study/Lecture for the youth and an address to the Black clergy.

Canon Samuel Van Culin was the Secretary General, Anglican Consultative Council. As a result of this contact, the rector's trip to England would soon include one more engagement: The Rev. Nan Peete became the first woman priest to address the bishops of the Anglican Communion. The invitation came from the Archbishop of Canterbury. Nan was to be one of two female priests who were to act as consultants to the bishop. In an interview with an Indianapolis newspaper, the rector said "I was shocked." At that time the British had no female priests. According to the November 1988 *Church Militant* (the diocesan paper later call *Tidings*), "Peete received a standing ovation for her moving confessional speech, as well as a good deal of international acclaim." A Reuters news service article was quoted in the parish newsletter:

> Rev. Peete, who is black, said she had turned to the church as a sanctuary from the pain of racism she suffered while growing up in the 1940s and 1950s. "Those feelings come back when I am not accepted as a priest, this time because of my sex and not my race," she said. "To many of you, I am a new phenomenon. To others, I am a familiar sight, And to others, I am a contradiction in terms. While I have been blessed with acceptance and support from many places, rejection is still painful."

Nan Peete was not the only person in Indianapolis involved in the issue. Bishop Jones was chair of a committee of the American Church's House of Bishops called to study women in the episcopate. The rector convened a group of the Episcopal Women's Caucus to respond to the report of the Jones committee. On April 1, 1987, the national Committee on Full Participation Of Women obtained a grant from St. Paul's, Indianapolis to study 12 dioceses, including Indianapolis. The study was to focus on attitudes, concerns, and issues about women's participation in the Church.

Yet another group on which Nan served was a sub-committee of the Standing Liturgical Committee charged with drafting new rites using more inclusive language.

Despite her focus upon women in the church, Peete continued to be active in other issues. On July 29, 1987, for example, she wrote a member of the national church staff about staff failure to invite black males to a conference. "It is very difficult and frustrating as an oppressed person in this society and this church to always be vigilant in the sin of racism. It makes the efforts seem responsive instead of intentional. For example the conference will be inclusive only as a reaction to its exclusiveness instead of its intentionality for inclusiveness."

The rector was invited to the Episcopal Divinity School in Cambridge, Massachusetts, to give an address during a Conference on Women in the Episcopate, January 11-13, 1998. She began:

About a year ago The Reverend Carol Cole Flanagan, President of the Episcopal Women's Caucus, called me and asked me if I would be willing to convene a group of women to be in dialogue with The Committee on Women in the Episcopate chaired by The Right Reverend Edward Jones. While there were women on the Jones Committee, the focus of their report was governed by the General Convention resolution which established the committee. Voices and perspectives of a variety of women needed to be heard and the discussion in The House of Bishops needed to be informed by the perspectives of women specifically … so the dialogue began between myself, Bishop Jones, his committee and the Ad Hoc Committee, as we called ourselves. I use the word dialogue loosely because the dialogue is a written dialogue between our reports. In keeping with the Anglican tradition: Scripture, Tradition and Reason were the framework of the report. However, we added a fourth, which filled in the picture and gave it life—Experiences of women in the ordained ministry in the Episcopal Church.

From Genesis which states "God created them male and female, in the image of God they were created"; to Galatians which states "there is neither Jew nor Greek, slave nor free, male nor female, for you are all one in Christ," we have recognized our mutuality and complementarity while living it imperfectly. We must hold fast to these biblical glimpses of male and female mutuality and resist ancient imperfect historical contexts to bind us to a greater imperfection in our own time.

One of the fundamental insights of feminist theology is that unity is neither static uniformity nor conformity. Pearls come from the tension caused when sand or grit rub against the flesh of the oyster.

"Sticks and stones may break my bones, but names will never hurt me." That is not true.
When is the word man or the men generic? When is it gender specific? Who decides? What are the criteria used in deciding? It if is always generic then the canonical change issue regarding Women in the Episcopate is non-existent.

Language about God is necessarily limited. God is more than Father. We must hold up the inclusiveness of God—male/female in God's image are we made.

Is Baptism enough? The answer is yes, according to the Baptismal formula in Paul (Galatians 3:28). Yet some people have concluded that Baptism is not enough. That the gifts for the ordained ministry lie in the maleness of the human being.

Another issue in which Baptism wasn't "enough" for some people in the church was homosexuality. Nan Peete continued to support the gay and lesbian members of the congregation. She routinely included Frs. Chastain and Honderich at the altar as a statement that Baptism was "enough" for participation in the Sacred Meal of the All Saints altar.

It was also during her rectorate that annual Services of Healing and Prayer for those affected by HIV/AIDS were instituted. The first was held in 1986. For the second on November 15, 1987, James Vesper wrote the following statement for the service leaflet:

A Time for Caring and Healing by James L. Vesper

While in San Francisco in March 1986 for the National Episcopal Church Conference on AIDS, I saw that a service of healing was to be a part of the conference. I didn't know what to expect. The closest I had gotten to faith healing was by watching some TV preacher on channel 40. At the service, held in the magnificent Grace Cathedral, I didn't see people throwing down crutches, unwinding bandages, or screaming and shouting. I did experience something profoundly powerful in a beautifully simple way.

The healing service had significant effects on all of us there—not just on those who went forward. For me, it helped to end some suppressed fears I had of AIDS. This freedom from fear helped me to talk, share communion, hug and cry with people who were dying such a painful death.

Since that time, I've learned that a service of healing could better be called a service to restore wholeness. This can happen to both an individual as well as all persons present.

Someone can be <u>not whole</u> for physical, emotional, and/or spiritual reasons. Part of it might involve feelings of unresolved guilt or feelings of hopelessness. During a service of healing, the clergy's hands are placed on the person to give them a real sense that there is a Christian community which can help them cope with their problems and help them become whole. This physical contact also symbolizes, as someone said, "being wrapped in the everlasting arms of Jesus."

Even though we come and worship each Sunday, we as a parish are not always whole—we don't always act with the same compassion, love, and selflessness described in the gospel. We need to become whole, also. The Eucharist, which follows "the laying on of hands," links us to each other and to Christ as well as to all other believers who have come before us. With this strength, we can go into the world and serve others and Christ.

Guest musicians playing flute, violin, viola, cello participated in the service. The sermon was a dialogue among James Vesper, Michael Shuff, and Nan Peete. A specially composed Litany was followed by the Laying on of Hands.

The Rev. Canon Earl Conner also attended the 1986 San Francisco conference mentioned in the Vesper article. He returned to Indianapolis determined to found a ministry to persons with HIV/AIDS. The result was an ecumenical ministry (and official institution of the Diocese of Indianapolis) called The Damien Center. The Center was located near All Saints on Pennsylvania Street at a former school building owned by the Catholic Archdiocese. Its first Executive Director was Michael Shuff.

The next AIDS service was held at All Saints on Sunday, November 13, 1988. Bishop Edmund Browning, the Presiding Bishop, had called the church to prayer in these words:

Our Church, praying and deliberating in Detroit, passed several resolutions concerning AIDS; its impact upon all of God's people; responses to this pandemic; and the appropriately Christian attitudes toward those of us who are living daily in the midst of sickness, death, grief, and discrimination.

Our mandated response is forthright, explicit, and begins at the altar. Sunday, November 13, will be the Third National Day of Prayer for Persons Living with AIDS and Those Who Minister with Them.

Persons with AIDS are extended a special invitation today, along with their friends, lovers, and families, to join us as we experience a wholeness, individually and collectively, only Christ can give.

The preacher on this occasion was The Reverend Wayne Olsen, Director of Metropolitan Indianapolis Campus Ministry. Following the Mass, Dr. Virginia Caine, Director of the Marion County Health

Department's Bell-Flower Clinic, led an adult forum on the latest AIDS medical and educational information.

This forum was held at the back of the nave because the parish hall was once again under construction for a new use—a homeless shelter. Addressing the needs of the homeless was another of the issues that marked the Peete years.

The city of Indianapolis began to be aware of an increasing population of homeless persons in the last half of the 1980's. Local news media, for example, reported the death of homeless man who had frozen to death. A shelter had operated near the parish at 16th and Delaware until March 1986. In the crisis, All Saints opened its doors to the homeless and allowed them to sleep on the pews and the floors. Volunteers were organized through the Metro Council, blankets were provided, and a meal was served to up to 70 persons a night beginning in October 1986. An *Indianapolis News* article estimated the number of homeless in the city on a typical night as 800. The article continued:

> While some of the homeless still fit the traditional image of the old wino, the most critical shortage is for women and children. The shortage of low-cost housing is a major reason for the growing problem. The solution has to involve long-term assistance, including help in finding jobs and living quarters.

The wire services picked up dramatic photos of the homeless asleep in the nave of All Saints. Once again the parish was making headlines.

The Christmas of 1986 would never be forgotten by those who attended Midnight Mass. After listening to the story of a homeless family forced to sleep in a stable, the congregation left the pews which would become beds for the modern-day homeless already gathering and preparing for sleep. One of the virtues of incense became very much appreciated when it masked the smell of not very clean bodies.

No long-term solution to the crisis had been found by the next winter. The Metro Council had proposed a 10,000 square foot addition to the Episcopal Urban Center building at 16th and Central, plus a remodeling of the kitchen in order to provide a permanent shelter. When the plans were submitted to the Indianapolis Historic Preservation Commission in the summer of 1987 (as required by the neighborhood's designation as Historic), neighbors in the Old Northside protested.

According to *The Indianapolis Star*,

> Neighbors of the church ... complain about the possibility of lowered property values and crime.

> Having a shelter in the church is a First Amendment right, says the Metro Council. Church officials also justify what they are doing with historical precedent: churches have been used as sanctuaries since medieval times.

When the plans were halted by a series of continuances which lasted into cold weather, the doors of the nave were once again opened to the homeless. There were rumors that the neighbors would try to block the parish from doing so with a court injunction, but that did not happen.

Stephen DeVoe, an attorney and volunteer from Trinity Parish, was quoted by the *Star*: "You have people with strong moral and religious convictions in conflict with the practical issues of running a city. You mix the segment of our society fallen on hard times with the concept of a stable neighborhood, and it's oil and water." Nan Peete said that during the summer when the proposal was introduced to the Historic Preservation Commission, some people "said a lot things that were really awful" and that a letter writing campaign was in progress to let the city know that those concerned about the homeless were not "just a small band of weird people."

The eventual compromise was not an addition to the building for a homeless shelter but a complete renovation of the Parish Hall to turn it into a homeless shelter for women and families (not single men). This program would become known as the Dayspring Center. The compromise, of course, would leave the parish without any program space (and even without bathrooms). Through the Metro Council, funds were made available for the construction of a new and much smaller Parish Hall for All Saints on the north side of the nave. There would be further struggles with the Historic Preservation Commission and the neighborhood over the design of this building, which would not be completed until 1991.

In the meantime, the number of homeless was growing. It was estimated at 1,540 on February 17, 1987, when the *Star* again featured the program at All Saints:

> The doors at All Saints Episcopal Church are unlocked at 7 p.m. and the guests begin to enter. They shuffle in quietly, asking few questions. They are, after all, "home," and they know the rules—odd rules, perhaps, for a home or a church: no booze, no weapons and no fighting.
>
> At the check-in table, they tell a volunteer their names and nothing more.
>
> They deposit their belongings in a plastic bag for safekeeping. One man wants to make sure his valuables will be cared for properly. He is assured that they will be. His valuables are two batteries. They are searched for weapons and alcohol and are asked to please deposit any matches or cigarettes.
>
> Because the shelter is free and includes a hot meal, its success is based on volunteers, a nightly crew of six men and women who check in the guests, serve them dinner, pass out blankets and watch over them as they sleep on church pews or the sanctuary's floor. There are about 200 volunteers from the Episcopal diocese and the city who take turns working at the shelter.
>
> At 6 a.m. lights are on, and coffee is served. Slowly, reluctantly, people begin leaving.

In the February, 1988 newsletter, the rector wrote:

> I would like to say how proud I am of all of you. The last year has not been an easy one with the Shelter and its attendant problems. A great benefit to a great number of guests, it has been at great cost to you. You have, with great grace, endured much. I do not know of any other congregation who would have so willingly—or even not so willingly—consented to such a crazy suggestion by their rector. This is not to say that we also have not benefited as well. But I want you to know I am aware of what the cost has been to you and how deeply grateful and appreciative I am for it.

All Saints life was not all about social issues, however, the organ project which was being talked about when Jack Eastwood was rector took some steps forward. Father Honderich reported for the January, 1988 newsletter:

> In late summer, the Organ Committee went to the Vestry to request permission for soliciting funds to purchase a new console for the organ. As a result of the generosity of the parish and its friends we raised over $5,400. Larry MacPherson, a local organbuilder and member of our parish, helped us acquire a relatively new three-manual console. By All Saints Day, Larry had rebuilt the bass pedal trombone. These pipes had stood silent for several years because of the deterioration of their wind chests and worn reeds. Enlisting help from David Hawn, Roger Whitehead, Win Tackett, Jim Anderson, and Graham Cook, Larry removed, washed, rebuilt, and replaced the trombone pipes. Work is progressing on the console now. This is a big project and will require the building of some scaffolding to lift the several-hundred-pound console to the gallery. Larry has been able to acquire the pipes for a much-needed three rank mixture to complete the Positive chorus. Graham and Larry had worked out a tonal design and schedule of work. Last September the Committee prepared a proposal to the Lilly Memorial Trust of St. Paul's. The Trust approved a grant of $7,000 to finance the work during 1988 and to allow us time to raise funds for 1989.

Jim Vesper wrote another report for a December newsletter:

> All the work has gone on without those of us in the pews noticing a disruption to the All Saints music program, thank to volunteers like Larry MacPherson (our organ builder "boss"), Tom Honderich, Graham Cook, Roger Whitehead, David Hawn, Jim Anderson, Brad King, and others. Recently, their dedication kept them up all night wiring and soldering connections so the instrument would be playable on Sunday morning.

Graham Cook was now the organist-choirmaster. A member of the parish for several years, he had retired as Director of Music at First Baptist Church.

The approval of a new Prayer Book by the Church in 1979 was followed by the introduction of a new Hymnal in 1982. David Bell, a seminarian at Sewanee who did an internship at All Saints during 1988, had worked with Dr. Marion Hatchett on preparation of the Hymnal. During his time at All Saints he presented a program on "the latest in church music and hymnody."

Informal House Masses were a feature of parish life in these years. During Lent of 1988 they were held on Friday evenings and also featured speakers on spirituality and prayer.

Another kind of liturgy was celebrated on at least two occasions—Solemnization of Holy Matrimony during the Sunday 10 a.m. Mass. Michael Romary and Catherine Albrecht were married on February 14, 1988. Laura Chastain and Marshall Gibson were also married during a Sunday service on May 15, 1988.

On April 24, 1988, there was no Sunday Mass at All Saints for the first time since the great snow of the Eastwood years. This time the reason was a diocesan-wide service at Market Square Arena to mark the 150th anniversary of the diocese. Alice Usher designed and Lynn Browning-Nance executed the design of the All Saints banner. All Saints' choir, acolytes and ushers participated in the service.

In 1988, Shawn Schreiner was accepted as a Postulant for Holy Orders. Shawn had been a member of the youth group before leaving for college. When she returned to Indianapolis she became active in parish life, maintaining the office while Nan Peete was traveling to fulfill her national and international commitments. Shawn enrolled in Seabury-Western Seminary in the fall of 1988.

For the February 1988 newsletter, Peete decided to list the names of some of the parishioners who routinely assisted parish life:

> Alice Usher comes faithfully each Wednesday to serve in the Feeding Program. Lynn Browning-Nance does a great job planning and arranging Informal Gatherings. Marc Sotkiewicz, John Phillips, and Penny Edwards all work long hours trying to see this place kept spic and span in spite of the tremendously high traffic in the building. George Hight, bookkeeper, and Cliff Henderson, treasurer, have kept us on the straight and narrow (with much difficulty). Birtie Smith keeps our pledge records up to date. Graham Cook edits the newsletter. Roger Whitehead not only sees to altar supplies and audio-visual needs, but also makes the coffee.

In 1988, the city decided to close down the steam line which had served All Saints. They offered some funding to assist in a replacement boiler. The boiler was placed in the Parish Hall building during reconstruction as the Dayspring Center. Pipes then ran to radiators in the nave. This system meant that heat in the church was controlled by Dayspring, a system that would lead to some very cold Sunday mornings in the church for years.

One of those cold Sundays soon came. The rector received a fan letter about the parish liturgy in the fall of 1988 from a visitor:

> I want to thank you and your congregation for your warm hospitality when I was in Indianapolis two Sundays ago (when there was no heat). The cabbie indicated that I would be lucky to get from the corner into the church alive, but I am so glad that I was able to worship with you.
>
> All Saints showed me what I have always wanted but never experienced: worship that is serious but not solemn, relaxed but not casual, and careful but not obsessive. High or Anglo-Catholic parishes in this part of the country tend to have what our rector calls a "porcelain" quality: you have the impression that if someone does something wrong (like swinging the censer too few or too many times), the whole thing will break. It makes for very solemn, dry, deadly liturgy.
>
> Your worship is so reverent but so warm.

By May 1988, the vestry had developed and approved a mission statement. It read: "All Saints Episcopal Church is a small, diverse Christian family, striving to live out Christ's love for us and stretching ourselves to share that love in the world. In serving Christ, we try to serve ourselves and those around us, including the excluded; the hurting, the broken, the poor in spirit, the hungry and the homeless."

Nan Peete did not get to see the opening of the new Dayspring Center and Parish Hall. Her last Sunday at All Saints was Christmas Day, 1988. She had resigned to become Canon to the Ordinary for the Bishop of Atlanta. (Later she would serve on the staff of Trinity Parish, Wall Street in New York, and then on the staff of the Bishop of Southern Ohio.) The *Church Militant* (November 1988) described her three years at All Saints: "She was instrumental in the development of her congregation into a caring community whose outreach and concern for the homeless, victims of AIDS, substance abusers, and otherwise marginalized individuals is empowered through worship."

In her letter to the parish, Nan summed up her time in the parish: "These past three years have seen many changes and many new opportunities. The new parish hall is a symbol of these new opportunities. The parish will no longer have the administrative responsibility for the Urban Center. You will be able to expand and develop ministries suited to the needs and interests of the parish and the community."

The old Parish Hall and its connections to the ministries which had been undertaken there, however, were very much missed. In the course of the construction of the shelter, the door which had led from the Michael Chapel to the Parish Hall was forever sealed off. Now that door led only to a closet for cleaning supplies. The old traffic pattern from parking lot into church and from church to coffee hour was no longer possible. Now that it was the access point to the new Parish Hall, St. Mary's Chapel no longer could be used as a space for weekday Masses. And it was not yet clear what new ministries would emerge to replace those that had been housed in the Urban Center. What would happen in that new Parish Hall, if and when it was completed?

Upon the rector's resignation, The Rev. Gordon Chastain had indicated that he would consider a call from the parish if the process should lead in that direction; and Father Honderich became priest-in-charge for the interim.

By May 1989, a search committee was in full swing. On May 7 the committee presented to the vestry the form to be sent to the national church computer describing the parish. In June, 35 names of potential candidates had been received from the computer. Additional names received brought the total considered to 72 candidates.

In the meantime, parishioner Kitty Burton had been accepted into a Venture in Mission Program in Honduras. The vestry endorsed her trip on May 21 and appealed for financial support from the parish, in addition to budgeting $500 to assist in expenses. She wrote the following description of the program for the June newsletter:

> I will be volunteering through Volunteers for Mission, a program of the National Church. I applied to VFM in the fall of 1988, and received my assignment in January of 1989. I had an interview with the VFM staff in

April in New York. I will be attending an ecumenical training session in Canada in July. In August, I will attend four weeks of language lessons in Guatemala. I will report to Holy Spirit School in Tela, Honduras on August 26, 1989. I have been assigned to teach kindergarten to 30 children (in groups of 15 at a time).

On June 18, Fr. Honderich included a commissioning and blessing of Kitty's ministry in the Sunday liturgy.

Plans continued for the new parish hall. At its June 1989 meeting, the vestry dealt with a list of corrections that were needed in the plans. Dust from construction was being tracked onto the nave floor and was difficult to clean. Concern about the situation led to an explanation of the problem in the newsletter. The new building was to be ready for occupancy by August 5, but a number of items on the parish "wish list" could not be included in the new building. A last minute appeal was issued in August for ceramic tile and vinyl wall fabric in bathrooms, blinds and window treatments, library bookcases, and carpet. It had been hoped that a new kitchen stove could be installed, but that was also beyond the budget.

The newsletter was now edited by Brad King and Kelly Lowe. In the June 1989 issue, they featured the Altar Guild: "The Altar Guild at All Saints lives by two simple rules: 1) if it doesn't move, and it's made of cloth, take it home, wash it, and iron it; and 2) if it doesn't move, and it's not made of cloth, polish it."

A group of parishioners was now gathering on Saturday mornings to say the rosary together. Another enrichment to personal spiritual life of parishioners was the Cursillo movement. Cursillo was an intense weekend experience with regular gatherings for participants to continue to reflect on their spiritual lives. Penny Edwards, Carol Ernsting, Brad King, John Orton, Irma Reinumagi, Shawn Shreiner, and Dona Young were listed as parish contacts for Cursillo in the September 1989 newsletter.

This same newsletter suggests that the construction project brought not only physical problems, but also communications problems. The Metro Council had let the contract for both the shelter renovation and the parish house. Parishioners were instructed to contact John Phillips, representative to the Council, and not the contractor or the president of the Council for matters dealing with the Council. For general concerns about buildings and grounds, they were to contact Larry MacPherson. Once again there was confusion about what was parish business and what was the proper concern of another agency in the same building complex.

The Metro Council construction projects did not involve the nave, but the changed traffic pattern created by the construction affected it. At the Annual Meeting on Sunday, September 17, 1989, Fr. Honderich presented proposed architectural changes: moving the brass eagle lectern to the front; moving the baptismal fonts so that one would be in the narthex; and moving the statue of the Our Lady Queen of All Saints (the Cirlot memorial) to St. Mary's chapel.

The Senior Warden during this period of transition was Dr. Frank Lloyd. He chaired the Annual Meeting. The Junior Warden was Alice Usher. She also represented the parish at the diocesan convention for 1989 and gave the following report in the next newsletter:

> Going north to Keystone-at-the-Crossing, where the convention was being held, seemed at odds with my All Saints, one-way-south-on-Central orientation. Seated finally at the All Saints table in the ballroom, with a sheaf of papers in variegated colors labeled from A to G and from 1 to 41, I did my best to keep up with the proceedings. There were amendments to the Constitution and Canons of the Diocese, resolutions bursting with Whereases and Therefore-be-its, comments from the floor, and much voting. We stood to receive our ballots, sat to fill them in, and stood to have them collected. It was diverting from time to time to glance at the mirrored and twinkling ceiling to view the proceedings in reverse. (My name isn't Alice for nothing.)

November 1989 was marked by several special events. The patronal festival was celebrated with its usual splendor on November 1. The year 1989 was the 125th Anniversary celebration of the parish, and All Saints Day marked the 78th anniversary of the dedication of All Saints Cathedral. Letters of greeting were received from state legislators, the Presiding Bishop of the Church, and the governor. On November 19, Jackie Slatter returned to the parish to give a vocal recital (as part of her work at the Indiana University School of Music). When asked why she had picked All Saints as the site for her recital, she said, "That's where I got my start." On November 16, the New World Chamber Orchestra presented a concert in the nave. This concert was also in the tradition of outreach to young people through music: it was composed of 55 young musicians (ages 11 through 18) from Central Indiana.

Finally, on December 10, 1989, the parish hall was as complete as it could be considering the limited funds available; and the parish could celebrate its dedication at an Evensong followed by a pitch-in dinner.

Cheryl Eiszner was now the choir director. She made one Christmas Eve especially memorable. During the Mass celebrating the birth of a Child, she had given her utmost vocally and emotionally even though she was eight months pregnant. She went with the choir to its annual post-Mass party and then went into labor. Cheryl, her husband John, Fr. Chastain, and Fr. Honderich celebrated Christmas around baby Sarah's incubator in the hospital. Regulars in the choir in 1989 were Lynn Browning-Nance, Kelly Lowe, Gloria Kemper, Irma Reinumagi, John Eiszner, Mark Gastineau, Jay Hering, Allan Miller, David Kubley, Larry MacPherson and Paul Nance. The organist was Jeff Donohue.

As a result of the search committee's work, the name of The Rev. Wayne R. Hanson, III, was placed in nomination for rector at a special vestry meeting on November 20, 1989. At another called meeting on November 24, 1989, the official vote of the vestry was taken. Fr. Hanson would be the next rector of All Saints.

The "parish profile" developed by the search committee had a concluding section called "Afterword." It described the parish and its hopes for its new rector:

> All Saints' begins and ends with contrasts. We are a church in which votive candles are lit before the statue of the Blessed Virgin, and a church that welcomes women in all facets of the ministry. We chant Gregorian propers, and follow them with hymns composed in 1980. The thurifer censes the congregation with pontifical incense while tennis shoes peep out from under his robe. We're an aided parish that distributes food baskets to the neighborhood. We have a small number of pledge units, yet our per capita giving is higher than that of several large parishes. The surface contrasts are

all there—but they are only on the surface. Despite the surface contrasts, it all meshes: the contrasts blend together, showing us God's love, and allowing us to show God's love to the world. We treasure All Saints' and we seek a rector who will treasure the church as we do.

As we search for a rector for All Saints', we look for someone to assist us in growing—both spiritually and physically. We'd like a priest who can educate us in our faith from the pulpit, in the classroom, and in the office. A priest who can preach the Gospel of our Lord, and who can help us to preach that Gospel in our own lives, in our own ways. What we are looking for is a priest who can empower us to show forth God's love, who can assist us in growing and developing as a congregation, and who can respect and maintain a tradition of worship and activism.

At the regular vestry meeting of December 17, Fr. Tom Honderich was thanked for his service during the interim. He announced that he and Fr. Chastain would absent themselves from the parish for about six months to allow the new rector an opportunity to forge his own relationships with the parish. Fr. Honderich also reported that he had been in conversation with the rector-elect about some proposed changes in the placement of lectern, etc. However, the old baldachino had been removed from St. Mary's Chapel, now that the chapel had become the major access between nave and new parish hall. A wrought iron fence still separated the chapel from the nave. (This fence had been installed as a security measure to protect the nave during some of the Carthy years when St. Mary's Chapel had been left unlocked.) Fr. Honderich requested that the fence be left in place until the new rector had an opportunity to make a decision about it.

Because Christmas Eve fell on a Sunday in 1989, scheduling was very tight. On Sunday morning, December 24, there was a Low Mass for Advent IV followed by the Greening of the Church. The Solemn High Mass of the Nativity began at 10:30 that evening. A Low Mass for Christmas was celebrated at 10 a.m.

Another rector and another call to extraordinary response would soon arrive.

The Rev. Nan Arrington Peete

# CHAPTER TWELVE

## A Plague on My House
## All Saints Parish: 1990-1994

In the January 1990 newsletter, The Rev. Wayne R. Hanson, II, introduced himself to the parish:

> I have seen some letters of this sort that I wish had never been written! I have seen letters from new rectors that coyly say, "I have no agenda in coming to this place." I have seen other such letters where, couched between the claptrap slogans of assured collaboration, one can detect that the new rector has designs on establishing his very own Byzantine bureaucracy.

> The focus of my vocation and ministry is the Altar of God. I will serve you out of my gifts, my background and experience, and my wounds. I will write and speak to you from my heart as informed and honed by my education which ranges from a couple of initial years in the Chicago Public schools, to graduation from York Community High School in Elmhurst (a Chicago suburb); from the excellent and broadly based liberal arts education I received at St. Olaf College to my brief encounter with Law School at Willamette University; from the highly structured curriculum of rigorous and doctrinal theological training I received during one year of studies at Luther Theological Seminary to the individually designed, tutorial-based, sometimes almost counter-cultural final two years of seminary I spent at the Episcopal Divinity School.

> Like any human being, I am not without my share of faults and shortcomings. Generally, I am quite outgoing ... During the first couple of years after my ordination I learned just how important it is to slow down as a result of several episodes of my back "going out." ... Over the years I have learned more and more patience ... yet I still have a certain, latent sympathy with the California bumper sticker which reads. "I want it all now!" I am a penitent; I can mark several momentous turns in the road of my life by confessions ... I grew up as a Lutheran (of the rather "high

church" variety), and was confirmed in the Episcopal Church in 1976 … I was drawn to the full, Catholic liturgical life of the Episcopal Church, and by the diverse spiritual expressions of this communion … Since I was ordained some five years ago, I have also come to be called, and happily respond to the address, "Father." Thus far, I have been charged with the cure of souls in two locations in the Diocese of Chicago—Grace Church, Oak Park, where I served as a curate, and St. John's Church, Lockport, where for the past three-and-a-half years I have served as vicar.

That considerably shortened selection was an authentic introduction to the new rector. He loved words and loved to use them. And he did "want it now."

Father Hanson began his ministry on February 1, 1990. In his second newsletter article, he said, "I find myself constantly stretched with the identity of being your rector, being a Hoosier, and being the 'current occupant' at 49th and Park." (Fr. Hanson and his partner, Fr. Don Melvin, had purchased a home at 49th and Park.) One thing, however, was familiar to Fr. Hanson: "Following the Liturgy my first Sunday here, I commented to several parishioners of feeling very much at home by saying, 'I felt like a fish swimming in a familiar aquarium.'"

He had arrived just in time for Lent and so announced the following Lenten schedule:

Shrove Tuesday—Mass followed by Pancake Supper
Ash Wednesday—7 a.m. said Mass; 7 p.m. Solemn Mass
Wednesdays—Stations of the Cross and Benediction
Fridays—House Eucharists
Sunday Forums—Discussion of the Liturgy.

As a way of getting to know the parish, Fr. Hanson and Fr. Melvin invited small groups of parishioners to dinner in their home. There was never any secret about the fact that Hanson and Melvin were life partners.

One of the new rector's first projects was a revision of the parish by-laws. Some would have preferred a different focus. He prepared a 10-page document dated August 8, 1990, on the subject; it included the following comment: "As I recently wrote to a member of the Vestry who had expressed to me some exasperations about the amount of effort being directed in this area: Why the heavy concern with the ByLaws? It is because I don't like conflict and confrontation any more than the next guy, and All Saints can ill afford such disruption at this point."

By the time of the Hanson rectorate, the Dayspring Center was operating independently of the parish and physically separated from the nave. Outreach to the neighborhood would now have to recognize that "gentrification" had happened and that the Old Northside organization was a leading player in the neighborhood. The parish offered to become a stop on the Old Northside Home Tour of September 1990. A brief history of the parish was prepared to share with tour participants. The organist, Jeff Donohue, gave brief programs of organ music at various times during the afternoon of the tour. At least one person, Billie Smiley, was attracted to the parish as a result of an Old Northside Tour. A similar event, sponsored by the Historic Landmarks Foundation and called a "Sacred Places Tour", included All Saints on September 22, 1991. It featured six downtown churches.

On the Feast of Corpus Christi in June 1991, the parish provided a much different kind of witness to the neighborhood—a Procession of the Blessed Sacrament. The route went down Central Avenue to 15th Street and back up Park to 16th Street. Clergy and acolytes were vested. The rector carried the monstrance under a specially crafted canopy. Prior to the event, neighbors received a flyer describing and explaining the event.

On another Feast of Corpus Christi, The Rt. Rev. James Montgomery, retired bishop of Chicago (and the bishop who had ordained Fr. Hanson), was the celebrant.

Fr. Hanson was an active letter writer, relishing a clever turn of phrase. In the parish archives, for example, are bits of correspondence between the rector and the governor, The Hon. Evan Bayh. On December 3, 1991, Hanson wrote with some sarcasm:

> What a splendid surprise it was for me—and all of Indianapolis, for that matter—to learn of your continued affiliation with The Episcopal Church of All Saints, as reported by Susan Hanafee in last Saturday's Indianapolis

Star. I have certainly been remiss, during these two years of my rectorate, for not having included you on the parish's mailing list, for not having invited you to dinner at the rectory ... and for not having paid a pastoral call to you and Susan at the Governor's Mansion. Please forgive my oversight.

As you know, this is the time of year when parishes are hard at work in planning next year's budget and trying to garner the wherewithal to meet upcoming expenses through the annual pledge canvass. I am taking the liberty of enclosing for your consideration our 1992 stewardship brochure ... along with a pledge card.

This letter was occasioned by a November 30 *Indianapolis Star* article giving details of the governor's scheduled appearance on a national religious television program and mentioning as an aside that he was affiliated with All Saints. His reply was dated December 9, 1991: "Many thanks for your kind and gracious letter concerning our affiliation with the Church of All Saints. We have a close association with the church over the years. Susan and I worshipped there on a regular basis while we resided at our condominium in Renaissance Place. Since our relocation to the Governor's Residence we have attended services at Holy Trinity."

At the time of Fr. Hanson's arrival, some of the decisions were still unsettled about the furnishing of the nave and Mary Chapel, as a result of changed traffic patterns to the new parish house north of the nave. Thanks to a bequest from a person Fr. Hanson had known in his previous parish, All Saints was able to complete the renewal of the sanctuary along with permanent placement of the furnishings. A loan from the diocesan loan fund supplemented the bequest so that the old red carpet of the sanctuary could be replaced with tile and wood. The original steps to the altar had been designed for celebrations "with back to the people." Although for many years the priest had been celebrating "facing the people," the arrangement of the sanctuary space made this somewhat awkward. A new area of wooden flooring created ample liturgical space. An ingenious design allowed the altar rails to be taken out relatively easily. (Fr. Hanson encouraged—or perhaps insisted—that the congregation stand during the 50 days of Easter both for the Prayer of Consecration and receiving of Holy Communion.) The chairs for presider and other ministers of the altar were moved from the sides of the sanctuary to the rear of the altar on the new raised platform. (Following Fr. Hanson's death, a commemorative plaque was placed on the wall at the entrance to the sanctuary to record in a permanent way his contribution to the beauty and functionality of the liturgical space.)

On March 13 and 14, 1992, the parish hosted a "School of Prayer." The sessions were led by The Rev. Martin L. Smith, SSJE (a member of the Society of Saint John the Evangelist). Fr. Smith entitled his presentations "Wanting Real Prayer: Exploring the Basics of Christian Prayer with Guidelines for a Fresh Beginning." Participants in the diocesan School for Ministry participated in Fr. Smith's sessions as a part of their curriculum, but the sessions were also open to the public.

Another workshop offered at All Saints to the parish and a wider public was billed as "Does the Building Fit the Prayer Book: A Workshop on Liturgical Architecture." The June 6, 1992, workshop was co-sponsored with Christ Church, Trinity, and the Worship and Music Commission of Diocese The featured presenter was Dr. Marion Hatchett of the School of Theology, University of the South (Sewanee). This presentation, in part a celebration of the completion of work in the sanctuary; was followed by a Solemn Evensong offered in thanksgiving for the workers and the work. On the following day (Pentecost), Dr. Hatchett preached at the All Saints' Sunday Mass rededicating the sanctuary.

In conjunction with the Hatchett presentation and the rededication, "A Brief Architectural History" was written:

> The Episcopal Church of All Saints, formerly the cathedral church of the Diocese of Indianapolis, was never completed to its original specifications.
>
> In 1964, when the "temporary" sanctuary structure at the east end of the building—in place since 1910—began to crumble, the current semi-circular apse was constructed as designed by architect Evans Woollen.
>
> Although a "free standing" altar was part of that 1964 construction, it had actually been designed to be used as an "east wall" altar (the celebrant offering the Eucharist facing away from the people). When a few years later, in the development stages of our current Prayer Book, the celebrant moved to face the people from "behind" the altar, all sorts of unanticipated problems of movement and safety began to develop.

In the recent renovation, as designed by architect Valentina Williamson, the All Saints sanctuary was "re-fitted" to accommodate the sort of liturgical celebration envisioned by the 1979 Book of Common Prayer.

In his letter of invitation to Dr. Hatchett, Hanson included what he called another "Brief History" of the parish and its architecture. The following quotations from this "Brief History" provide not only a good idea of the rector's thoughts on these subjects, but also a good sample of his fulsome writing style:

The Episcopal Church of All Saints, from 1911 until 1948 the Cathedral Church of Indianapolis, is a unique and stunning edifice among the churches in this diocese. Its basic neo-Gothic architecture with a basilica-like apse appended in 1964, its soaring height and incomparable acoustical properties are treasures known and appreciated by the entire diocesan family. Since original construction in 1910-1911, All Saints has had only one episode of major maintenance and restoration, centered around the construction of the new sanctuary.

The Episcopal Church of All Saints, Indianapolis, has a rich heritage of Catholic liturgical life coupled with concern for social action. This parish, at one time, would have unapologetically described itself as "Anglo-Catholic", but that sort of nomenclature has become increasingly problematic. All Saints was the site of the first canonical ordination of a woman to the priesthood (the Rev. Jacqueline Means, 1 January 1977), and the Rev. Canon Nan A. Peete (now in Atlanta) was my immediate predecessor as Rector. All Saints' "Anglo-Catholic" heritage and reputation have prompted inquiries and visits from representatives of the E.S.A. I can only respond to these overtures with a certain ironic glee in pointing to our history and our affirmation of the actions of the General Convention with regard to women's ordination and ministries.

All Saints' Catholic liturgical perspective prompted its relinquishing of cathedral status in a conflict with the Ordinary in 1948. All Saints was, for some time, the only parish in the diocese which was fully committed to the celebration of the Holy Eucharist as the principal act of worship of the People of God on the Lord's Day. All Saints was the first parish in the diocese to begin celebrating the Mass at a free-standing altar. This was in the mid 1960s during the tenure of the Rev. Frank Carthy, who coined the parish's motto: "Altar Centered Social Concern." Although the Diocese of Indianapolis has now become thoroughly eucharistic in its worship, and although the gentrifying environment of the All Saints' neighborhood has pulled us into new perspectives of ministry and "social concern", this parish still takes seriously its role of liturgical leadership.

In the past several years, All Saints has undergone some very significant liturgical renewal. The Liturgy is still celebrated with full ceremonial, but it has been simplified with the removal of arcane or unclear gestures and actions. An important addition to the Sunday Liturgy in the parish has been the Sacrament of Healing—anointing and laying-on of hands. This Sacrament, each week, is available in the transept chapels during the distribution of Holy Communion. We regularly have 30 or more persons in the congregation who avail themselves of this Sacrament. This sacramental ministry is made possible by the presence in the parish of four non-stipendiary priest-affiliates. All Saint's growth and activity affords each of these priests ample opportunity to exercise the ministry to which they were ordained, and the presence of these priests affords to All Saints a richness, variety and depth of preaching and an availability of clerical ministry which no rector alone could offer.

The composition of the All Saints' worshipping congregation is as diverse as one could probably find in the Episcopal Church. Located in the central city, the congregation is drawn from throughout all of Marion County. The parish is composed of persons who are black and white, rich and poor, married and single, straight and gay, old and young (although concentrated in the 35-55 year-old range). As the congregation has experienced growth in the past couple years, the ratios between these groups within the parish have remained remarkably the same.

Wayne Hanson's arrival upon the All Saints scene coincided with a wave of deaths related to HIV/AIDS. Although the parish had observed annual Days of Prayer and Healing for AIDS during the rectorate of Nan Peete, awareness of the disease went back to the closing years of Fr. Eastwood's ministry. Another connection with HIV/AIDS was through the Damien Center. The Damien Center (named after the Fr. Damien who, literally, devoted his life to the lepers of Hawaii) was established at a former Roman Catholic school building on Pennsylvania Street, just a few blocks from All Saints. In 1990, Fr. Gordon Chastain became the Executive Director of the Center. (Canon Earl Conner, the founder of the Center, also helped to found the National Episcopal AIDS Coalition, a national network of AIDS ministries; Fr. Chastain became a board member of that organization in 1991.) Clients of the Damien Center were welcomed at All Saints. Parishioners became both clients and volunteers of the Center. Fr. Hanson appointed Jim Anderson as an official liaison between the parish and the Center.

In the first year or so of Fr. Hanson's rectorate many funerals at All Saints of persons who died of AIDS-related illness took place at All Saints. Although not all those buried from All Saints were regular parishioners, the rector calculated that approximately 10% of his flock had died in a short period of time. Despite the grief, the parish was not devastated by illness and death. The funerals became glorious witnesses to faith stronger than death. Some were memorable for the glory of the music. The requiem for Gordon Dove, for example, brought together on a New Year's Day (filling the church as it had not been filled since January 1, 1977) eight clergy and 55 choir members from All Saints, Christ Church, St. Paul's, and the Indianapolis musical group known as Pro Musica. Gordon had sung with all those groups.

Making not only the funerals, but all the services, glorious were Irma Reinumagi and Mark Gastineau, the faithful Sacristan and Master of Ceremonies for Fr. Hanson. Kelly Lowe was the parish secretary.

Some funerals were memorable for reasons that immediately made them a part of All Saints' legend. There was, for example, the funeral of a man who had been crowned "Mr. Indiana Leather." His funeral flowers were red roses in a biker's boot. His pall bearers were a women's motorcycle group from Chicago, and one of the pall bearers got her leather chaps close enough to the flames of the bier lights to cause smoke and pain. At another funeral a relative of the deceased was brought from prison manacled to a guard. Fr. Hanson yelled out to the guard to get rid of his gun before entering the church.

Despite the fact that the parish had lived so much in the shadow of AIDS for so long, it would soon find that it had yet another connection when Fr. Hanson announced in March 1993 that he, too, had the disease. The announcement was reported on page one of *The Indianapolis Star*:

> After Mass on Sunday, the Rev. Wayne Hanson stood at the front of The Episcopal Church of All Saints and matter-of-factly told his parish he has AIDS. The announcement sent waves of shock and grief through the church ... The emotions came not because parishioners have never dealt with the deadly disease, but because they now know another dear friend has acquired immune deficiency syndrome. Nine of the 11 deaths recorded in the 100 member parish in the past three years were AIDS-related. And Father Hanson dealt with each one with the silent knowledge that

he, too, might succumb to the disease ... That recognition unleashed an outpouring of support that enveloped the priest as he revealed his illness, parishioners and church officials said ... Father Hanson said he decided to inform church officials and parishioners of his illness because it had started to affect the way he does his job ... "I don't have the stamina I used to have," he acknowledged ... Fr. Hanson said he knew he had HIV ... when he was hired as rector of All Saints in 1990 ... He said he did not share that information with parishioners or church officials until recently because of a national policy that forbids discrimination in the hiring of people with AIDS. "I don't want people to think I was hiding anything," Father Hanson said. "I simply placed my faith in church policy."

The announcement came after consultation with diocesan staff, and both Canon Robert Hansel and Canon Sue Reid were present when it was made. Hansel was quoted by the *Star* as saying, "I believe he has handled himself very admirably." Hansel also met with parishioners to help with questions they might have about the rector's status or the future of the parish. Vestry member Brad King was also quoted by the *Star*, "Despite our familiarity with this disease, nothing really helps all that much in dealing with the grief and the sense of loss that it brings ... This latest announcement just causes us to continue a grieving process that has become all too frequent an occurrence."

The rector himself prepared an article, which he called "A Plague on My House", to be published in *The Tidings* in order to avoid "gossip, rumor, or innuendo" as a result of "leaving a whole lot of unanswered questions:"

> *Question: How long have you known?* I have known myself to be HIV-positive since January, 1987.
> *Question: How did you get HIV?* There seem to be three methods for contracting HIV/AIDS: 1) IV drug use; 2) tainted blood transfusions; and 3) unprotected sexual encounters. I have never had a blood transfusion and I have never used IV drugs. I did, however, have a period of "sowing my wild oats"—a period which came rather abruptly to a halt as the information on transmission of HIV became known. Looking back, I suspect is most likely that I contracted HIV in the late 1970's or early 1980's ... While engaged in the process leading to my call as Rector of All Saints, in late 1989, I agonized over the issue of my health ... My health at that time remained good, but I knew it would some day begin to fail. Would it be two years, three years, five or even ten? I decided to take the risk ... I felt I had several good years left and that All Saints was the sort of place where I could challenge and be

challenged. Both have been true. Above all I felt *called* to All Saints—felt that I was the right priest at the right time.

Fr. Hanson then talked of how each of the AIDS deaths he had faced at All Saints had affected him personally:

> In each of these tragedies, I have felt the grief of dealing with untimely death; I have also felt a deep stab of pain as each of these deaths has brought me face to face with my own mortality. I am certain that the hand of God was involved in my coming to All Saints … From a personal angle, repeatedly facing HIV, AIDS and death as pastoral issues for others has provided me a powerful spiritual preparation for the challenges I myself am likely to encounter in the future. From a pastoral perspective, I believe God was at work in calling me to All Saints because my own woundedness has assisted me to lead the parish through a difficult period of grief, loss and change … I have seen the people of All Saints face down death by welcoming the dying into their midst. I have assisted several parishioners to approach death as a *holy* event—the gate of everlasting life … Now it is known that All Saints is a place where HIV-positive persons are welcome, where the Lord of life is celebrated, where death is know to be defeated by resurrection, where the communion of saints is a reality. All Saints is still a small parish, but—in part, as a result of its response to AIDS—it is larger than it was in 1989. It is larger not only in numbers, but also in spirit.

Although Wayne Hanson's announcement had been precipitated by his awareness of declining stamina, he was *not* announcing his retirement. On March 19 he sent a letter to the parish reviewing the publicity surrounding his announcement and concluding:

> What comes next? I really don't know … nobody does! I do know that I would like to remain as Rector of All Saints as long as I can. I dare to hope that disability retirement, which even now is an option to me, is still well in the future. The unpredictability of the disease, however, could change this situation rather quickly. Please know that I have already received an overwhelming outpouring of support from my Bishop, from parishioners, for friends in the diocese, and from my family.

There were, however, indications that the rest of the world and parts of the church were not supportive. A church-related group outside the parish had arranged to hold a meeting at All Saints prior to the announcement. The convenor of the group (a member of another parish) contacted Fr. Hanson on March 21. As he reported to the

Bishop, "she informed me that on account of the recent newspaper article … [we] will make arrangements elsewhere … They're not all Episcopalians, you know." Then the rector added in his own emphatic style, "What **that** has to do with anything is beyond me."

As time went on, the parish received yet another blow when it learned that Fr. Hanson's partner, The Rev. Donald Melvin, also had AIDS. Fr. Melvin was a frequent preacher and celebrant because the rector had arranged for all the Priest Associates (also including two other life partners, Tom Honderich and Gordon Chastain) to share in the altar and pulpit. Fr. Melvin also contributed significantly to the musical life of the parish. He had composed a Mass setting and the "Melvin Mass" became part of the regular rotation of musical settings. He also set to music the hymn "Jesus, Son of Mary" and named the tune *Hanson* in honor of Fr. Hanson. The parish has continued the use of *Hanson* on All Saints Day.

Wayne's retirement on disability was not as far in the future as he had hoped it might be. As he became more and more ill, teams of parishioners helped the household with offerings of meals and presence and providing pastoral care for the pastor.

The parish was again in the papers in July 1994, when Fr. Hanson's own glorious funeral was reported in the *Indianapolis News*:

> The revelation that one of its ministers had AIDS might have split apart another church, with all the reproachments and red herrings the disease usually brings to the fore. And the inevitable questions: How did he get it? Is he gay? Those things didn't matter at All Saints. Even after his announcement, Hanson, 41, continued his work for some months. He felt no compunction to talk publicly about his sexual orientation, and apparently the people in his congregation shared that feeling. They filled the pews for his funeral service Sunday in the lofty sanctuary of the church … They had embraced him as a brother as well as a priest … The local Episcopal Bishop, the Right Rev. Edward T. Jones, spoke at Hanson's funeral. The arms of God's mercy, Jones told the mourners, are wider than the narrow ways of humanity.

The Rev. Jim Leehan was asked to serve the parish as the interim priest. Jim had recently come from the Diocese of Ohio to work in the pastoral counseling program of Christian Theological Seminary. With the assistance of The Reverends Tom Honderich, Gordon Chastain, Mary Campbell, Don Melvin, and John Dorr, services and activities continued. Mary Campbell was, of course, not unknown to All Saints. Like John Dorr, she was now also a retired priest of the diocese.

Shortly after Fr. Hanson's funeral, the General Convention of the Episcopal Church met in Indianapolis. All Saints was featured in a special *Indianapolis News* background story on August 23, 1994, for the convention, which was expected to be discussing ordination of gay clergy and blessings of same sex relationships, along with continuing looks at racism and the status of women. A color picture showed The Rev. Mary Campbell celebrating and Katie Day at her side as the Sub-deacon. The headline read: "All Saints offers lesson to Episcopal Church."

> Those issues—homosexuality, racism and the ordination of women—are non-issues to the people of All Saints Episcopal Church, an 83-year-old parish in near-Downtown Indianapolis ... If anyone can explain this kind of parish Gloria Kemper can. She has been attending church at the corner of 16th Street and Central Avenue since 1924. Kemper, 73, remembers when many of the city's middle-class and wealthy families attended services. Back then, All Saints served the Indianapolis diocese as the cathedral, a place where tradition reigned. But as early as the 1940's, All Saints began to change in ways that often alienated traditionalists. Young members wanted to see a return to a regular celebration of Holy Communion. More conservative church members felt that this was too much like the Roman Catholic Church, Kemper said ... When the Civil Rights movement gathered momentum during the 1950's, All Saints parish had no trouble declaring itself a place where color didn't matter. Without fanfare, church members nailed a sign above the front door—"Everyone is Welcome." They were code words that declared the church to be an integrated house of worship. It made sense to be that kind of parish because the near-Northside neighborhood surrounding the church was changing, becoming more black as white residents began migrating farther north.

The *News* article then draws upon the memory of Annie Mae Greene (who is pictured under the "Everyone is Welcome" sign):

> Annie Mae Greene, 69, joined the parish in 1963, after moving to Indianapolis from her rural hometown of Crystal Spring, Mississippi. She came to be near family and to find work. Greene found work cleaning homes and in restaurants; she found a house on the near-Northside; and

despite being raised in a Baptist tradition, she found a new church home at All Saints. "It was church with doors open; it didn't matter what color I was, what kind of clothes I wore," Greene said. What a contrast from church communities in Mississippi, where churches were either black or white. Rarely were they both. "If you were working for a white family and they wanted you to go to church with them then that's what you did and you would sit in the back," Greene recalled. "All Saints was different." Because it was different, Greene said, she has grown accustomed to change at the parish.

A litany of the changes followed: ordination of a woman, the coming of a number of gay and lesbian parishioners in the 1980's, the hiring of a black woman rector. Annie Mae Greene was then quoted: "A lot of people did leave because of all the change. They didn't like what was going on, couldn't tolerate the change or understand why … Me? I can deal with most anybody. As long as they are kind and friendly to me, I do the same for them. They are what they are and I am what I am." The final statement was from Gerry St. Amand Senior Warden: "If the delegates take a look at the parish, they're looking at a place that has worked through a lot of these issues of racism, sexism, and sexuality, and we're still here."

The delegates did have a chance to take a look at the parish. To coincide with the convention, Gerry St. Amand put together a committee to plan a special Reunion Mass for all those who had known and loved All Saints and who might be in Indianapolis for the convention. R. Stewart Wood, now bishop of Michigan, agreed to celebrate. Other former rectors in attendance on August 27 were Jack Eastwood and Nan Peete. The propers chosen for the day were for the Mission of the Church. At the conclusion of the Mass, the Senior Warden announced that a call had been issued and accepted. The Rev. Gordon Chastain would be the next rector of All Saints.

All Saints Day, 1994 not only marked another splendid celebration of the Patronal Feast, it was also the Celebration of a New Ministry with a new rector. The preacher was not new, however. Shawn Schreiner returned to speak about how the parish had "put the *All* in All Saints." She concluded with a charge to keep that "*All* in All Saints."

Here, then, is an appropriate place to end the story—for now. It would be immodest or foolish for the teller of the tale to talk too much about his own part in it. And we leave the story with the voices of Gloria Kemper, Annie Mae Greene, Gerry St. Amand, and Shawn Schreiner still echoing:

"Everyone is Welcome"
"They are what they are and I am what I am"
"We're still here"
"Keep the *All* in All Saints."

# AFTERWORD

## "All saints and a sinner: A long trip to find what's near" by Harrison C. Ullman

Note: The following article appeared in *Nuvo Newsweekly*, February 3-10, 2000, page 10. Harrison Ullman died a few months later. His funeral was another of the "glorious funerals" in the history of All Saints.

A few weeks ago I wrote about the time long ago when I left the church. It was just a church, as I wrote, not The Church. I also wrote about the reasons for my leaving, though they should not matter in your own thoughts about whether or not to be churched.

As it happened I took myself to a church a few days later for reasons that had nothing to do with weddings or Baptisms or grandchildren. The church we chose was All Saints Episcopal Church at 16th and Central, just a short drive down my street. There are a lot of churches on my street—17, if I've counted well—and we chose All Saints for no particular reason.

There has been a church at 16th and Central for most of the city's history. The church that's there now is a pile of red brick, stacked high in the American Gothic style. The building is old, but there's a soaring new apse that was designed by Evans Woollen. The Woollen contribution fits well with the old nave and its side chapels. I have looked up these words—nave and apse and some others—but maybe you should look them up yourself. I am not well-informed about churchly stuff. But I like the architecture.

I also like the services. The rituals at All Saints are "high church," in Episcopalese, ancient and Eastern with much singing of psalms and chanting of prayers. Incense is regularly swung about to purify the place and the participants. There is much bowing and blessing among the priest and his companions around the altar. And they all wear the formal robes of the church, though I see jeans and khakis and sandals and running shoes beneath the hems.

There are also women at the altar, often serving Communion. Other Episcopal congregations in our city have women for their priests. An interesting and wonderfully intelligent woman is the bishop for the city's Episcopal churches. I mean no offense, at least not with this column, but I think women and men should have equal opportunity to serve God.

I also like the music. The choir and congregation at All Saints hold a lot of fine voices from the Indianapolis Men's Chorus and the Indianapolis Women's Chorus. The Men's Chorus began here, though it now needs a much larger hall. There is a good organist at work in the choir loft. When he plays the recessional, we all sit and listen and then applaud before we recede into our own lives.

I also like the diversity I find at All Saints. There are some of the usual Episcopalians, comfortable and confident and white like me. There are also some young families from the neighborhoods around All Saints, some of them gentrified and some of them still in their traditional poverty (I am writing about the neighborhoods here, not the families). There are a few blacks in the pews, mostly women and sometimes a child or two. There are also some gays. This is an important church in the gay community. There is diversity in these demographics, but I sense a comfortable unity in the congregation they have made.

I came to All Saints as a spectator, not as a participant. I had lost any useful memories of the kneelings and recitations of the Episcopal service and I soon learned that the choir and congregation had no need of my help for the hymns. So I sat and watched. And then I wept.

At first I though it must be the music. Music works for me, sacred or profane. I can get wet eyes from Bach and Chopin or Rogers and Hammerstein or "Pomp and Circumstance" and sometimes from the Boston Pops playing the "1812 Overture" and, every time, the "Stars and Stripes Forever." But it wasn't just the music.

So I though it might be the majesty of the rituals. I can be entirely awed by a good ritual, like one of those wonderful weddings for the royals. I also think we should restore some majesty to our lives, or at least to the important passages—births and Baptisms, marriages and perhaps also divorces, and also death. We could also stand more majesty in our courts and legislatures, which have become too ordinary to be taken seriously by even their own dignitaries.

But this is only preference, not a recommendation. I don't know if the majestic rituals at All Saints meet with any Godly approval. But I suspect hat if there is a God, a good God, then there would be many ways for a proper worship and that most of those ways would not be Christian ways. We waste too much goodwill among ourselves arguing about the ways God wants us to do our Baptisms or Communions. I think it's the spirit that matters and not the form of the ritual. So, I do not write that you should want it this way, but only that I like it this way, which is a way full of a majesty that probably does not really matter.

There's a moment in the All Saints Communion service when part of the party around the altar leaves the table and carries the Bible into the congregation. As they walk down the aisle, bearing crosses and candles as well as the book, there is a heavy use of incense to purify the sinners who are about get the word. And the Gospel is read.

There was a Sunday when a woman carried the Bible into the congregation. She held it above her head, as high as her arms could reach, and her face was lit from within with her own devotion. It was only an old book, for all I knew, and the Gospels are only words, for all I know. But for her, it was The Bible and it holds The Word. I wept for the look of her devotion.

However, it was not the majesty, any more than it was the music that put me to tears.

I thought for a time that it might be the congregation. There are many gays here. There are also many prayers for those with AIDS and for those who have died too soon, and perhaps learned too soon whatever truth their faith might really hold.

I watch those men and women while they wait for their turns at the Communion rail. They are comfortable in the hospitality of this church. They have recently come and will soon return to a community that is inhospitable to gays, for no reason that we can find in the Bible nor for any reason that we should put in our laws. Here, for an hour on Sunday, is the small community that we should make of our larger community.

So I kneel at their Communion rail and I share their chalice. This is their house. I am their guest.

Most Sundays there are also one or two very old black women who walk slowly, carefully up the aisle to take their bread and wine.

They are old enough to recollect from their own memories how there was a time when it was not enough to be Christian in our Christian community, not if you were also black. It wasn't so long ago that we let black Christians have only the neighborhoods, the schools and the churches that white Christians didn't want. These old black women remember those times, and I suppose they would tell us what we have forgotten if we ever wanted to know it again. If I wept for these women, it would be with tears of shame.

But finally I knew it is not the people I find here who make me weep. I weep only for myself.

I don't claim any epiphany from the tears. There has been no great light nor any thundering voice to set me right. If there was a voice, it was only my own, and it was a voice that I was slow to hear.

Slow to hear, I suppose, because I was also slow to know that I wept for joy and not for grief.

As the Sundays wore on, I began to feel that I was in the right place, not just in their church but also in my disorderly life.

I recollect enough of Christian history to know the faith was given first to the poor, the weak, the afflicted, the despised, the outcast. When the faith came to the rich and the powerful, it was a faith that required their service to the poor and rest of the least.

So, I believe I am in the right place, not just in this church, but also in places like this one, where I write about our city and the community we so rarely share. I am a noisy person by inclination, but I believe now that I am also a noisy person by way of obligation.

I know no more about God than I knew before we ever drove down Central Avenue to stop at All Saints. It doesn't matter. I am old now, closer to my end than I am to my beginning, and I will know soon enough if there's anything or only nothing to know when the darkness falls. For now, I am in no hurry to have the mystery solved.

This column will come as a surprise to the congregation of All Saints and I hope I have not abused their hospitality. I thought for a time that I would not name their church, but in the end I felt a greater obligation to you than to them and so I gave the name. I meant no harm. But I never do mean it, even when I've done it.

In any case, I am grateful for what I have found in their church, though I think it was only me that I found. But maybe there's nothing more to God than what we can find in ourselves.

# APPENDIX

## In loving memory of the bishops, clergy and laity

### Bishops (of Indiana until 1899, of Indianapolis thereafter)

| | |
|---|---|
| Jackson Kemper | 1835-1849 |
| George Upfold | 1849-1872 |
| Joseph Cruikshank Talbot | 1872-1883 |
| David Buell Knickerbacker | 1883-1895 |
| John Hazen White | 1894-1899 |
| Joseph Marshall Francis | 1899-1939 |
| Richard Ainslie Kirchhoffer | 1939-1957 |
| John Pares Craine | 1957-1977 |
| Edward Whitker Jones | 1977-1997 |
| Catherine Maples Waynick | 1997- |

### Vicars, Curates, Associates, Rectors and Deans

| | |
|---|---|
| Martin W. Averill | 1865-1867 |
| Charles B. Davidson | 1867-1871 |
| Warren H. Roberts | 1871-1874 |
| Harvey O. Judd | 1874-1877 |
| Jonas B. Clarke | 1878-1881 |
| William Richmond | 1881-1883 |
| Augustine Prentiss | 1884-1887 |
| George E. Swan | 1887-1891 |
| Christopher S. Sargent | 1891-1896 |
| Edwin Johnson | 1896-1897 |
| Edgar F. Gee | 1897-1898 |
| John H. McKenzie | 1898-1898 |
| Robert E. Grubb | 1899-1900 |

| | |
|---|---|
| Roger H. Peters | 1900-1902 |
| Frederic O. Granniss | 1902-1906 |
| George Huntington | 1906-1910 |
| Henry Lodge | 1910-1911 |
| Charles S. Lewis | 1912-1914 |
| Willis D. Engle | 1912 |
| Rush R. Sloane | 1914-1916 |
| John White | 1917-1920 |
| Herbert M. Denslow | 1921-1925 |
| A.L. Skerry | 1922-1924 |
| Henry A. Hanson | 1925-1929 |
| Robert C. Alexander | 1929-1940 |
| Francis H. Tetu | 1933-1941 |
| John C.W. Linsley | 1940-1941 |
| John M. Nelson | 1941-1944 |
| J. Willard Yoder | 1944-1945 |
| John T. Payne | 1945-1948 |
| William E. Ashburn | 1948-1949 |
| Felix L. Cirlot | 1949-1955 |
| Frank V.H. Carthy | 1956-1970 |
| Henry Atkins | |
| Alden W. Powers | 1962-1966 |
| Peter C. Moore | |
| Harris C. Mooney | 1970-1972 |
| R. Stewart Wood | 1972-1976 |
| John Harrison Eastwood | 1973-1985 |
| Jacqueline Means | 1976-1980 |
| Joe Riggs | 1977-1983 |
| Gordon L. Chastain | 1978-2001 |
| Thomas E. Honderich | 1978- |
| Nan Arrington Peete | 1985-1988 |
| Wayne Hanson, II | 1990-1994 |
| Donald A. Melvin | 1990-1995 |
| John Dorr | |
| Ian Douglas Mitchell | 1994- |
| Mary Lockwood Campbell | 1994- |
| Thomas Stoll | |

## Wardens and Officers

| | |
|---|---|
| J.O.D. Lilly, Sr. Warden; Nelson Kingman, Jr. Warden | 1868-1870 |
| J.O.D. Lilly, Sr. Warden; George W. Geiger, Jr. Warden | 1871-1873 |
| J.O.D. Lilly, Sr. Warden; Harry Taylor, Jr. Warden | 1874 |
| W.H. Thurston, Sr. Warden; George W. Geiger, Jr. Warden | 1875-1876 |
| Willard Nichols, Sr. Warden; Dr. J.F. Johnston, Jr. Warden | 1879 |
| P.B. Thurston, Sr. Warden; Dr. J.F. Johnston, Jr. Warden | 1880-1881 |
| Deloss Root, Sr. Warden; William Edmunds, Jr. Warden | 1885 |
| Deloss Root, Sr. Warden; F.T. Monroe, Jr. Warden | 1886 |
| Frank M. Curtis, Clerk and Treasurer | 1887 |
| Ralph St. John Perry, Clerk and Treasurer | 1888 |
| William Wilkinson, Clerk; John Voorhees, Treasurer | 1889 |
| Deloss Root, Nelson Kingman, Albert Michie, Auditing Committee | 1890 |
| J.O. Cooper, Treasurer | 1891 |
| A.P. Lewis, Clerk; A.B. Coffey, Treasurer | 1892 |
| A.P. Lewis, Clerk; Albert Michie, Treasurer | 1893 |
| Frederik Pain, Clerk; William Archdeacon, Treasurer | 1894 |
| Albert Michie, Sr. Warden; A. P. Lewis, Jr. Warden | 1895 |
| Albert Michie, Sr. Warden; A.B. Coffey, Jr. Warden | 1896 |
| E.A. Munson, Clerk; William Archdeacon, Treasurer | 1897 |
| E. A. Munson, Sr. Warden; William H. Archdeacon, Jr. Warden | 1898-1903 |
| Louis Howland, Sr. Warden; George W. Ladley, Jr. Warden | 1909-1911 |
| *Cathedral Chapter administers so no vestry* | *(1912-1940)* |
| C.W. Holmes, Sr. Warden; J.L. Rainey, Jr. Warden | 1941 |
| Fred Phillips, Sr. Warden; H. Taylor, Jr. Warden | 1942-1943 |
| J. Wilson Miller, Sr. Warden | 1944 |
| Henry Hull, Sr. Warden; Dr. Roy Robbins, Jr. Warden | 1945 |
| Louis Huss, Sr. Warden; Henry Hull, Jr. Warden | 1946 |
| Henry Hull, Sr. Warden | 1947 |
| Rufo Lutes, Sr. Warden; Henry Hull, Jr. Warden | 1948-1951 |
| Jerry Belknap, Sr. Warden; Rufo Lutes, Jr. Warden | 1952 |
| Rufo Lutes, Sr. Warden; Bob Nowicki, Jr. Warden | 1953 |
| Rufo Lutes, Sr. Warden; Phillip Smith, Jr. Warden | 1954-1956 |
| Bob Nowicki, Sr. Warden; Leighton Hutchings, Jr. Warden | 1957 |
| Bob Nowicki, Sr. Warden; Walter Pliley and Dr. John Russell, Jr. Warden | 1958 |

James Blande, Sr. Warden; Dr. John Russell, Jr. Warden          1959

Bob Nowicki, Sr. Warden; Dr. John Russell, Jr. Warden          1960

Jerry Belknap, Sr. Warden; Aldo Bertorelli, Jr. Warden          1961

Jerry Belknap, Sr. Warden; Dr. John Russell, Jr. Warden          1962

Dr. John Russell, Sr. Warden; Phillip Smith, Jr. Warden          1963

Jerry Belknap, Sr. Warden; Dr. John Russell, Jr. Warden          1964

Jerry Belknap, Sr. Warden; Paul C. Salsbury, Jr. Warden          1965

Jerry Belknap, Sr. Warden; Dr. John Russell, Jr. Warden          1966

Dr. John Russell, Sr. Warden; L.H. Bayley, Jr. Warden          1967

Ed McPherson, Sr. Warden; Don Bose, Jr. Warden          1968-1969

L.H. Bayley, Sr. Warden; Ida Edelen, Jr. Warden          1970

L.H. Bayley, Sr. Warden; William S. Coleman, Jr. Warden          1971

L.H. Bayley, Sr. Warden; George Hight, Jr. Warden          1972

Culver Godfrey, Sr. Warden          1977

Nancy Shaw, Sr. Warden; Bill Scott, Jr. Warden          1981

Nancy H. Shaw, Sr. Warden; Dr. John L. Tofaute, Jr. Warden          1982

Louise Jones, Sr. Warden; Charles White, Jr. Warden          1983

James L. Vesper, Sr. Warden; Roger Whitehead, Jr. Warden          1984-1985

Win Tackett, Sr. Warden; Culver C. Godfrey, Jr. Warden          1986

Win Tackett, Sr. Warden; Gordon Dove, Jr. Warden          1987

Maurice Edelen, Sr. Warden; Gordon Dove, Jr. Warden          1988

Dr. Frank Lloyd, Sr. Warden; Marc Sotkiewicz and
    Alice Usher Jr. Wardens          1989

Dr. Frank Lloyd, Sr. Warden: Marc Sotkiewicz, Jr. Warden          1990

Dr. Frank Lloyd, Sr. Warden: Marc Sotkiewicz, Jr. Warden          1991

Gerry St. Amond, Sr. Warden: Irma Reinumagi, Jr. Warden          1992

Gerry St. Amond, Sr. Warden: Katie Day, Jr. Warden          1993

Gerry St. Amond, Sr. Warden: Katie Day, Jr. Warden          1994

## Communicants Reported

- 1865     41
- 1875     96
- 1882     22
- 1885     41
- 1889     135
- 1912     233
- 1920     196
- 1938     243

- 1950     215
- 1955     133
- 1959     119
- 1965     318
- 1970     287
- 1975     134
- 1979     102
- 1981     144
- 1983     104
- 1985     120
- 1986     114
- 1987     132
- 1988     116

Episcopal Cathedral of All Saints, from Central Avenue, looking East
(November 1911).

Interior of All Saints, looking to the East and the high altar
(November, 1911).

Interior of All Saints, photo of the high altar (November, 1911).

Interior of All Saints, looking toward the Michael Chapel and the organ, located to the right of the altar (November, 1911).

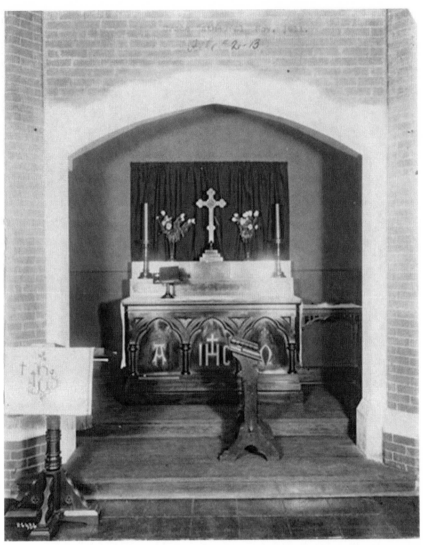

Interior of All Saints, Michael Chapel altar (November, 1911).

Interior of All Saints, looking west toward the rear of the church
(November, 1911).

Exterior of All Saints, looking south from 16th Street, showing the back of the "Bishop's House," the temporary wooden structure on the back of the church containing the sacristy and altar, and a corner of the original wooden structure used for Grace Church (November, 1911).

Image of the "Bishop's House" that stood at the corner of 16th and Central Avenue. Construction had not yet begun on the church building to the south, so this photo was taken before 1910. The brick structure to the right of the house is Knickerbacker Hall.

CPSIA information can be obtained at www.ICGtesting.com
Printed in the USA
LVOW041151101011

249856LV00001B/2/P